Eisenhower's Fine Group of Fellows

Eisenhower's Fine Group of Fellows

Crafting a National Security Policy to Uphold the Great Equation

Valerie L. Adams

LEXINGTON BOOKS

A Division of
ROWMAN & LITTLEFIELD PUBLISHERS, INC.
Lanham • Boulder • New York • Toronto • Oxford

LEXINGTON BOOKS

A division of Rowman & Littlefield Publishers, Inc.
A wholly owned subsidiary of The Rowman & Littlefield Publishing Group, Inc.
4501 Forbes Boulevard, Suite 200
Lanham, MD 20706

PO Box 317
Oxford
OX2 9RU, UK

British Library Cataloguing in Publication Information Available

Library of Congress Cataloging-in-Publication Data

Adams, Valerie L., 1970-
  Eisenhower's fine group of fellows : crafting a national security policy to uphold the
great equation / Valerie L. Adams.
    p. cm.
  Includes bibliographical references and index.
  ISBN-13: 978-0-7391-0958-8 (cloth : alk. paper)
  ISBN-10: 0-7391-0958-8 (cloth : alk. paper)
  1. National security—United States. 2. United States—Military policy. 3. United
States—Politics and government—1953-1961 I. Title.
UA23.A5235 2006
355'.03357309045—dc22   2006009982

Printed in the United States of America

♾™ The paper used in this publication meets the minimum requirements of American
National Standard for Information Sciences—Permanence of Paper for Printed Library
Materials, ANSI/NISO Z39.48–1992.

In Memory

of my father,

James C. Dunham

Contents

Preface

This project initially came about from my interest in presidential science advising. As a doctoral student, I envisioned a dissertation on the development of the Special Assistant to the President on Science and Technology, a role James Killian first filled in 1957. As many dissertations go, I changed the focus of my topic enough times to concern my advisor. Then I found inspiration and focus from the Winter 2000 issue of *Diplomatic History*. In it, Gregg Herken suggested a comparison study between the Killian Committee and the Gaither Committee. I added the Solarium Committee because not only did it give the project the desired ability to examine the entire Eisenhower period, it also set up Eisenhower's national security policy. Looking at these three influential ad hoc committees gave me exactly what I wanted in terms of a strong focus on science and technology, but also a focused project on Eisenhower's leadership style and his national security policy.

In the original dissertation Eisenhower's Great Equation played a supporting role. However, as I began revisions to the dissertation, I simultaneously watched the War on Terror be unleashed. I watched a president with little military or foreign policy experience take the United States down a road that looked in many ways like the Cold War. I heard myself muttering to the president on television, "Prepare for the long haul." I soon realized that my book had to have its main focus on the Great Equation. In these troubling times we need to remind ourselves that we can not overreach our defense spending and expect to maintain the high morale and fiscal soundness that provides Americans with the coveted American Dream. If we lose the ability for social mobility, or the ability to deploy strong, professional armed forces, or the ability to speak freely about our government, we will lose the War on Terror. Eisenhower understood this concept perfectly and was a determined leader to win the Cold War without creating a garrison state at home. This book is my small attempt to remind policymakers history matters and that we do not have to reinvent the wheel for each crisis.

In producing this book I have many people to thank. I would like to thank the Graduate School of the University of New Hampshire for their financial help throughout my tenure as a doctoral student. Two Summer Teaching Assistant Fellowships enabled me to travel to the necessary archives to complete my research and the generous Dissertation Writing Fellowship allowed me the time to finish writing the dissertation. In addition, financial support to travel to professional conferences gave me the opportunities to present parts of the dissertation in front of my professional peers for comment. Without this assistance from the Graduate School, the dissertation would have been indefinitely delayed.

I was able to travel to the Eisenhower Library through the generous support of The Eisenhower World Affairs Institute's Eisenhower Presidential Library Travel Grant. Their support financed a two week research trip that was imperative to the dissertation. I also have to thank the staff at the Eisenhower Library for their impressive dedication and knowledge. The staff has a reputation among scholars for being one of the best and friendliest of the Presidential Libraries and they did not disappoint. In particular, a special thank you to staff archivist Barbara Constable, who pointed me in directions I would not have thought to take on my own.

The Department of History at the University of New Hampshire had also provided invaluable financial assistance in the form of tuition scholarships, teaching assistant funding, and research support through the Gunst-Wilcox fund. In addition to financial assistance, the Department had been helpful in advising. I owe a special debt to my advisor, Kurk Dorsey, whose critical eye, intellectual pursuit, and unmatched support have improved the overall quality of this dissertation. Few advisees have been as fortunate as I to have had the guidance of such an outstanding scholar and mentor.

In addition, Harvard Sitkoff, Thomas Trout, Robert Mennel provided much needed and heeded advice as members of my committee. I thank you for your support along the way. In particular, a special thank you to committee member Allan Winkler for agreeing to serve on a committee so far away from Ohio. Your advice and support was invaluable.

As this moved towards a manuscript, I would like to acknowledge my colleagues in the Department of Global Studies at Embry-Riddle Aeronautical University in Prescott, Arizona. Phil Jones, Archie Dickey, Robin Sobotta, Ricardo Carreras and Richard Bloom have all offered support and encouragement, even reading sections of the manuscript on top of all their other work. The collegial nature of this department is perfect for a junior faculty to actually accomplish the daunting task of rewriting the dissertation. I am also thankful for the financial support the department and College of Arts and Sciences have provided, allowing me release time and travel expenses to finish the research.

I must thank Rebekka Brooks at Lexington Books for her enthusiasm in my project and patience with deadlines. She found a unanimous reviewer who kindly pointed me to my weaknesses, but encouraged my strengths. The entire group at Lexington has my utmost respect and thanks.

I am indebted to Thomas Jones, a brilliant aeronautical engineer undergraduate who found my history classes "fun" and who has since helped me as an assistant. Most helpful has been his ability to place this manuscript in a camera ready format. I am also indebted to the talent of Mollyssa Kuper, who copy edited the manuscript and allowed a powerful voice for Eisenhower's fine group of fellows. Of course all the errors within are mine.

I have to thank my father, James C. Dunham, for his constant enthusiasm about history. Hardly a family summer vacation went by when we did not visit some historical monument or museum. His love for history was contagious and I am so glad I caught that bug. Thanks Dad.

Finally, I thank my entire supporting cast. Gretchen Adams and Kate Larson served as sounding boards and critical analysts during many revisions of my dissertation. Governor, Franklin, and Dallas all provided much needed breaks during the writing process. Hunter James Adams was kind enough to wait until I was finished writing the dissertation before making his entrance into this world. Although, Troy Bryan Adams delayed the process of revision to manuscript, but his birth was a welcomed delay. I am amazed that Hunter will be five and Troy will be three before I see this in finished form! And my husband, Bryan Adams, gave me the emotional, spiritual, and intellectual support I needed to complete this task. Without his confidence and love I could never have completed this journey in my life. I will always be indebted.

Introduction

In the fall of 1912 at West Point a young man was determined to excel at sports, particularly football. During a stunning year, the young Dwight D. Eisenhower led his team to victory after victory until a devastating knee injury prevented him from playing again. Instead of leaving football, Eisenhower participated in the game as a cheerleader and eventually coach of the junior varsity team. As biographer Stephen Ambrose wrote, "coaching brought out his best traits—his organizational ability, his energy and competitiveness, his enthusiasm and optimism, his willingness to work hard at a task that intrigued him, his powers of concentration, his talent for working with the material he had instead of hoping for what he did not have, and his gift for drawing the best out of his players."[1] During his career in the Army, Eisenhower's techniques as a leader were often compared with those of a good football coach. In fact, it was his dedication to teamwork and his ability to build those teams that made him a natural choice to be Supreme Commander of the Allied Forces and to oversee the Normandy Invasion during World War II. As Eisenhower reflected towards the end of his life, "I believe that football, perhaps more than any other sport, tends to instill in men the feeling that victory comes through hard—almost slavish—work, team play, self-confidence, and an enthusiasm that amounts to dedication."[2] Eisenhower never forgot those lessons.

As President of the United States, Eisenhower drew upon his experiences with football to coach his team to victory. First and foremost he urged teamwork among the fine group of fellows he assembled to craft a coherent national security policy that withstood the long haul of the Cold War. The eight years that Eisenhower was president were anxious years in terms of hostilities between the United States and the Soviet Union. However, they were also eight years of unprecedented economic growth and relative peace. How he crafted a national security policy while promoting prosperity and a high public morale is the story of this volume. It is a story that has much relevance to today, as the United States fights a war on terror while trying to balance the budget and keep public spirits high. It is a story with many lessons, the first one being on presidential leadership.

"He [Eisenhower] wanted to get, as we came later to express it, all of the responsible people in the room, take up the issue, and hear their views," explained his good friend General Andrew Goodpaster. "If somebody didn't agree, he was obliged to speak his mind and get it all out on the table or in the Oval Office; and then in light of all of that, the President would come to a line of action, he wanted everybody to hear it, everybody to participate in it, and then he wanted everybody to be guided by it."[3] As Goodpaster's remarks indicate, Eisenhower was against a "one-man" government. Although there can be little doubt that Eisenhower made the final decisions regarding national security policy, he did assemble a fine group of fellows that included the usual suspects like his secretaries of State and Defense, but also included his national security advisors and the often unseen men of various ad hoc committees. In fact, Secretary of State John Foster Dulles saw that Eisenhower's ability to build this organization of able men would be what history recorded as one of the "greatest achievements of his career."[4]

Of course, assembling a fine group of fellows was not enough. The team had to be guided by certain principles that ensured a sound national security policy and national fiscal health. While visiting Eisenhower at a Denver hospital in November 1955, Dulles recalled that the President was concerned about the future; in particular, he worried "that the country might fall into the hands of persons who had no real principles and who just believed in 'give away' for the purpose of trying to buy votes and favor at home and abroad."[5] Eisenhower explained to Dulles that he had "worked very hard to introduce new and solid principles," and he did not want to see them destroyed. He hoped that he could get the American people to understand and accept these principles before he left office and also hoped that his successor was someone from "within the inner circle of his Administration so that such a successor would be imbued by the existing spirit and also be able to keep much of the same team that he had created, and of which he was very proud."[6]

The guiding principles that shaped Eisenhower's thinking are captured in what he called "the Great Equation." To win the Cold War and prosper as a nation, the United States had to adhere to a set of principles that safeguarded national security while ensuring that the American way of life was preserved, and one cannot understand Eisenhower as a decision maker or grand strategist without comprehending the emphasis that he placed on this 'Great Equation.' As Eisenhower himself remarked, "we could lick the world if we were willing to adopt the system of Adolf Hitler." Unwilling to resign to this approach, Eisenhower had a different vision for national security policy, and he brought together a remarkable team to develop that vision.

Eisenhower's vision for a national security policy that could survive what he called the "long haul" was based on a number of beliefs that translated into the "new and solid principles" he spoke to Dulles about. They included keeping a sound economy, and a strong military, as well as promoting high morale—a spiritual resolve—within the public. Prior to the 1952 election, Eisenhower explained to a friend the importance of those factors to security: "Spiritual force, multiplied by economic force, multiplied by military force, is roughly equal to security. If one of these factors falls to zero, or near zero, the resulting product does likewise."[7] This 'Great Equation' was central to his decision making. Eisenhower was not about to sacrifice security for a balanced budget or any other reason. Neither, though, was he willing to sacrifice a sound economy for a large and unnecessary military force. Likewise, to guarantee security, the public had to be spiritually centered and educated about the dangers involved in the Cold War so as to remain sensible, calm, and motivated to participate in preserving the American way of life. Crafting a national security policy that upheld the 'Great Equation' allowed the United States to win the Cold War without having to fight World War III.[8] As such, it was clear to Eisenhower that the panic-rhetoric and enormous defense spending of Truman's national security policy following the Korean War had to be curbed.

To accomplish this change, Eisenhower looked at policy broadly and considered the bigger picture. That meant considering relations with allies, the economy, military service needs, and so forth. This is not to say he did not pay attention to narrower problems. As Goodpaster remarked, Eisenhower "liked to have very thorough, comprehensive evaluations made, targeted ultimately on specific options and specific lines of policy," but after such evaluations were made, Eisenhower placed them within a larger context.[9] This became very apparent with civil defense and the question of a federally sponsored national shelter program. Eisenhower did not deny that a fallout shelter might save some lives. However, he had bigger questions to consider: Should American tax dollars pay for a shelter program when the government did not currently provide for protection against other disasters such as hurricanes, tornadoes, or floods? Would that money be better spent on other means of security? If one did survive a nuclear war, what kind of world would be left? Was survival merely enough? What type of message would such a program send to American allies and to the Soviet Union? Could the economy and public spirit withstand such a large project? Recognizing such questions was the first step in making Eisenhower an effective leader able to oversee eight years of peace and prosperity. In today's political debates involving the budget and national security, many lessons can be drawn from the 1950s.

Understanding that the aforementioned questions were not easy to answer in an era of rapidly changing science and technology, Eisenhower realized the value of an intelligent team and sound advice in the volatile time of the Cold War. For example, after leaving office, Eisenhower explained that assuring the nation's security was the "primary duty" of the president and that "situations of actual or probable conflict change so rapidly and the weaponry of modern military establishments increase their destructiveness at such a bewildering speed that he [the president] will always need the vital studies, advice, and counsel that only a capable and well-developed staff organization can give him."[10] To secure the studies, advice, and counsel that he sought, Eisenhower reorganized the National Security Council (NSC) and tasked various ad hoc committees of civilian advisors to report directly to the NSC on matters of national security.

Although Eisenhower was certainly not the first president to call upon civilian advisors, his presidency is unique in that he frequently asked for civilian advice on matters of national security. Three such occasions deserve special attention for what they illuminated about the formation of a sound national security policy that upheld the Great Equation, the effectiveness of ad hoc civilian committees, the importance of recruiting experts in an era of rapidly changing science and technology, and the leadership style of Eisenhower. The Solarium Exercise in 1953, the Killian Committee in 1954-55, and the Gaither Committee in 1957 exemplify these four characteristics.

The Solarium Exercise was a response to an immediate concern of Eisenhower in 1953 to formulate an organized, systematic blueprint guiding American foreign policy that was less expensive than Harry Truman's adopted policies. Creating three separate task forces, Eisenhower conducted an exercise to evaluate the merits of various policy options, including preemptive war, so-called rollback of communism, and containment. The outcome of this exercise led to what became known as the "New Look," NSC 162/2. This national security policy incorporated all the vital elements of the Great Equation that Eisenhower desired, and guided American foreign policy for eight years.

A year later, faced with the growing possibility that the Soviet Union might launch a surprise attack against the United States as a result of advancing science and technology, Eisenhower once again turned to civilian experts to examine national security issues. James Killian was tasked to chair the Technological Capabilities Committee, which was to apply science and technology to guard against a surprise attack. He put together a smart, efficient group whose efforts significantly improved American national security while staying true to the principles of the Great Equation. The committee's recommendations included prioritizing the development of Intercontinental Ballistic Missiles (ICBM), Intermediate Range Ballistic Missiles (IRBM), and Submarine Launched Ballistic Missiles (SLBM), as well as creating the top-secret high altitude reconnaissance plane, the U-2.

Facing increasing political pressures from Democrats against his foreign policy and increased public awareness about the dangers of nuclear fallout, Eisenhower again turned to an ad hoc committee in 1957 to investigate the wisdom of implementing a recent Federal Civil Defense Administration (FCDA) recommendation to spend nearly 40 billion dollars on a national fallout shelter program. Rowan Gaither was asked to chair this committee of which Eisenhower had little interest. For Eisenhower, such spending on passive defenses did not make sense within the Great Equation. He believed 40 billion dollars would be better spent on improving active defenses. The committee was formed as a response to outside pressures, unlike the other two committees that were formed internally and carefully overseen by Eisenhower himself. The Gaither Committee concluded that the United States was in grave danger and recommended that large monies be spent on both passive and active defenses. When Eisenhower did not respond favorably to their recommendations, many members leaked parts of their report to the press—they did not act as the team players Eisenhower expected. In fact, their "disloyalty" and ensuing weeks of banter became a bitter source of irritation for Eisenhower and abated his enthusiasm for ad hoc committees.

Overall, civilian committees benefited Eisenhower on many levels. First, they allowed Eisenhower to build the consensus he desired. Second, particularly in regard to the Killian Committee, they provided him with valuable insight; Eisenhower was not an expert on all things, and the technological advances being made during the Cold War called for expert advice in the fields of science and technology. Third, by including outsiders, such as Democrats, in the decision-making process, his policies had a stronger footing. By allowing critics to serve on committees, Eisenhower made them complicit in the decision-making process, giving his policies more weight. Fourth, when Eisenhower did not agree with the committee's recommendations, such as with the Gaither Committee, he claimed he had had an open mind and had carefully considered the recommendations, but ultimately found them unpersuasive. In fact, the success of a civilian committee depended in part on how well its recommendations reflected the ideas of the 'Great Equation' and the elements of Eisenhower's strategic thinking. If a civilian committee recommended a path that differed with Eisenhower's thinking, it was rejected by the President.

Using civilian committees was an integral part of Eisenhower's decision-making process. They brought to the NSC deliberations a "fresh, frequently changing civilian point of view" which allowed the president and his national security staff to hear all sides of a debate.[11] Serving as educators, the committee members often recommended innovative solutions to national security problems. They served without being burdened by political or interservice rivalries. And Eisenhower used them deliberately as part of developing a coherent national security policy that stayed true to the 'Great Equation.' Eisenhower crafted the use of civilian experts to achieve the greatest possible understanding of technical security issues for himself and his staff. When he employed these committees for his own use, under a veil of secrecy, they were wildly successful. When the committees were formed in the public arena to pacify a public debate, they were troublesome and unproductive. The lesson is that internal ad hoc committees can provide valuable, politically unbiased advice, but committees brought on by outside political pressures are more susceptible to failure. Present and future leaders would do well to learn from this lesson.

Another lesson comes from Eisenhower's use of the NSC. Since every president has used the NSC differently since its inception in 1947, it is worthwhile to closely examine how Eisenhower reorganized it into an efficient advising body. A top priority in the first months of his presidency was to make the NSC an efficient decision-making body. He used the NSC to set national security policy for the Cold War and he attended over 300 of the meetings, encouraging debate and discussion. The process may very well have controlled any other president through its bureaucracy, but his NSC was orderly and tamed by his national security advisors and himself.[12] For Eisenhower, it was a perfect setting in which to build a consensus for his foreign policy vision. In step with William Whyte's "Organization Man," Eisenhower sought to create an atmosphere that appeared to welcome old virtues of individualism and freethinking, but really expected loyalty to the company. Teamwork was valued above all else. Teamwork was the key to national security. The famous words of George Kennan to the American people that the "entire security as a nation depended on them pulling themselves together and accepting the responsibilities of moral and political leadership that history plainly intended them to bear" were not lost on Eisenhower.[13] He understood Kennan's charge and he continually worked to get his staff and the American people to buy off on his national security policies.

It may seem ironic that Eisenhower spent so much time on building a consensus and team players when it was he who devised strategy. As historian Richard Immerman has noted, "for all his famed deliberations and 'staffing out' procedures, he seems consistently to have approached a problem with his mind all but made up."[14] Immerman even called Eisenhower his own secretary of defense. Eisenhower himself believed that important national decisions had to be made by a single authority. "Any attempt to use a voting system," he wrote, "would be futile because a single man, the head, carries all the responsibility."[15] Yet, Eisenhower did value advice and this emphasis on seeking out advice is not ironic when one understands Eisenhower's decision-making process.

Rather than appear as the "head" who had his mind all but made up, Eisenhower realized the value of soliciting advice from many people, including civilian expert advisors. He cultivated a climate to solicit advice for his own understanding and for winning support for his policies. Eisenhower believed his policies to be more successful if he listened to all sides of a debate and had the full support of his national security staff. Walter Bedell Smith, Eisenhower's Chief of Staff during World War II and Under Secretary of State for Dulles, explained:

> His personality is such that it impresses itself immediately upon senior subordinates as completely frank, completely honest, very human and very considerate . . . . He has great patience, and he disdains no advice regardless of source. One of his most successful methods in dealing with individuals is to assume that he himself is lacking in detailed knowledge and liable to make an error and is seeking advice. This is by no means a pose, because he actually values the recommendations and suggestions he receives, although his own better information and sounder judgment might cause them to be disregarded.[16]

This observation of Eisenhower's ability to sincerely include everyone in the decision-making process explains why he chose to "staff-out" problems while acting as his own secretary of defense. He sought advice for the advice itself, but also to develop a consensus for his policies. Those consulted tended to accept Eisenhower's policies readily because, as Greenstein explained, they felt that "whatever line of action Eisenhower embarked upon had been informed by consultation with them."[17] Eisenhower learned the art of making friends and influencing people in the military and continued to lead that way as president.[18] In particular, he used this decision-making process to gain support from his staff for developing a national security policy that reflected both the 'Great Equation' and his strategic thinking.

Eisenhower's strategic thinking can be broken down into three elements: (a) deterrence based on nuclear weapons, (b) second strike capabilities, (c) a rejection of limited war. His strategic thinking rested in part upon his understanding of the military strategist Claude von Clausewitz. Eisenhower learned military history and theory and read Clausewitz's *On War* three times while stationed in Panama during the 1920s as staff officer for General Fox Conner. Conner questioned the young officer closely on the material he read and Eisenhower quickly became fascinated by the subject.[19] Eisenhower had come to decide that, in the nuclear age, there was no room for limited war. This was based on Clausewitz's idea that no military commander would surrender if he still had more powerful weapons at his disposal. In other words, Eisenhower believed that a limited war inevitably led to a general war because it could not be won without using nuclear weapons. However, that did not mean Eisenhower was against building a nuclear arsenal.

For Eisenhower, deterrence meant a strong nuclear force that allowed America to demobilize its conventional forces, thus saving money. He used the specter of nuclear weapons in the policy of Massive Retaliation and he used the weapons to keep the Soviet Union on guard. "Nuclear saber rattling," was a way to get and keep Moscow's attention.[20] The value of nuclear weapons was symbolic—to remind the Soviets that such a war was suicidal.[21] In addition to a nuclear deterrent, protecting second-strike capabilities was central to Eisenhower's strategic thinking. Ensuring that, should war come, American forces could retaliate was imperative. These ideas, along with the concept of the 'Great Equation,' permeated Eisenhower's NSC within months after taking office.

For example, a NSC memorandum identified the two principal threats to the survival of American traditions and values as "the formidable power of the Communist world led by the USSR, and the weakening of our economy which may result from the cost of opposing the Soviet Union."[22] To counter these threats an integrated political, military, and economic system had to be maintained. That meant balancing the budget, eliminating waste, educating the public about the nature of the Communist threat, and improving the readiness of U.S.

military forces to meet the Soviet threat. Continental defense and offensive capabilities, coupled with continued research and development in special weapons, were key.[23] These themes reappeared time after time. The Joint Chiefs also reflected part of Eisenhower's strategic thinking, concluding in October 1953 that the principle deterrent to a Soviet air attack was to convince the Soviets that such an attack could not achieve their military objectives in war—by ensuring the massive air capabilities of the U.S. and the effectiveness of the U.S. air defense.[24] These examples captured Eisenhower's thinking.

With his vision for crafting a national security policy based upon his strategic thinking and the 'Great Equation,' Eisenhower led the country through eight years of peace and prosperity. After leaving office he boasted, "the United States never lost a soldier or a foot of ground in my administration. We kept the peace. People ask how it happened—by God, it didn't just happen, I'll tell you that."[25] This is the story of how it happened—how an able leader built a team to craft a national security policy that survived the long haul in the face of the challenges of the Cold War.

Notes

1. Stephen E. Ambrose, *Eisenhower: Soldier and President,* (New York: Simon and Schuster, 1990), 27.

2. Dwight Eisenhower, *At Ease: Stories I Tell to Friends,* (New York: Double Day, 1967), 16.

3. "Project Solarium: A Collective Oral History with General Andrew Goodpaster, Robert Bowie, and Ambassador George Kennan," 2/27/88, Princeton University, Mudd Library, Woodrow Wilson School, Box 93, folder 10, p.20.

4. Memorandum of Conversation with the President at Fitzsimmons Hospital, Denver, 10/11/55, EL, JFD Papers, WH Memorandum Series, Box 3, "Meetings with the President, 1955 (2)."

5. Ibid.

6. Ibid.

7. Eisenhower to Lucius Du Bignon Clay, 02/09/52, *The Papers of Dwight D. Eisenhower,* ed. Louis Galambos, 13 vols. (Baltimore, 1970-), quoted in Richard Immerman, "Confessions of an Eisenhower Revisionist: An Agonizing Reappraisal," *Diplomatic History,* 14 (Summer 1990), 328.

8. Eisenhower's psychological strategist C.D. Jackson said Eisenhower "was one of the few who not only believed but understood that it would be possible to win World War III without having to fight it." Jackson Memorandum to the President, 09/21/53, EL, C.D. Jackson Papers, Time, Inc. File, "DDE Correspondence through 1956 (2)," quoted in Immerman, "Confessions of an Eisenhower Revisionist," 341.

9. "Project Solarium: A Collective Oral History," 10-11.

10. Dwight D. Eisenhower, "The Central Role of the President in the Conduct of Security Affairs," in Col. Amos A. Jordan, Jr., ed. *Issues of National Security in the*

1970s: Essays Presented to Colonel George A. Lincoln on His Sixtieth Birthday, (New York: Praeger, 1967), 205-206.

11. Letter Lay to Coller, 7/25/55, EL, WHO OSANSA, NSC Series, Administrative Sub series, Box 4 "Consultants- NSC July 1954-Aug 1956] (4)."

12. Anna Kasten Nelson, " 'The Top of the Policy Hill': President Eisenhower and the National Security Council," *Diplomatic History*, 7 (Fall 1983), 307-26.

13. George Kennan, "Sources of Soviet Conduct," in *American Diplomacy*, (Chicago: University of Chicago Press, 1979), 128.

14. Immerman, "Confessions of an Eisenhower Revisionist," 323.

15. Dwight D. Eisenhower, "The Central Role of the President in the Conduct of Security Affairs," in Col. Amos A. Jordan, Jr., ed. *Issues of National Security in the 1970s: Essays Presented to Colonel George A. Lincoln on His Sixtieth Birthday*, (New York: Praeger, 1967), 213.

16. Walter Bedell Smith to General Maxwell Taylor, 2/1/56, EL, Walter Bedell Smith Papers, quoted in Fred Greenstein, *The Hidden Hand Presidency: Eisenhower as Leader*, (New York: Basic Books, 1982), 34.

17. Ibid., 34.

18. See ibid., 31-35.

19. Dwight D. Eisenhower, *At Ease: Stories I Tell to Friends*, (New York: Doubleday & Co., 1967), 182-186. For more on the influence of Clausewitz on Eisenhower see Marc Trachtenberg, *History and Strategy*, (Princeton: Princeton University Press, 1991), 138; John Lewis Gaddis, *Strategies of Containment*, (New York: Oxford University Press, 1982),135; Saki Dockrill, *Eisenhower's New Look National Security Policy, 1953-61*, (New York: St. Martin's Press, 1996), 4.

20. Immerman, "Confessions of an Eisenhower Revisionist," 340.

21. Richard Immerman put it this way: Eisenhower "never considered the nuclear option viable, except in the sense that one considers suicide viable." See Immerman, "Confessions of an Eisenhower Revisionist," 326.

22. Memorandum for the Vice President, 6/8/53, EL, WHO NSCS, Special Staff File, Box 1, "Basic National Security Policy, 1953-54 (3)."

23. Ibid.

24. Decision on JCS 1924/76, "Magnitude and Imminence of Soviet Air Threat to the United States- 1957," 10/30/53, NA, RG 218, Box 65, "CCS 350.09 USSR (12-19-49) sec 5."

25. Eisenhower quoted in Ambrose, *Eisenhower*, vol. 2, *The President*, 626.

PART ONE

The Debating Club Meets National Security Needs:
The Solarium Project (1953)

CHAPTER ONE

The Three C'S:
Containment, Cost Cutting, and the "Chance for Peace"

"The issue of Soviet-American relations is in essence a test of the over-all worth of the United States as a nation among nations. To avoid destruction the United States need only measure up to its own best traditions and prove itself worthy of preservation as a great nation."[1] This challenge, written by George Kennan in 1947, inspired a generation of public servants to support its country during the Cold War. After defeating the totalitarian regimes of Germany and Japan in World War II, Americans felt invincible and righteous in their desire to spread to the peoples of the world the democracy and freedoms their Constitution guaranteed. Standing in their way was the Soviet Union. Despite being wartime allies, relations between the two countries quickly deteriorated into a Cold War in part because of Soviet expansion into Eastern Europe and in part because of the hard line the Truman Administration took against the Soviets. Harry Truman had to fight a cold war against the Soviets while balancing American post-war economic needs. To accomplish this task, he followed a policy of containment first proposed by Kennan, which emphasized political and economic maneuvering. Although containment was successful in the short term, the Soviet detonation of an atomic bomb in 1949, the outbreak of the Korean War in 1950, and Truman's authorization for developing a hydrogen bomb that same year resulted in a redefinition of containment by Paul Nitze. Nitze militarized containment, which resulted in higher defense budgets and a more dangerous Cold War.

Dwight Eisenhower entered the presidency on January 20, 1953 in the midst of this Cold War and on the eve of the thermonuclear revolution. He inherited from Truman high budget deficits, massive military spending, a nuclear arms race, and a foreign policy that seemed to lack any cohesion. Clearly Eisenhower could not craft a national security policy that upheld the 'Great Equation' with Truman's policies. Eisenhower first prepared to maintain peace, practicing a policy that avoided any war, since even limited war, he believed, would inevitably lead to a general nuclear war.[2] In addition to avoiding world destruction, ensuring American fiscal solvency was equally essential for Eisenhower's national security policy. Eisenhower wanted to bring the budget within reasonable limits not because the nation could afford to relax in the face of the Soviet threat, but because a strained economy over the long haul would weaken American strength, require government economic controls, and ultimately ruin America's free economy.[3] This "Great Equation" was an idea that Eisenhower never lost sight of, and, throughout his tenure, he placed great importance on a sound economy, strong military, and high public spirit. Finally, he sought to ease Cold War tensions heightened during the previous administration. Feeling that the Truman administration fell short of its potential to defend the homeland, Eisenhower reevaluated national security policy while calling upon the Soviets to take a chance for peace.

An Unlikely Alliance

World War II began on September 1, 1939 when Hitler's army invaded Poland. Bound by a Non-Aggression Pact signed earlier that year, the Soviet Union aided Germany in her conquest of Poland by invading the country from the east. It seemed an improbable marriage, but Nazi Germany and Communist Russia were for a time allies. Hitler, however, wished to conquer all of Europe and invaded the Soviet Union in June 1941 forcing the Soviet Union to join forces with the British. In trying to explain the unlikely alliance between Great Britain and the Soviet Union, Prime Minister Winston Churchill remarked that he had only one goal: the destruction of Hitler. He explained to a friend, "If Hitler invaded hell I would make at least a favorable reference to the Devil in the House of Commons."[4] Speaking to the British people, Churchill, a long-time anti-Bolshevik advocate, promised that "any man or state who fights against Nazidom will have our aid. . . . It follows therefore that we shall give whatever help we can to Russia and the Russian people."[5] The American president, Franklin Roosevelt, felt the same way. Explaining the significance of the fight against Hitler, Roosevelt said in his Arsenal of Democracy fireside chat in December 1940, "Never before, since Jamestown and Plymouth Rock has our American civilization been in such danger as now. . . . If Great Britain goes down, the Axis powers will control the continents of Europe, Asia, Africa, Australia, and the high seas. . . . It is no exaggeration to say that all of us . . . would be living at the point of a gun."[6] With the Soviet Union joining the British in the Allied fight against Hitler, Roosevelt extended over one billion dollars in American aid under the Lend-Lease program to Russia in the autumn of 1941 to ensure its survival. By his audacious gamble, Hitler had converted suspicious ideological rivals into unlikely military allies.

After the Bolshevik Revolution in 1917, President Woodrow Wilson refused to recognize the communist nation. He worked to defeat communism, in Russia and at home, committing U.S. troops to fight in Russia from 1918 to 1920 and authorizing the Attorney General to investigate and deport suspected communists during the Red Scare of 1919. Wilson viewed the new government in Russia as the antithesis to American liberal-capitalism and V. I. Lenin's call for the proletariat to rise up and overthrow its oppressors as dangerous. As historian John Lewis Gaddis explains, "The events of 1917-18 created a *symbolic* basis for conflict between communism and capitalism by setting the self-proclaimed objectives of the United States and Soviet Russia against one another in the most fundamental way."[7] This ideological difference between the two powers did not create immediate conflict, but it did reemerge as a central source of tension during the Cold War.

President Roosevelt was the first American president to recognize the Soviet Union, establishing diplomatic relations with Moscow in 1933.[8] However, charges of Communist influence in the New Deal and rumors of the slave camps, famines, and purges in Russia under Joseph Stalin only reinforced the average American's suspicions of the Soviet Union. In fact, it took a wave of propaganda after the Nazi invasion of Russia to convince Americans to support Stalin. For example, *Mission to Moscow*, written by Ambassador Joseph Davies and produced by Warner Brothers in 1943, excused Stalin's actions and proclaimed that the Soviet regime was based "on the same principle of the 'brotherhood of man' which Jesus preached."[9] And *Time* magazine honored Stalin as its Man of the Year in 1943, featuring him on the cover as a clear-eyed man of determination portrayed as almost God-like, descending from the heavens. Although American perception of Stalin temporarily shifted during the war, Roosevelt still had a challenging time negotiating within the Grand Alliance.

The single shared goal of the Grand Alliance was the defeat of Hitler. From there, agendas differed between the three. Roosevelt believed that the Soviet Union could be manipulated by kind treatment and ironically spent more time fighting with Churchill than with Stalin. He also placed winning the war above all else, putting post-war planning on the back burner.[10] When it came down to working out the details of the post-war world at Yalta in February 1945, it was clear that the Allied forces were going to defeat Hitler soon. Victory in the Pacific was not as certain and Roosevelt came to Yalta seeking Stalin's help in the Pacific war. Stalin finally agreed to help in the Pacific war in return for Manchuria and Mongolia and an occupation zone in northern Korea. The issue of Poland was also resolved at Yalta by redrawing its borders, recognizing the communist Lublin Poles as the legitimate government, and securing Stalin's promise to honor free elections in that nation. Stalin also agreed to guarantee all Eastern European countries the right to choose their governments and leaders in free elections. Although Roosevelt was criticized for "giving away" Poland and the rest of Eastern Europe, the Red Army and Communist partisan forces in Eastern Europe held control of almost all of this territory. Churchill wanted the Allied forces under Eisenhower to continue pushing east to stop the Red Army from acquiring more territory, but Eisenhower ordered General Patton to pull back, letting the Russians liberate Czechoslovakia, eastern Germany, and Berlin. As such, when the war was over, Stalin had retained all the lands he grabbed under the 1939 Nazi-Soviet Non-Aggression Pact, the Polish borders he desired, and much of northern Asia.

Despite the concessions Churchill and Roosevelt made to Stalin at Yalta, Roosevelt believed an American-controlled United Nations and his own personal hand could solve problems related to these issues as they arose. Roosevelt biographer James McGregor Burns explains, "Holding only weak hands in the great poker game of Yalta, Roosevelt believed he had won the foundations of future peace. It was with hope and even exultation that he and his party left Yalta for the long journey home. Above all, he left with confidence that whatever the problems ahead, he could solve them through his personal intervention."[11] It was not that Roosevelt thought he could charm Stalin; it was that Roosevelt believed he could outwit Stalin, as Walter Lippmann observed, but outwit him within the framework of cooperation.[12] Therefore Roosevelt viewed the survival of the Grand Alliance as vital to post-war peace, a view his successor did not hold as dear.

The Haberdasher from Missouri

Despite President Roosevelt's best efforts to ensure longevity of the Grand Alliance after World War II, any chance of cooperation between the United States and the Soviet Union disappeared on April 12, 1945 when Roosevelt died from a massive stroke. Harry S Truman, a former haberdasher from Missouri and the Vice Presidential compromise for the 1944 election, took a different approach towards the Soviet Union after he took office. Taking a harder line towards the Soviets than Roosevelt, and priding himself on being a no-nonsense, telling-it-like-it-is guy, Truman placed a plaque on his desk in the Oval Office which read "The buck stops here!" Immediately after taking office, Truman relied on Roosevelt's advisors, who urged a more forceful approach towards the Soviets but, Truman soon steered American participation in the Grand Alliance away from the conciliatory nature Roosevelt had cultivated. One of the more infamous exchanges between Truman and Soviet Foreign Minister V. M. Molotov illustrates this point. When Truman harshly reprimanded Molotov for Soviet violations of the Yalta agreement in Poland, Molotov complained to Truman that he had "never been talked to like that in my life." Truman, unmoved, responded, "Carry out your agreements and you won't get talked to like that."[13] But despite Truman's outward appearance, he knew that he had a formidable task ahead of him in ending WWII and dealing with the Soviets. "Boys if you ever pray, pray for me now," Truman asked a group of reporters after taking office. "I don't know whether you fellows ever had a load of hay fall on you, but when they told me yesterday what had happened, I felt like the moon, the stars, and all the planets had fallen on me."[14]

Truman knew little about foreign policy in general and Roosevelt's war policies in particular. Roosevelt had made no attempts to include the Vice President in any policy discussions. As Truman wrote in his diary on April 12th, "I knew the President had a great many meetings with Churchill and Stalin. I was not familiar with any of [them.]"[15] Truman certainly did not know about the massive government project to develop an atomic weapon, code-named the Manhattan Project. Following a brief Cabinet meeting after the swearing in, Secretary of War Henry Stimson stayed behind to tell Truman little more than that the project existed. It was not until another meeting between the two men on April 25th that Truman was given the details. Truman agreed to continue the policy decisions set in motion by Roosevelt and authorized the use of the bombs used on Japan in August 1945, bringing the world into the atomic age.[16]

Truman certainly hoped that American atomic superiority kept the Soviets in their place and hoped that the bomb might convince Stalin to be more cooperative. However, although Truman saw atomic weapons as a kind of diplomatic tool, he did not intend to place them in the same category as conventional weapons and actually use them liberally. As he stated publicly in 1953 "atomic weapons [were] in a moral category separate from so-called conventional weapons and perhaps separate from biological and chemical methods of warfare."[17] He believed atomic weapons murdered civilian populations "by wholesale," and he understood the gravity of a decision to use atomic weapons.[18] However, Truman did not dismiss entirely the use of atomic weapons and conceded that there were certain circumstances in which the use of atomic weapons might be authorized. He never specifically outlined what those certain circumstances might be, leaving it purposely vague.

Historian S. David Broscious explains this apparent paradox by looking towards Truman's early interest in international controls over atomic energy. Truman hoped that an international agency might eliminate the threat of atomic war while promoting peace. Yet, as the Cold War progressed and international cooperation over atomic energy seemed impossible, Truman was willing to use atomic weapons to ensure world freedom and democracy in the face of Soviet aggression. Truman primarily relied on the deterrent value of American atomic superiority, banking on Soviet unwillingness to risk war with an atomically superior United States. Once the Soviets successfully tested an atomic bomb of their own in August 1949, Truman's fundamental beliefs dictated that development of the hydrogen bomb begin in order to ensure the deterrent value of nuclear weapons.[19] "As you know," explained Truman at a Blair House meeting, "we have made every effort to obtain international control of atomic energy. We have failed to get that control—due to the stubbornness and inferiority contrariness of the Soviets. I am of the opinion we'll never obtain international control. Since we can't obtain international control, we must be strongest in atomic weapons."[20]

Truman's legacy, therefore, was in part to immerse American national security policy into a continuous arms race with the Soviet Union.

Truman was not wrong to think a meaningful international control agency was futile. According to Russian historian Vladislav Zubok, Stalin never trusted America's good intentions to establish international control over atomic weapons. Suspicious of America, Stalin also believed that Truman was practicing atomic diplomacy right from the beginning with Hiroshima, trying to blackmail the Soviet Union. This was particularly evident, in Stalin's mind, with the Bikini tests in July 1946 when American officials decided to invite Soviet observers to the atomic tests at the Bikini atoll. The Kremlin viewed the invitation as "another attempt at atomic intimidation of the USSR, and," according to Zubok, "the veterans of the Soviet atomic project believe this even today."[21]

Rather than deter Stalin, America's atomic monopoly energized the Soviet atomic program that began in earnest after WWII. Unable to afford committing resources to an atomic program during the war and strapped with devastating losses after the war, the decision to commit tremendous resources to an atomic program was not one that Stalin made quickly. It was not until the Americans became an atomic power that the costs and risks seemed worthwhile to Stalin.[22] Once the atomic program began however, Stalin defined it as a "patriotic deed," and elevated the role of science and scientists in the Soviet Union to the high stature that the scientific community enjoyed for decades.[23] It was this elevation of science in Soviet society that captured the attention of many Americans in the fall of 1957 after the Soviets beat the Americans to space with the launching of *Sputnik I*.

Regardless of whether the Soviets had or did not have the atomic bomb, Stalin was not eager to immediately engage in a war with the United States. Stalin firmly believed that war would occur eventually. The peace after WWII was only a respite for the Soviet Union to gain strength before the next war. Atomic weapons did not deter Stalin. It may have made the prospect of this future war horrifying, but atomic weapons did not negate the chances of a future war. Since it was inevitable that the peace was only an interim between wars, Stalin's security policy was based on preparedness for war at all times.[24] Stalin's security strategy was also based on post-war plans drawn up in January 1944 by Ivan Maisky, commissioned to look at post-war reparations. He wrote that the Soviets' specific goal was to create a post-war world that assured Soviet security in Europe and Asia "for a durable term" so that the Soviet Union might "become so powerful that it would not have to worry about any hostile strategy in Europe and Asia," and so that Europe might "become socialist, thereby excluding the very possibility of generating war in this part of the world."[25] Maisky's report reflected the primary goal of Stalin for dominance in Eurasia. Maneuvering through the end of the war in ways to achieve this dominance, the Soviet Union appeared ready to carry out Maisky's recommendations. This was not lost on one American serving in Moscow.

Defining Containment I: Kennan

After studying at Princeton, George Kennan chose a career in the Foreign Service. His fluency in the Russian language and knowledge of Russian literature, culture, and history, coupled with his previous Foreign Service assignments in Eastern Europe, made his assignment as counselor to the American embassy in Moscow nearly inevitable. While serving in Russia, Kennan developed a loathing for Bolsheviks, Marxism, and Communism. Fearing the susceptibility of Europe to communism if Germany did not remain strong, Kennan opposed the Allied strategy of Nazi Germany's unconditional surrender. Kennan believed that Germany was the key to a balance of power in Europe that checked the expansion of communism, so he saw the destruction of Germany as an opening for Soviet expansion. By the summer of 1944, after the Allies had opened up a second front and were racing the Soviets towards Berlin, Kennan expressed this concern when he said that the "jealous eye of the Kremlin can distinguish, in the end, only vassals and enemies; and the neighbors of Russia, if they do not wish to be one, must reconcile themselves to being the other."[26] To Kennan, the Soviets desired a sphere of influence, and, without Germany to challenge them, they would proceed to realize that goal. In fact, Soviet plans for the postwar, which had been developed during WWII agreed with Kennan's analysis. The Soviets saw no threat to their power in Europe or Asia. The United States was not a threat either, as it was assumed America would retreat back into its traditional isolationist policy.[27] Kennan continued to emphasize the need for a strong Europe, particularly a strong Germany, in the post-war years.

Needing to reevaluate its own policy, the State Department requested that Kennan submit an evaluation of recent Soviet policy. On February 22, 1946 Kennan sent an 18-page, 8,000-word "Long Telegram" to the State Department. Its timing was perfect. As Kennan himself said, had it been sent six months earlier, it would have received "raised eyebrows and lips pursed in disapproval. Six months later, it would probably have sounded redundant."[28] What it sounded like to Truman, according to Gaddis, was "precisely the intellectual justification needed for [a] reorientation of policy" in light of recent events.[29] Communist-led regimes had taken hold by early 1946 across Eastern Europe despite Stalin's promise at Yalta to hold free elections. The Soviets also seemed to be probing in Greece, Turkey, Iran, China, and Korea. In addition to Soviet expansion, Stalin proclaimed on February 9, 1946 that cooperation between the West and the Soviet Union was impossible; a week later, twenty-two Soviet spies involved with the Manhattan Project were arrested in Canada. Truman responded to these events by confiding to Admiral Leahy on February 20 that he was unhappy with the existing policy of appeasing the Russians and was determined to assume a stronger position at once.[30] Furthermore, Senator Arthur Vandenberg and Secretary of State James Byrnes indicated the need for a more aggressive foreign policy the following week. Even Winston Churchill expressed grave concern over current policy, warning a group of Americans in a March 5 speech of an "iron curtain" descending upon Eastern Europe. By mid March, most Americans did not trust the Communists and believed U.S. policy towards Russia was "too soft."[31] Kennan's policy of containment was the tougher policy the State Department needed.

"At [the] bottom of Kremlin's neurotic view of world affairs," Kennan wrote, "is traditional and instinctive Russian sense of insecurity. . . . And [Russian leaders] have learned to seek security only in patient but deadly struggle for total destruction of rival power, never in compacts and compromises with it."[32] In addition to Soviet paranoia, Kennan explained that negotiation with the Soviets was impossible because Stalin exploited capitalistic themes to justify his oppression at home. A truce with the West would undermine his totalitarian rule. The Soviets also sought to expand wherever they found weakness. If, for example, a Persian government became "friendly" towards the Soviet Union, Moscow might ask for a Russian port on the Persian Gulf. Colonial areas were also susceptible to Communist schemes of weakening the colonial power to create "a vacuum which will favor communist-Soviet penetration."[33]

Despite the gloomy outlook, Kennan assured the American policymakers the Soviet Union was inherently weak and could be checked with American mobilization. The Soviets would back down in the face of force. Yet although the Soviets were not looking for a military confrontation with the West immediately, they did seek to undermine Western power covertly, through efforts to "disrupt national self-confidence, to hamstring national defense, to increase social and industrial unrest, [and] to stimulate all forms of disunity."[34] Certainly the Soviets, Kennan wrote, sought to disrupt the United States in that way and concluded there could be no permanent *modus vivendi* with the Soviets. They worked without fixed plans, took no unnecessary risks, and were impervious to logic of reason. They were, however, "highly sensitive to logic of force."[35] If the West were to confront the Soviets with "strong resistance" at any point, Kennan believed the Soviets would back down because they were still the weaker force. Furthermore, they could be contained through economic and political initiatives that undermined Soviet propaganda. Since the Soviets were weak and did not seek immediate confrontation with the United States, Kennan concluded the Soviets were not a direct military threat to American security. It was important, therefore, not to overspend on a military build-up that would jeopardize the "health and vigor of our own society." Much depended, said Kennan, on our "courageous and incisive measure to solve internal problems of our own society, to improve self-confidence, discipline, moral and community spirit." To achieve this at home would be "a diplomatic victory over Moscow worth a thousand diplomatic notes and joint communiqués."[36]

Kennan's telegram was widely read and praised throughout the national security policy circles. Its conclusions that Russia could not be negotiated with were startling and flew in the face of American policy to organize the postwar world in their vision established in the various wartime conferences.[37] Yet, while it was startling, Kennan's policy was appealing because it explained the actions of Stalin while placing the blame for the Cold War squarely on the Soviet Union. Kennan's analysis "provided a unifying theme to U.S. foreign policy."[38] The theme identified the Kremlin as the enemy with whom negotiations could not be made; therefore, this enemy had to be contained.

Truman made containment an official policy through his Truman Doctrine. After the British announced their inability to continue supporting Greece and Turkey, two countries that faced Communist pressure, Truman took heed and addressed Congress on March 12, 1947. Truman divided the world into two ways of life. One way was "based upon the will of the majority" and guaranteed freedoms; the other way was based "upon the will of a minority forcibly imposed upon the majority," relying on terror and oppression.[39] He told his audience that it was up to the United States to support those people who were free but fighting against the pressures of the second way of life, like those in Greece and Turkey. One "only had to glance at a map," Truman explained, to see the strategic importance of those countries to the stability of the Middle East. He suggested that the United States send economic aid and civilian and military personnel to ward off the Communist advances and secure freedom in Greece and Turkey. To fail in this leadership role, Truman warned, would "endanger the peace of the world" and "the welfare of this Nation."[40] The Truman Doctrine was a success in that it mobilized Americans in general and Congress in particular to support a policy of economic and material aid to contain Soviet aggression on a global scale. In the same spirit of containment through economic aid, the Marshall Plan was implemented in 1948, aiding Western European recovery so that it would be less vulnerable to Communist overtures.

The Truman Doctrine and the Marshall Plan both reflected the essence of Kennan's definition of containment, a policy based not on militarization, but on psychological, economic, and diplomatic strategies. Kennan's policy was intended to instill a sense of self-confidence in countries threatened by the Soviets and to instill that same self-confidence in the United States. It was also based on what Gaddis called "the ability of national leaders to make and maintain rational distinctions between vital and peripheral interests, adversary capabilities and intentions, negotiations and appeasement, flexibility and direction."[41] For the most part, Truman exhibited that rational ability to balance economic solvency at home with the needs of national security.[42] However, as world events quickly deteriorated in 1949, pressure to change containment from a political policy into a military policy increased from within the State Department. American policy was about to take an even more aggressive turn.

Defining Containment II: Nitze

On January 31, 1950, Truman directed the secretaries of State and Defense "to undertake a reexamination of our objectives in peace and war and of the effect of these objectives on our strategic plans, in light of the probable fission bomb capability and possible thermonuclear bomb capability of the Soviet Union."[43] Masterminded by Paul Nitze, a trained economist and young blood in the State Department, the resulting NSC-68 was a departure from Kennan's conception of containment.[44] Written to shock the Truman administration into dismantling the $13.5 billion defense-spending ceiling and to militarize Kennan's policy of containment, Nitze's NSC-68 succeeded with a little help from his friends and the Soviets.

By late 1949, Truman faced severe pressure from more militant-minded officials to increase defense spending. Cautious about overspending on defense at the expense of domestic programs, Truman fought over the budget each year.[45] However, events in 1949 strengthened the arguments for increased military spending. The Communist victory in China and the Soviet detonation of an atomic bomb indicated to many that the Americans were losing ground in the Cold War. Senator Stuart Symington, for example, warned that the Soviets' atomic capability threatened "the survival of the United States" and Secretary of State Dean Acheson complained, "During the last six to nine months there had been a trend against us which, if allowed to continue, would lead to a considerable deterioration in our position."[46]

Acheson was at odds with Truman over the direction American policy should take. Acheson argued that an even tougher line had to be taken against the Soviets, which included increased military preparation. By the end of 1949 Kennan, who was head of the State Department's Policy Planning Staff, disagreed strongly with Acheson's policy of strength over diplomacy. Acheson accused Kennan of having lost his appetite for standing up to the Soviets.[47] Frustrated, Kennan decided to resign from the Policy Planning Staff. In his final memo to Acheson, he reiterated that containment could be successful as a political policy and pleaded not to alter containment into a military policy.[48] Acheson ignored Kennan's pleas and replaced him with Paul Nitze, a man who passionately shared Acheson's views. Acheson called Nitze "a joy to work with because of his clear, incisive mind," and the two were in sync as soon as Nitze entered the State Department.[49]

Nitze was deeply suspicious of the Soviet Union, despite the fact he had never been to the Soviet Union, nor had he any formal training in Soviet affairs like his predecessor. He had worked in Washington since 1940 and observed the destruction resulting from the atomic age first-hand, examining the rubble of Hiroshima and Nagasaki as a member of the U.S. Strategic Bombing team surveying A-bomb damage.[50] Impressively, having only been involved in national security matters since early 1949, Nitze was considered one of the leading military specialists in the State Department. Yet he deeply believed that the Soviets would stop at nothing to achieve world domination. Stalin was simply another Hitler. In his own words, Nitze believed the chance of war with the Soviets was great and that "the antipathy of slavery to freedom explains the iron curtain, the isolation, the autarchy of the society whose end is absolute power."[51] It did not matter to Nitze that the CIA concluded that predicting Soviet intentions with certainty was impossible or that Soviet experts George Kennan and Charles Bohlen believed the Soviets were not seeking immediate war with the West.[52] For Nitze, and Acheson, the need to gain the upper hand again against the Soviets was never greater. In February alone, Alger Hiss and Klaus Fuchs had been accused of being Soviet spies; Mao Tse-tung, the communist leader of China, had signed a treaty with the Soviets; and Republican Senator Joseph McCarthy accused the State Department of being riddled with communists. Acheson and Nitze were keenly aware that a change in policy was needed and they were ready to put pressure on Truman.

The drafting of what became NSC-68 was a long, tedious process, and something Acheson called "a difficult pregnancy" in his memoirs.[53] Headed by Nitze, the small committee organized to review basic national security consisted of like-minded people who rejected the defense-spending ceilings placed by Truman.[54] Drafts of the paper emphasized the views Nitze held of the Soviet Union as aggressive, oppressive and determined to achieve world domination. Whereas Kennan had stressed that military preparedness had to be only sufficient enough to check the Communists at the key industrial centers to maintain the balance of power, Nitze argued that American preparedness levels had to be high enough to check the Communists at all points along the perimeter. In other words, Kennan saw containment only applying to the five industrial regions of the world—the United States, Great Britain, the Rhine valley, the Soviet Union, and Japan. Nitze enlarged that geographical limitation to include any region that faced Communist threats. Nitze also warned that the Soviets had not sought war with the West because they had no assurances of winning. Nitze estimated that by mid-1954, what he labeled the date of maximum danger, a Soviet arsenal of at least 200 atomic bombs would exist, enough to devastate the United States. Adding to the danger was the stark fact the Soviets were devoting a greater percentage of their economy to defense spending. Whereas the United States spent 6.5 percent of its Gross National Product (GNP) on the military, the Soviet Union was spending 13.8 percent of its GNP. And where the United States spent 13.6 percent of its GNP on defense-related investments, the Soviets allocated 25.4 percent for the same purpose. The American economy was capable of spending more, insisted Nitze. By taking a page from World War II, Nitze reminded his audience that when operated at levels of full efficiency, the American economy "can provide enormous resources for purposes other than civilian consumption."[55] If the people were educated about the threat the Soviets posed to their freedom and democracy they would embrace any sacrifices necessary. Finally,

NSC-68 advocated the need for greater atomic capabilities and a stronger conventional force to counter the current inadequacies of the military. Instead of demobilizing, the nation had to break tradition and maintain a powerful armed force despite the lack of a hot war. In short, the message of Nitze's paper was one of panic and buildup. Kennan had stressed patience and emphasized the American upper hand; Nitze stressed action and a time of maximum danger. While Acheson mostly approved of the paper, drafts were circulated for comment.

Dr. Robert Oppenheimer, director of the Manhattan Project and Chairman of the General Advisory Committee of the United States Atomic Energy Commission, was the first outside consultant asked to review a draft of NSC-68. Oppenheimer had mixed reviews. He was sympathetic to the dangers of the Cold War but critical of both the role atomic weapons played and the portrayal of the Soviet-American conflict as black and white. Oppenheimer asked if the paper might "present a recognizable picture to the average citizen of the Soviet Union," so that the comparison was not "one between jet black and pure white."[56] Nitze did not think that was the impression given, but over the years Nitze would hear that criticism again and again.

Dr. James Conant, President of Harvard University and also a member of the General Advisory Committee, was the next outside consultant to review the paper. Conant was more critical than Oppenheimer of many sections. In sentiments similar to those that Eisenhower expressed as President, Conant wondered if the consequences of winning World War III might be the loss of American freedom. He suggested that a reevaluation of the risks of defending Europe be made, as well as the risks of a policy of "restoring freedom" to the peoples of Eastern Europe and the Soviet Union itself. Conant believed that rather than a policy of rollback, the United States ought to try to live "with the Soviet Union on tolerable terms," while avoiding war.[57] Oppenheimer and Conant were the only two outside consultants who had criticism of the drafts; but, it is as notable to identify who the review group ignored. Neither George Kennan nor Charles Bohlen, America's two leading experts on the Soviet Union, were asked their opinion, and the two certainly had opinions.[58]

Kennan and Bohlen were both familiar with what Nitze was writing. In fact, George Kennan admitted that one of the reasons he left the Policy Planning Staff at the end of 1949 was his disagreement with Paul Nitze and the assumptions of NSC-68.[59] Bohlen thought Nitze's assessments of Soviet intentions were way off the mark, and he argued that the internal situation in the Soviet Union was the single most important factor in Soviet foreign policy and NSC-68 ignored that reality.[60] The policy also seemed to reject Kennan's assertion that the Soviet Union was a cautious power that was not actively seeking confrontation with the United States. But Bohlen and Kennan's views went unheeded and the final draft was presented to Truman on April 7, 1950.

President Truman was initially skeptical of the report, and, since the House was currently in the middle of tearing up Truman's "skimpy" defense budget for FY51, he asked a subcommittee of the NSC to review the report from a budgetary point of view. Truman was not alone as concerns rang through the State Department that NSC-68 required a "full time mobilization of the economy," and "a gigantic armament race."[61] The subcommittee moved slowly against its enormous task of estimating the cost of implementation of the report, and Truman was in no rush. Still at an impasse, Nitze and Acheson finally saw NSC-68 implemented with the Soviet-backed North Korean invasion of South Korea on June 25, 1950. The aggressive nature of the Soviet threat seemed to be proved. It was the kind of event that proved that the authors of NSC-68 were correct in their assessment that the United States needed a new defense policy, and Truman finally approved their report in September. The final version of NSC-68 downplayed much of the cold war rhetoric that had dominated earlier drafts and instead concentrated on the question of how much money would be appropriated to what programs. Nitze did not see all of his recommendations approved, but spending did increase for civil defense, psychological warfare, accumulation of atomic weapons, assistance to NATO countries, and military personnel.[62]

Nitze and Acheson had succeeded in writing a shocking report in order to implement their vision of American defense. With the Korean War raging on for the remainder of his term, Truman was unable to keep military spending in check. By the 1952 election, the American people were immersed in a Cold War defending the American way of life against the dangers of Communism and spending whatever it cost. It seemed that defeating the Soviets superseded more traditional concerns over inflation, deficits, and government controls. In this transformation, a coherent policy got lost. Truman was successful in waging the Cold War between 1946 and 1950 following Kennan's policy through the Truman Doctrine, the Marshall Plan, the Berlin airlift, the creation of NATO, and the reconstruction of Germany and Japan.[63] By 1950, after the Korean War broke out and NSC-68 took hold, Truman's policy became confused and less coherent.[64] It became impossible to balance the objectives of NSC-68 with budgetary realities. Europe was secure, but NSC-68 had expanded American commitment globally and places like Iran, Indochina, Guatemala, and Egypt looked vulnerable. Eisenhower, an active participant in the fight against the Soviets during the Truman administration, saw the positive legacy of containment and wished to extract that from the muddled confusion that plagued the last year of the Truman administration.[65] It was up to Eisenhower to create a coherent strategy that maintained the peace and American economic security at the same time. In short, Eisenhower had to redirect strategy so that it would be sustainable for the long haul—so that national defense did not jeopardize the "health and vigor" of American society that Kennan spoke of in 1946.[66]

Planning for the "Long Haul"

Long before Eisenhower entered office, he held major reservations about the Truman defense policy, fearing that the high costs placed an unbearable burden on the nation's fiscal health. Eisenhower wrote after the election that a defense policy must be sustainable over the long haul, something he did not see Truman's policy achieving.[67] Eisenhower believed that the costs of a defense policy had to be weighed against the strain it would put on the economy. High deficits stifled growth and caused inflation. Not naive to the dangers the Soviet Union represented, Eisenhower nevertheless wanted to achieve a balance between a strong military able to meet the Soviet threat and a sound economy.[68] His 'Great Equation' required as much.

Eisenhower inherited a situation that made that balance difficult. Truman's 1952 budget saw a $4 billion deficit, and the estimates for Fiscal Year (FY) 53 and FY54 projected deficits of $5.9 billion and $9.9 billion respectively. It was projected that an estimated $81 billion of authorizations to spend government funds had to be raised from future revenues, and most of the programs had already been started and could not be easily readjusted. In addition, tax revenue estimates by the Truman administration appeared high and tax revenue was expected to fall by about $2.1 billion in FY54 and $5.9 billion in FY55. In short, without any reductions in expenditures by the Eisenhower administration, deficits over the next four years could be as high as $37 billion, making any tax reductions impossible.[69] Deficits that high were unacceptable to Eisenhower and he sought to reduce the deficit problem immediately.

Eisenhower believed he could achieve this in part through defense cuts that targeted waste and duplication. In talking to his speechwriters during the campaign, Eisenhower told them, "I know better than any of you fellows about waste in the Pentagon and about how much fat there is to be cut."[70] Cutting fat was a key part of his presidency. For example, while campaigning, he promised to turn in the Presidential yacht, Williamsburg, which he thought was an unnecessary luxury. He explained to a friend a few months after the election, that "the very word 'yacht' created a symbol of luxury in the public mind that would tend to defeat some of the purposes I was trying to accomplish."[71] The Navy did not wish to relinquish any possessions but, despite its protest, the Williamsburg was decommissioned shortly after he assumed office.[72] For the same reason of committing to "an Administration of economy," Eisenhower gave up the Presidential quarters in Key West and "kept only the little camp in the Catoctins," renaming it from "Shangri-La" to "Camp David," because the former name was "just a little fancy for a Kansas farm boy."[73] Giving up a yacht and presidential retreat was a start, but the real lard was in the Defense budget. However, before slashing defense, Eisenhower needed to establish the framework on which to build what he promised in the campaign: a Cold War strategy that was "unified and coherent."[74]

President-elect Eisenhower went to task immediately after the election. On his return trip from Korea in December, Eisenhower had his close advisors meet with him aboard the *USS Helena* to discuss the budget, his first State of the Union address, and national defense. John Foster Dulles, Eisenhower's nominee to be Secretary of State, led the discussion on national defense, assessing the Soviet threat as one which would "extend our resources and our patience and divide us internally by mounting a series of local actions around the world at times and places of their choosing."[75] Foreshadowing his Massive Retaliation doctrine, Dulles believed that the appropriate response was for the U.S. to "seize the initiative" and "beat him [the Soviets] at his own game."[76] Whether Eisenhower was ready to accept the risks involved with such action was not the issue at this series of meetings. Rather, Eisenhower immensely enjoyed the dialogue and debate that the *Helena* trip inspired among his advisors. Remarking that he had the "most satisfactory conference of his life" on board the *Helena*, Eisenhower revealed that the meetings went as he had planned.[77] Eisenhower designed the trip to introduce his staff to each other so that they might feel comfortable in free exchanges and debates and learn to work as a team. Historians Bowie and Immerman put it succinctly: "only if he [Eisenhower] was exposed to vigorously articulated competing diagnoses and prescriptions, and only if he received candid information and advice, could he make the sound and informed decisions on which a consistent and coherent national strategy depended."[78] Eisenhower also saw the *Helena* retreat as a way for his advisors to understand fully and back the decisions being made so that he could "efficiently mobilize and orchestrate the resources necessary to implement the decisions over an extended period of time."[79] The *Helena* trip allowed Eisenhower to set the stage for a reevaluation of national security policy with the enthusiastic support of his staff.

Upon his return, Eisenhower drafted a memorandum for discussion with the Senate leaders on December 30 in which he expressed the administration's first objective to be a balanced budget. To cut waste, reorganizing the Defense Department also had to be a priority. Running the Pentagon like a business, to avoid costly duplications and to achieve maximum efficiency, made sense to Eisenhower and certainly explains his appointment of Charles Wilson, president of General Motors, to Secretary of Defense.[80] However, reorganization alone would not produce the defense cuts that Eisenhower desired. A major revision in strategy was also needed. As Defense Secretary Wilson stated in a February 24, 1953 meeting of the NSC, either a major overhaul in the "basic objectives" of the nation's national security policy or a slower implementation of the Truman budget was needed as there was "no possibility" for the $5 billion cut that Secretary of the Treasury George Humphrey insisted had to be made in order to balance the budget. Eisenhower replied to the secretary's remarks that talking in generalities was irrelevant as "the decisions could be made only when the Council had the facts before it and could see precisely what was involved."[81] The next day the

NSC met again and Robert Cutler, Special Assistant to the President for National Security Affairs, explained in his review of basic national security policy "if major reductions in the budget were to be made they would have to be made in the large programs of the Department of Defense and the Mutual Security Administration." The President agreed, but wanted a further breakdown on where duplication occurred and whether there were avoidable costs. He was clearly disturbed by the inability of the Bureau of the Budget and the Pentagon to reach similar projections in the budget. Without cooperation between the two offices, Eisenhower complained, the NSC would be paralyzed. He insisted "his Administration had got to get the right answer on these problems."[82] He was not about to slash the budget or military preparedness arbitrarily, putting American national security at risk. To get the answers, Eisenhower proposed to bring together a panel of experts of "distinguished Americans" to review basic national security policies and report their findings to the NSC.[83]

The Council agreed to establish a seven-man ad hoc committee of civilian consultants to the National Security Council to "study and advise the Council on basic national security policies and programs in relation to their costs." Establishing this sort of committee was something Eisenhower had promised to do during his campaign. In a September 1952 speech, Eisenhower proposed "at the earliest possible date next year . . . [the creation of] a commission of the most capable civilians in our land to restudy the operations of our Department of Defense" in regards to the "most economical way to fill the demonstrated needs of the nation."[84] After being in office for only one month, Eisenhower had his committee.

Chairing the group was a Texas Democrat and attorney, Dillon Anderson. Anderson could hardly refuse to serve when Eisenhower told him that the committee, which was "being sought on a matter of national urgency," would "be of great help to me and to the Council in dealing with a very serious and basic national issue."[85] Choosing Anderson to chair the group allowed Eisenhower to point to the group as a bipartisan committee, proving the President's willingness to hear all sides. The other members represented a broad range of professionals and academics, creating a diverse, well-respected group. Business, finance, education, science, and even labor were all represented.[86]

Senator Joseph McCarthy, who was in his third year of hunting for suspected communists in the government, seized upon a *Washington Post* report announcing the establishment of this advisory council in March. The paper reported that a "group of business, labor, and educational leaders" had been named as consultants to the NSC to "provide more civilian direction of the nation's defense program to end stop and start military planning."[87] It went on to say that the group was to be briefed by "key government agencies" including the CIA and was likely to have "intimate association with the Administration's deepest cold war secrets."[88] As the list of consultants was printed in the article, it did not take Senator Joseph McCarthy long to investigate the names. Contacting the

White House, an anonymous caller from McCarthy's office expressed grave concerns over the participation of David B. Robertson on this civilian advisory board since Robertson was "unfit to have access to such security information, owing to personal weaknesses."[89] After Cutler briefed the NSC on the phone call, Eisenhower told Cutler that what advice was solicited from consultants was the President's business alone. Eisenhower warned, "If Senator McCarthy proposed to take on the National Security Council, he was taking on the President."[90] McCarthy was notified of the President's position by phone, and, with the matter closed, Robertson remained a member.

The group assembled on March 1 and Cutler explained that the task before them was not so much determining the strengths or weaknesses of the Soviet military threat, but rather "a judgment as to American capabilities and desires as a people."[91] The consultants then met for three weeks with various heads of departments and carefully examined the nation's defense posture. When Cutler called the group back to the NSC on March 31 to give its final report, the committee had concluded that the United States had "bitten off more than we can chew."[92] Anderson, speaking for the consultants, confirmed what Eisenhower believed, that there was much duplication among the three services and that excess spending would continue until there was a clarification of the role and the mission of the three Services. In addition, the consultants believed that "the grave fiscal situation" was in part due to the very general basic security objectives and that national security policy "ought to be re-examined with the greatest care." Specifically, the consultants criticized the "profligate" use of military manpower, recommended the government be more selective in research and development projects, place scientific programs of the Department of Defense under an Assistant Secretary, and reduce American commitments to "shore up the whole non-Soviet world." Scaling down the Mutual Security budget was a must for Anderson as was assisting other countries based on "concrete defense implications and results," since it was "impossible to purchase the loyalty and friendship of other nations." In short, an immediate reappraisal of American commitments had to be made.[93]

Eisenhower agreed with the consultants as to the dangers a high defense budget posed to the economy, but he was hesitant just to slash funding for developing policies and programs. Rather, Eisenhower suggested, the Administration needed to make a move towards balancing the budget over time instead of making drastic cuts to balance it now.[94] Eisenhower's unwillingness to look only at the financial side of the problem was reflective of his deep belief in the 'Great Equation,' which said that military force could not be sacrificed for a balanced budget, or vice versa. Each side had to be brought into balance or overall security would be lost. Debate continued throughout the meeting as to the fine points of how to achieve the balanced budget. The end result was NSC 149/2, "Basic National Security Policies and Programs in Relation to Their Costs."

Drafted by the Policy Planning Board three days after the meeting with the civilian consultants, NSC 149 reflected the Civilian Consultants' concern for a balanced budget, but rejected their recommendations for drastic military cuts. The NSC report began by stating, "The survival of the free world depends on the maintenance by the United States of a sound, strong, economy. For the United States to continue a course of Federal spending in excess of Federal income will weaken and eventually destroy that economy."[95] In response to Eisenhower's concerns about the timing of balancing the budget without drastically cutting vital programs, it went on to say, "As rapidly as is consistent with continuing our leadership in the free world, and barring an emergency, the United States will annually balance its Federal expenditures with its Federal income."[96] So although Eisenhower had help from outside experts in stressing the necessity for a strong economy, he still prudently maintained a strong military against external threats.

By allowing a diverse group, which included Democrats, to participate as civilian consultants, Eisenhower included them in the decision-making process. If he accepted their conclusions, they were directly involved in the final decision. If he rejected their conclusions, he could say he had had an open mind to all sides, but ultimately found their argument unpersuasive. Eisenhower was able, even if he had already made a decision, to use the process to paint a picture of an open-minded leader who wanted to build a team consensus through educated debates within the NSC. So even though Eisenhower had a clear vision of how he wished to run the country, his decision-making process allowed him to operate not as a dictator or closed-minded military officer, but as the team captain and democratic leader he had the reputation for being. Civilian advisors complimented this process well.

With the approval of NSC 149/2 on April 29, 1953, Eisenhower believed that he had a policy covering both the external threat of the Soviet Union and the internal threat of overspending—a side of the equation he thought Truman's policies had not considered.[97] As C.D. Jackson said, the meeting's conclusions reflected "not . . . retrenchment or cuts, but [a] competent, positive, efficient, forward-moving program."[98] It reflected the ideas behind the Great Equation. There were more budget cuts and more reviews of national security policy to be made, but with NSC 149/2, Eisenhower had a framework to maintain the nation's military and economic strength while planning for the long haul.

The Chance for Peace

Coinciding with the new policy planning that was going on, Eisenhower's team had a remarkable opportunity for a new chance for peace upon the death of Soviet dictator Joseph Stalin on March 5, 1953. Stalin's death immediately prompted Eisenhower to reevaluate the U.S. position towards the Soviet Union. In a Cabinet meeting the next day, Eisenhower commented that it was striking what had not been done in preparation for Stalin's death by the Truman administration. Although there had been talk about what to do if Stalin died since 1946, the president remarked the "net result of 7 years is zero. There is no plan, there is no agreed upon position."[99] Eisenhower decided to bring in C.D. Jackson, his special assistant for psychological warfare, to write a speech that Eisenhower aimed towards the Soviets.[100]

Jackson went right to work, seeing it as a great opportunity to create discord inside the Soviet Union while rallying the peoples of Eastern Europe around an American "vision." This was another opportunity to implement containment in the way Kennan had envisioned, via psychological warfare, not military build-up. However, the speech, which Jackson wrote with MIT professor Walt W. Rostow, mentioned a reconvening of the Council of American, Soviet, British, and French Ministers who had not met since 1949. The speech proposed that at such a meeting, the Americans would be willing to discuss measures to end the Korean War, unify Germany, end the Austrian occupation, and control arms.[101] Eisenhower and Dulles had major reservations towards these overtures. An aggressive initiative before the corpse was even cold, Dulles feared, would only serve to unite the Soviets. And calling for a Council meeting without first settling on a negotiating posture with our allies would certainly result in disaster. Eisenhower agreed with Dulles, but was still drawn to Jackson's assertion that Stalin's death was a great opportunity to do something dramatic.[102] After all, the obvious way to reduce defense spending was to reduce the tensions of the Cold War. Eisenhower suggested that the speech be rewritten to reflect "the simple theme of a higher living standard for all the world," a theme Eisenhower hoped would have "universal desire," and which reflected part of his 'Great Equation.'[103] But neither Jackson nor Rostow produced a speech that satisfied Eisenhower.

To complicate matters, Georgi Malenkov, the newly appointed chairman of the Soviet Council of Ministers, used his eulogy at Stalin's funeral as a stump for his own peaceful overture on March 15. In essence, Malenkov beat Eisenhower to the punch, delivering a speech calling for the two superpowers to reach a détente. He proclaimed that the two countries' disputes should "be decided by peaceful means, on the basis of mutual understanding."[104] Eisenhower, upset that he had not given his speech before Malenkov, realized a speech focusing on a higher standard of living was no longer appropriate.[105] He had to deliver more substance.

Eisenhower turned over the task to his speechwriter Emmet Hughes. Hughes recalled the meeting with a passionate Eisenhower in late March. Eisenhower explained to Hughes that he wanted to tell the people of the world that money and resources ought to be spent on butter, not guns. "The jet plane that roars over your head," he said to Hughes, "costs three-quarters of a million dollars. That is more money than a man . . . is going to make in his lifetime. What world can afford this sort of thing for long? We are in an armaments race. Where will it lead us? At worst, to atomic warfare. At best, to robbing every people and nation on earth of the fruits of their own toil."[106] Eisenhower wanted Hughes to write a speech that assumed Malenkov was a reasonable man with whom the U.S. had serious differences to iron out. It seemed to Eisenhower that, although there "was no ground to anticipate a basic change in Soviet policy toward the Western powers," there was ground to hope that the new Soviet leaders were realizing that a larger share of their nation's resources had to be distributed to the people, raising standards of living and squelching internal discontent. Some kind of *modus vivendi* might be possible.[107] Hughes went to work with the assistance of Paul Nitze from the State Department's Policy Planning Staff, whom Dulles—not persuaded by Eisenhower's point of view—appointed to the task.[108]

Immediately the two ran into obstacles as Nitze, speaking for the PPS, objected to nearly every section of the speech drafted by Hughes. As Nitze complained to Dulles about the lack of progress being made, Dulles became convinced that no speech could be given that would serve U.S. interests and he had objections with every draft.[109] Eisenhower was furious with the State Department's unwillingness to seize this great opportunity for what it was: to test the new Soviet government's intentions. At one point Eisenhower exploded in frustration, "I don't know what I've got State Department advisors for."[110] Aware that the substance of the speech would be continuously debated, Eisenhower decided to oversee the writing of the final draft himself. He rejected Dulles' objections and wrote a speech that was moderate and sincere. A few days prior to delivering the speech before the American Society of Newspaper Editors on April 16, Eisenhower entitled the speech "The Chance for Peace."

Eisenhower recorded later that the proposals he set forth in the speech "were deliberately specific . . . I felt it wise to put the nation's deepest aspirations in the record, where they could be examined and studied by all the world, including the Russians."[111] Examined they were. The speech was translated into 45 languages and broadcast throughout the free world. Even *Pravda* gave the speech a six-column article on the front page and included a complete and accurate translation of the speech.[112] In the speech, Eisenhower called for the Soviets to back their peace offering with specific deeds such as releasing POWs held since 1945, concluding the Austrian treaty and reunifying Germany, instituting "an honorable armistice" in Korea, and ensuring the "full independence of the East European nations." The United States, in turn, would sign an arms limitation treaty and accept an international agency under the supervision of the UN to control atomic energy. Eisenhower went beyond specific, rather old-hat, demands. He took this opportunity to preach to the world fiscal responsibility in regards to the Cold War:

> Every gun that is made, every warship launched, every rocket fired, signifies, in the final sense, a theft from those who hunger and are not fed, those who are cold and are not clothed. This world is not spending money alone. It is spending the sweat of its laborers, the genius of its scientists, the hopes of its children. The cost of one modern heavy

bomber is this: a modern brick school in more than thirty cities. It is two electrical power plants . . . It is two fine, fully equipped hospitals. We pay for a single fighter plane with a half-million bushels of wheat. We pay for a single destroyer with new homes that could have housed more than eight thousand people. This is not a way of life at all, in any true sense. Under the cloud of threatening war, it is humanity hanging from a cross of iron.[113]

Eisenhower concluded by promising to devote a percentage of savings induced from an arms' reduction treaty to a fund for world aid so that the "monuments to this new kind of war would be these: roads and schools, hospitals and homes, food and health."[114] The President explained these overtures in his memoirs. Reflective of the spirituality part of the 'Great Equation,' he believed that to be an effective leader of the free world, the American people and their government "should always . . . display a spirit of conciliation without appeasement, confidence without arrogance," and, most important, demonstrate a leadership "based on honesty of purpose, on calmness and inexhaustible patience in conference."[115] In these ways he hoped to influence allies and potential enemies. The Chance for Peace was the Great Equation.

Not surprisingly, the Soviets never did bite at Eisenhower's proposals. Certainly much of the speech was pure propaganda. However, as Ambrose observed, the tone was "reasonable and moderate [and] Eisenhower's sincerity so apparent" that the speech did outline early on in the administration central issues in Eisenhower's thinking.[116] Although suspicious of the Soviets, he was willing to negotiate on certain terms. He deeply believed a continued arms race would strangle the fiscal health, and ultimately the democratic freedoms, of the United States.

The first three months of the new administration were indeed productive and set the tone for the next eight years. Eisenhower reevaluated the policies outlined in NSC-68 to formulate a more balanced national security policy. He set the wheels in motion to fight for budget restraints in military spending, a fight that would continue every year he was in office. And Eisenhower made a grand gesture of peace towards the Soviets, demonstrating his sincerity in working towards a world that did not have to fear nuclear annihilation. With this framework in place, Eisenhower was ready to call upon some of the most respected minds of the day to work out a national security plan that reflected his strategic thinking and the 'Great Equation.'

Notes

1. George Kennan, "The Sources of Soviet Conduct," in *American Diplomacy*, (Chicago: University of Chicago Press, 1984), 128.

2. Campbell Craig, *Destroying the Village: Eisenhower and the Thermonuclear War*, (New York: Columbia University Press, 1998), 69.

3. Letter Eisenhower to General Alfred Gruenther, 5/4/53, EL, AWF, DDE Diaries, Box 3, "December 52-July 53 (3)."

4. Winston Churchill, *The Second World War,* Vol. 3 "The Grand Alliance," (New York: Houghton Mifflin, 1950), 370.

5. Ibid., 371-372.

6. Franklin Roosevelt, *Papers of the President 1940,* December 29, 1940.

7. John Lewis Gaddis, *We Now Know: Rethinking Cold War History,* (New York: Oxford University Press, 1997), 6.

8. Roosevelt formally recognized the Soviet Union against the wishes of American labor and his own State Department. For a full account see Ronald Powaski, *The Cold War: The United States & the Soviet Union, 1917-1991,* (New York: Oxford, 1998), 35-37.

9. Walter McDougall, *Promised Land, Crusader State: The American Encounter with the World Since 1776,* (Boston: Houghton Mifflin, 1997), 154.

10. Gaddis Smith, *American Diplomacy During the Second World War, 1941-1945,* (New York: John Wiley & Sons, 1965).

11. James McGregor Burns, *The Crosswinds of Freedom,* (New York: Knopf, 1989).

12. LeFeber, *The American Age,* 442.

13. Harry S Truman, *Memoirs,* vol. 1, *Year of Decisions,* (Garden City,NJ: Double-Day, 1956), 80-82.

14. Truman, *Year of Decision,* 19.

15. Robert Ferrell, ed., *Off the Record: The Private Papers of Harry S Truman,* (New York: Harper and Row, 1980), 16.

16. Martin Sherwin, *A World Destroyed: Hiroshima and the Origins of the Arms Race,* (New York: Vintage Books, 1987), 150, 160-163.

17. S. David Broscious, "Longing for International Control, Banking on American Superiority: Harry S Truman's Approach to Nuclear Weapons," in John L. Gaddis, Philip Gordon, Ernest May, Jonathan Rosenberg eds., *Cold War Statesmen Confront the Bomb: Nuclear Diplomacy Since 1945,* (New York: Oxford University Press, 1999), 17.

18. Ibid., 17, 20.

19. Ibid., 20-21, 36-38.

20. Statement by President Truman at a Meeting at Blair House, Washington, 7/14/49, *FRUS,* 1949, 1:481.

21. Vladislav M. Zubok, "Stalin and the Nuclear Age," in John L. Gaddis et al., *Cold War Statesmen,* 45, 52, 61.

22. Ibid., 43, 45.

23. Ibid., 48.

24. Ibid., 40; 60-61.

25. Ibid., 41.

26. Quoted in Walter Hixson, *George Kennan: Cold War Iconoclast,* (New York: Columbia University Press, 1989), 22.

27. Zubok, "Stalin and the Nuclear Age," 41.

28. Quoted in John Lewis Gaddis, *The United States and the Origins of the Cold War,* (New York: Columbia University Press, 1972), 304.

29. Ibid.

30. Ibid.

31. "A February poll showed that only one third of Americans now trusted the Communists, and 60 percent in a March poll thought U.S. policy toward Russia "too soft." McDougall, *Promised Land*, 161.

32. Incoming Telegram to Secretary of State from George Kennan, 2/22/46, NA, RG 59, Records of the Policy Planning Staff, 1947-63, PPS Members Chronological File, Box 48, "George Kennan Speeches," 5-6.

33. Ibid., 9.

34. Ibid., 12.

35. Ibid., 15-16.

36. Ibid., 16-17.

37. John Lewis Gaddis, *We Now Know*, 193-194.

38. Melvyn Leffler, *A Preponderance of Power: National Security, the Truman Administration, and the Cold War*, (Stanford: Stanford University Press, 1992), 108.

39. Harry Truman, "The Truman Doctrine, 1947," in Thomas Patterson, *Major Problems in American Foreign Relations*, Vol. II, 4th ed., (Boston: DC Heath, 1995), 259-261.

40. Ibid.

41. John Lewis Gaddis, *Strategies of Containment: A Critical Appraisal of Postwar American National Security Policy*, (New York: Oxford University Press, 1982), 88.

42. For an excellent account of how Truman's budgets reflected this rational ability and his desire to keep defense spending down see Michael Hogan, *A Cross of Iron: Harry S. Truman and the Origins of the National Security State, 1945-1954*, (New York: Cambridge University Press, 1998), 289-293.

43. The President to the Secretary of State, January 31, 1950, *FRUS*, 1950, 1:141-142.

44. For further information on Nitze, see Paul Nitze, *From Hiroshima to Glasnost: At the Center of Decision*, (New York: Grove Weidenfeld, 1989); Strobe Talbott, *The Master of the Game: Paul Nitze and the Nuclear Peace*, (New York: Knopf, 1988); David Callahan, *Dangerous Capabilities: Paul Nitze and the Cold War*, (New York: HarperCollins, 1990).

45. For who and why Congressmen and the press opposed Truman's budget cuts see Hogan, *Cross of Iron*, 285-291.

46. Symington and Acheson quoted in Hogan, *A Cross of Iron*, 292.

47. LeFeber, *American Age*, 504-505.

48. Draft memorandum by Kennan to Acheson, 2/17/50, *FRUS*, 1950, 1:160-167.

49. Dean Acheson, *Present at the Creation: My Years in the State Department*, (New York: Norton, 1969), 373.

50. Nitze came to Washington as an aide to the Wall Street businessman, James Forrestal, as part of six special administrative assistants to Franklin Roosevelt who were assembled in an attempt to rebuild FDR's relations with the business community. Since then, Nitze held various jobs in Washington, helping to write the Selective service Act of 1940, helping Nelson Rockefeller in the Office of the Coordinator of Inter-American Affairs, and helping to write the final report on the Pacific War for the U.S. Strategic Bombing Team. After the war, Nitze accepted an offer from Will Clayton to join the State Department as deputy director of the Office of International trade Policy. See Nitze, *From Hiroshima to Glasnost*, 3-81; Callahan, *Dangerous Capabilities*, 94-98.

51. Record of Eighth Meeting of PPS, 2/2/50, *FRUS*, 1950, 1:142-143.; A Report to the President Pursuant to the President's Directive of January 31, 1950, *FRUS*, 1950, 1:240.

52. Callahan, *Dangerous Capabilities,* 99, 137.

53. Acheson, *Present at the Creation*, 373.

54. Hogan, *A Cross of Iron*, 295.

55. A Report to the NSC, NSC 68, 4/14/50, *FRUS*, 1950, 1:234-292.

56. Record of the Meeting of the State-Defense Policy Review Group, Monday, February, 27, 1950, *FRUS*, 1950, 1:168-175.

57. Record of the Meeting of the State-Defense Policy Review Group, Thursday, March 2, 1950, *FRUS*, 1950, 1: 176-177.

58. David Callahan, *Dangerous Capabilities*, 109.

59. "Project Solarium: A Collective Oral History," Princeton University Mudd Library, Woodrow Wilson School, Box 93, folder 10, 18.

60. David Callahan, *Dangerous Capabilities,* 110, 137.

61. Quoted in Hogan, *A Cross of Iron*, 302.

62. A Report to the NSC, NSC 68, 4/14/50, *FRUS*, 1950, 1:234-292.

63. George Kennan was actually against the creation of NATO, feeling that its presence drew solid lines between the East and West, reducing the possibilities of peaceful negotiation.

64. Robert Bowie and Richard Immerman, *Waging Peace: How Eisenhower Shaped an Enduring Cold War Strategy,* (New York: Oxford University Press, 1998), 39.

65. During the Truman Administration, Eisenhower was appointed Chief of Staff of the Army in 1945, but "retired" (as a five-star general he was on active duty for life by law) in February 1948. That June he became president of Columbia University. Truman called upon Eisenhower in January 1949 to act as a military consultant to the first Secretary of Defense, James Forrestal. In the spring, Eisenhower was asked by Truman to serve as the informal chairman of he JCS. As a part time chairman, Eisenhower had lots of exposure, but little influence and became frustrated over the constant bickering among the Joint Chiefs and the defense budget wars within the Administration. By late summer 1949, Eisenhower left the Truman Administration. Truman called Eisenhower again in October 1950 to serve as NATO commander, a position he held until 1952, when he retired to campaign for the presidency. For a further account, see Stephen Ambrose, *Eisenhower: Soldier and President*, (New York: Simon and Schuster, 1990), 233-245; 249-50.

66. Bowie and Immerman, *Waging Peace*, 40.

67. Samuel Wells, Jr. "The Origins of Massive Retaliation," *Political Science Quarterly*, 96(1981), 40-41.

68. Robert Ferrell,ed., *The Eisenhower Diaries*, (New York: W.W. Norton, 1981), 209-13.

69. Notes on the Fiscal Problem and Tax Program prepared by Dodge, 5/20/53, EL, WHO OSS, L. Arthur Minnich Series, Box 1, "Misc-B (1) [Jan 1953-Jan 1954];" Letter Eisenhower to Caffey, 7/27/53, EL, AWF, DDE Diary, Box 3, "December 1952-July 1953 (1)."

70. Quoted in Emmet John Hughes, *The Ordeal of Power: A Political Memoir of the Eisenhower Years*, (New York, 1975), 28.

71. Eisenhower to Captain E.E. Hazlett, Jr., 7/21/53, EL, AWF, DDE Diary Series, Box 3, "December 1952-July 1953 (1)."

72. Cabinet Minutes, 2/25/53, EL, WHO OSS, Cabinet Series, Box 1, "C-2 (2) February 25 and March 6 1953;" Memo, 8/12/57, EL, Evan Aurand Papers, Box 5, "Parsons, Dr. Edger A(1)."

73. Eisenhower to Hazlett, 7/21/53, EL, AWF.

74. Letter Cutler to Eisenhower, 12/27/52, EL, AWF, Administrative Series, Box 10, "Cutler, General Robert 1952-53 (5)."

75. Summary of J.F.D. remarks at meeting with Eisenhower, et. al., 12/11/52, John Foster Dules Papers, Princeton, Mudd Library, Subject Series, "S.S. Helena Notes," quoted in Bowie and Immerman, *Waging Peace,* 84.

76. Bowie and Immerman, *Waging Peace,* 84.

77. Cabinet Minutes, 2/25/53, EL, WHO OSS, Cabinet Series, Box 1, "C-2 (2) February 25 and March 6 1953."

78. Bowie and Immerman, *Waging Peace*, 85.

79. Ibid.

80. Memorandum for Discussion with senate leaders, 12/29,52, EL, AWF, Legislative Meetings, Box 1, "Legislative Leaders, 12/29/52."

81. Memorandum of Discussion of 133rd Meeting of the NSC, 2/24/53, EL, AWF, NSC Series, Box 4, "133rd Meeting of NSC, 2/24/53," 4-5.

82. Memorandum of Discussion of 134th Meeting of the NSC, 2/25/53, EL, AWF, NSC Series, Box 4, "134th Meeting of NSC, 2/25/53," 10-12.

83. Ibid.

84. Eisenhower address in Baltimore, Maryland, 9/25/52, EL, AWF, Speech Series, "Sept. 15, 1952-Sept. 25, 1952," quoted in Bowie and Immerman, *Waging Peace*, 101.

85. Letter Eisenhower to Anderson, 2/27/53, EL, AWF, Administrative Series, Box 10, "Cutler, General Robert, 1952-53 (5)."

86. James Black, president of Pacific Gas and Electric, Eugene Holman, president of Standard Oil of New Jersey represented business and finance. Charles Thomas, president of Monsanto Chemical Company, represented the scientific community as a member of the Science Advisory Committee. David Robertson, president of the Brotherhood of Railroad Firemen and Enginemen, represented labor. John Cowles, a Midwestern newspaper publisher, and Deane Malott, president of Cornell University, rounded out the group. Letter Dr. Lee DuBridge to Cutler, 3/19/53, EL, WHO OSANSA, Special Assistant series, Subject Sub series, Box 7, "Science and Research- General (1)[March-April 1953]."

87. Seven Named as Security Council Aides, *Washington Post*, 3/12/53, EL, WHO OSANSA, NSC Series, Administrative Sub Series, Box 4, "Consultants- NSC [Feb-March 1953] (1)."

88. Ibid.

89. Memorandum of Discussion at the 141st Meeting of the NSC, 4/29/53, EL, AWF, NSC Series, Box 4 "141st Meeting of NSC, 4/28/53."

90. Ibid.

91. Bowie and Immerman, *Waging Peace,* 104.

92. Memorandum of Discussion at a Special Meeting of the National Security Council, 3/31/53, *FRUS*, 1952-54, 2:268.

93. ibid., 268-269; Views of the Consultants to the National Security Council, EL, AWF, NSC Series, Box 4, "Documents Pertaining to Special NSC Meeting, 3/31/53."

94. Memorandum of Discussion at NSC, 3/31/53, *FRUS,* 1952-54, 2:269.

95. Draft Memorandum Prepared for the National Security Council, *FRUS,* 1952-54, 2:281.

96. Ibid., 281-82.

97. Bowie and Immerman, *Waging Peace,* 107.

98. March 31, 1953 entry, EL, CD Jackson Papers, Box 68, "Log- 1953(1)."

99. Cabinet Minutes, 3/6/53, EL, WHO OSS, Cabinet Series, Box 1, "C-2 (2) February 25 and March 6 1953."

100. C.D. Jackson's official title was Special Assistant to the President for Cold War Operations.

101. W. Walt Rostow, *Europe After Stalin: Eisenhower's Three Decisions of March 11, 1953,* (Austin: University of Texas Press, 1982), 84-90.

102. Bowie and Immerman, *Waging Peace,* 114-115.

103. Paper Prepared by W.W. Rostow, 5/11/53, *FRUS* 1952-54, 8:1180.

104. Quoted in Stephen Ambrose, *Eisenhower: Soldier and President,* (New York: Simon and Schuster, 1990), 323.

105. Memorandum of Conversation, 3/16/53, EL, JFD Papers, Chronological Series, Box 1, "March 1-17, 1953 (1)."

106. Hughes, *The Ordeal of Power,* 103-105.

107. Memorandum Discussion at the 139th Meeting of NSC, 4/16/65, EL, AWF, NSC Series, Box 4, "139th Meeting of NSC, 4/8/53."

108. Memorandum by Bonbright to Smith, 3/18/53, *FRUS* 1952-54, 8:1133-34.

109. Memorandum for Hughes, 4/10/53, EL, JFD Papers, Chronological Series, Box 2, "April 1-31, 1953 (3)."

110. Emmett J. Hughes Papers, Princeton, Mudd Library, Diary entry for April 11, 1953, "Diary Notes 1953," quoted in Bowie and Immerman, *Waging Peace,* 118.

111. Eisenhower, *Mandate for Peace,* 148.

112. Memorandum Discussion at 141st Meeting of the NSC, 4/29/53, EL, AWF, NSC Series, Box 4 "141st Meeting of NSC 4/28/53."

113. Address "The Chance for Peace" Delivered Before the American Society of Newspaper Editors, 4/16/53, *Public Papers of the President,* 1953, (US Government Printing Office, 1960), 179-188.

114. Ibid.

115. Eisenhower, *Mandate for Change,* 148.

116. Ambrose, *Eisenhower,* 326.

CHAPTER TWO

Talk About 'Liberty' Doesn't Stop People From Becoming Communists: Organizing A National Security Policy

On May 8, 1953, in an exchange between Dwight Eisenhower and John Foster Dulles regarding national security planning, Dulles argued that it was vital for America to obtain a success somewhere in the world to stop the momentum of the Soviet Union, even if that meant risking war. His argument, thought Eisenhower, seemed to reflect the radical thinking of Paul Nitze and NSC-68. Eisenhower repeated his "Chance for Peace" message to Dulles, reminding him that the United States ought to rely less on pure military might and more on "improving the standards of living in the other countries as the way to gain true indigenous strength." He explained that when people saw "freedom and communism in their true lights," success would come in Eastern Europe and the rest of the world. Dulles quipped back that "talk about 'liberty' doesn't stop people from becoming communists," but a persistent Eisenhower disagreed, reminding Dulles that it was the people's "minds and hearts that must be won."[1]

This May exchange between Dulles and Eisenhower reflected the thinking of his 'Great Equation'—not only were military preparedness and a balanced budget necessary to security, so was a sense of spirituality and moral leadership. Eisenhower had expressed that philosophy while campaigning in the fall of 1952. He told Americans that "as a nation everything we say, everything we do . . . will have its impact in other lands; it will affect the minds of men and women there."[2] This was similar to George Kennan's original containment policy. Kennan too believed that the preservation of liberty and the spread of ideas, not simply a military build-up, would thwart communism.[3] However, Dulles argued for a stronger military message to the Soviet Union under the guise of Eisenhower's rollback campaign pledge. Wanting to bring Dulles on board with his own vision for strategy in order to keep his campaign promise of adopting a "unified and coherent" Cold War strategy, Eisenhower suggested a debate about a variety of strategic plans, carefully thought out in terms of risk and costs by a handful of distinguished outside consultants. He carefully oversaw the membership selection for the subsequent Solarium Exercise and was able to predetermine an outcome he desired. The end result was a basic national security policy in NSC 162/2 that defined his strategic thinking.

Reorganizing the NSC

"One of my first responsibilities," recalled Eisenhower, "was to organize the White House for efficiency."[4] Calling the Truman NSC nothing more than a "shadow agency," Eisenhower immediately focused attention on creating a more dynamic and efficient NSC.[5] To carry out the reorganization, Eisenhower turned to his Special Assistant for National Security Affairs, General Robert Cutler.

Cutler was a good friend of Eisenhower and had a keen mind and sharp wit. One friend described Cutler as "a raconteur, par excellence, of risqué stories, which he does best with a scotch and soda in hand."[6] An intellectual with a flair for writing, Cutler graduated cum laude from Harvard in 1916 and Harvard Law in 1922 and was the poet of his undergraduate class. By the time he was 23, he had published two novels about love, commenting, "What else would a boy of twenty write about?"[7]

A veteran of both World Wars, Cutler served as a Special Assistant to Secretary of War Stimson and received the Distinguished Service Medal and the Legion of Merit during WWII. During the Truman Administration he served as a deputy director of the Psychological Strategy Board on the NSC. In 1952, he pressed Eisenhower to run for president and Eisenhower asked him to act as his personal assistant on NSC affairs during the campaign and write some of his speeches. After winning the election, Eisenhower asked the Boston lawyer to serve in the administration, helping him to reorganize the NSC. Cutler was reluctant to take the job, deeming his "talents unworthy of his position."[8] Cutler was being modest. His talents were well suited for the position, beginning with his exceptional organizational skills.[9] As president of the Old Colony Company of Boston, he was an experienced leader and knew how to run an efficient team. He had experience in Washington with the Truman NSC and he spent months campaigning with Eisenhower, learning Eisenhower's views on national security. In short, Eisenhower found everything was looking for in Cutler.

Once Eisenhower took office, Cutler went to work on reevaluating the structure and function of the NSC. Since its formation in 1947, suggestions had been made to improve the function of the NSC, and Eisenhower strongly believed it could be further improved.[10] Eisenhower envisioned a forum in which ideas could be discussed freely by both statutory and invited members, and then developed into an organized policy paper for Council consideration.[11] It was vital, in Eisenhower's mind, to have an efficient system for national security planning because the volatility and rapid weapon advancements of the Cold War forced the president to rely on "the vital studies, advice, and counsel that only a capable and well-developed staff organization can give him."[12] Eisenhower admitted that "organization cannot make a genius out of an incompetent," but, he went on to say, "organization makes more efficient the gathering and analysis of facts, and the arranging of the findings of experts in logical fashion. Therefore organization helps the responsible individual make the necessary decision, and helps assure that it is satisfactorily carried out."[13] It was creating this efficient and organized system that kept Cutler busy for the next two years.

After returning from Korea in early December 1952, Eisenhower appointed his brother, Milton Eisenhower, as well as Arthur Flemming and Nelson Rockefeller to study how to make executive operations more competent. This President's Advisory Commission for Government Organization (PACGO) interviewed various Washington staff members and presented its report to Eisenhower and his senior staff at their January 12th and 13th pre-inaugural retreat at his Commodore Hotel headquarters. Cutler, after being introduced as Eisenhower's appointee as Special Assistant for National Security Affairs, outlined for the audience the history of the NSC and the future role the Council and, in particular, Cutler would play. Armed with their recommendations, Cutler then solicited Truman NSC veterans to create study groups to report back to him their recommendations.[14] After reviewing all the reports and testimonies, and using his own personal experience on the NSC, Cutler presented his final report for reorganization on March 16, 1953.

In accordance with Eisenhower's wish for the NSC to function parallel to the Cabinet in importance and accessibility, Cutler submitted recommendations to overhaul the NSC into a fine-tuned advisory board on national security affairs.[15] Noting that the NSC had two functions, a policy-planning function and a supporting staff function, Cutler recommended that the supporting staff be a permanent staff which would not change with new administrations so that it could "furnish both a necessary continuity in highly sensitive matters and also maximum staff assistance to the policymakers."[16] The policy-planning function was to be made up of the highest security advisers to the President and a Planning Board. The Special Assistant for National Security Affairs was to act as executive officer at the Council meetings and, as part of the administration, would serve at the president's pleasure.

To keep the Council meetings efficient and productive, Cutler suggested that the number of formal Council members be limited to eight. One of those permanent members was to be the president himself. Truman rarely went to Council meetings, which had been a serious weakness of the NSC according to former Secretary of State George Marshall.[17] Eisenhower, on the other hand, attended over 90 percent of the meetings, and, when he was not there, he had his "bright, quick, . . . loyal and cooperative" Vice-President Richard Nixon preside over the meeting.[18] In addition to the participation by the president, the Treasury Department and Bureau of the Budget were brought in to the fold. Headed by George Humphrey and Joseph Dodge respectively, both men were staunch fiscal conservatives.[19] Humphrey was the president of the Mark Hanna Company of Cleveland, a large conglomerate, and Dodge was a Detroit banker who played no small role in the reconstruction of post-war Japan.[20] The presence of Humphrey and Dodge reflected the importance the budget played in Eisenhower's national security planning.

In addition to the regular members, the president could invite any Government officials he deemed appropriate. As it became obvious the NSC was a valuable and important tool for Eisenhower, many government officials sought an opportunity to attend the meetings and an invitation extended by the President was never refused.[21] Civilians without departmental responsibilities were not to be invited, but civilian ad hoc consultants or committees were to be called upon "in order to bring the Council deliberations a fresh, frequently-changing civilian point of view and to gain public understanding of national security problems through the use of civilians of stature."[22] Cutler understood the role Eisenhower saw for civilian consultants within the NSC. While campaigning, Eisenhower had stated his desire to see the membership of the NSC include "civilians of the highest capacity, integrity, and dedication to public service, who have no other official duties."[23] And in fact, one of the first things Eisenhower had Cutler do was to organize the ad hoc group of Civilian Consultants in February 1953, which advised Eisenhower and the NSC on the budget and national security policy.[24] Civilian consultant groups like that one were utilized to good effect thirteen times by the NSC during Cutler's tenure and proved invaluable to Eisenhower.[25]

Cutler rejected suggestions to place a few well-qualified civilians on the Council's permanent membership. He did so on two counts. First, keeping attendance small was important to Cutler to ensure a forum for vigorous, frank, fruitful discussion. Explaining that the "pow-wow element" of a meeting was invaluable, Cutler believed "that element disappears when over a certain number of persons sit about the Council Table . . . [and] people do not discuss and debate; they remain silent or talk for the record."[26] Second, and more important than attendance, Cutler worried about permanent civilian members being "Nestors" - elder statesmen whose views would be theoretical. With nothing but time to think, these members would not be privy to the daily march of world events faced by department heads. Therefore, their views might not hold up to current realities, but, because of their stature, their views might dominate Council meetings. For Cutler, the essence of the NSC was to bring Eisenhower the views of the men who would be carrying out his national security policies in a "give-and-take . . . questioning and being questioned" forum.[27] "Nestors" had no permanent place. Instead, their most efficient use was through ad hoc committees. These committees had access to relevant classified documents and departmental briefings to bring the consultants up to speed, and such committees could objectively research a specific issue of national security without being clouded by department agendas or rivalries.

Cutler also sought efficiency by recommending the Council meet every week at a specific time.[28] This enabled the regular members to plan their schedules around the weekly meeting. By instituting a regular meeting time, seeing that the president attended each meeting, and keeping attendance small, Cutler was able to work out some of the major problems faced by the Truman NSC. George Marshall, in recalling the Truman years, complained that it was too "evanescent," and that the meetings were "of busy men who had no time to pay to the business before them, and not being prepared, therefore took refuge in nonparticipation or in protecting their own departments."[29] Cutler eliminated these inefficiencies. He made it clear that the NSC was strictly an advisory body and every member ought to come to the meetings prepared. To help with preparation, Cutler placed great weight on the Planing Board of the Council.

Cutler recommended renaming the "Senior Staff" of the Truman NSC to the "Planning Board." A small group made up of the Special Assistant to the President, the Director for Mutual Security, and one person each from the Office of Defense Mobilization and the departments of State, Defense, and Treasury, the Planning Board had the difficult task of anticipating and identifying "problems and situations affecting the security objectives, commitments, and risks of the United States."[30] They were then to take action, analyzing the situation and drafting a policy paper for the Council members to consider. Unlike the Truman policy papers that offered no alternatives, the Policy Board's papers identified all possible alternatives and discussed all differences for Council consideration.[31] In order for the Board to accumulate all this information, it was imperative that the Board members be as prepared as the Council members. Cutler explained that each Board member had to be "prepared promptly to state to the Board the views of his department," in order for the Board to function efficiently.[32] In addition, the duty to the Board of each member overrode all other duties while maintaining a sufficient degree of activity within his department "so as to be capable of representing its views."[33] Certainly Cutler saw the Planning Board as the lifeline of the Council, providing an invigorating forum for some of the top government officials to meet at least twice a week to make vital contributions to the policymaking process.[34] Eisenhower agreed.

The day after Cutler's presentation, Eisenhower sent him a letter approving the recommendations and requested that Cutler forward to him the names recommended to be members of the Planning Board so that he could finalize their appointments and get the Board functioning immediately. Eisenhower explained to Cutler that he placed "great emphasis on the selection of men of high caliber for these positions, able to devote plenty of time to their Planning Board functions; for thereby the Council will be better able to operate promptly and effectively."[35] As Eisenhower viewed it, the Planning Board did the thinking for the Council members—thinking that they did not have time to do on their own. Therefore, Eisenhower recommended to his Council members that they "should therefore appoint individuals in whom [they] have complete confidence."[36] He also told them he wanted "new faces" that were not associated with the policies of the Truman administration because he, and the members of his administration, "were all trying to take a new look at existing policies and programs."[37] Getting the freshest faces of the highest character on the Planning Board was the key to efficient policy making and one step towards establishing a New Look for Eisenhower's foreign policy.

By April, the NSC was reorganized into an effective advising council. Dulles commended Eisenhower a few years later for "building a team which was so harmonious, which was so imbued with principles, and which had so good a backlog of forward thinking, as embodied in NSC papers."[38] One of its first papers, NSC 149/2, served as the first step towards a new national security policy. Although satisfactory to Eisenhower for the short term, the more fiscally conservative Republicans, led by Senator Robert Taft, wanted to see more cuts, and many Democrats thought the cuts were too deep, severely undermining American security. Eisenhower, barely three months into his first term, was past the honeymoon period.

Facing Political Pressures

Getting the approval for NSC 149/2 in April 1953 was a political success for Eisenhower.[39] It did not, however, please everybody and caused political headaches for Eisenhower in the next few weeks. Republican Senator Robert Taft was one of the loudest critics. Taft, the leader of the conservative wing of the Republican party and Eisenhower's competition for the Republican nomination in 1952, had urged Eisenhower during the campaign to make budget cuts a priority, particularly in defense.[40] Taft wanted the last Truman budget of $78 billion to be cut by at least $8 billion. As Senate Majority leader, Taft was concerned that Secretary of Defense Wilson did not share his views on defense cuts. Frustrated, Taft said in February that the administration "must make drastic economies forthwith . . . I give them until about May first to make the recommendations which will bring about a substantial reduction."[41]

When the new policy was introduced to the Republican legislative leadership on April 30, Taft criticized NSC 149/2 for not implementing the budget cuts he felt were necessary. Taft worried that Eisenhower's new budget looked just like Truman's and that public perception would be that the Administration was not reversing the Truman trend of increased spending. Such a perception, Taft believed, was disastrous for the Republican chances in the 1954 Congressional elections. "With a program like this," Taft yelled at Eisenhower, "you're taking us down the same road Truman traveled. It's a repudiation of everything we promised in the campaign."[42] Eisenhower defended his position, reminding Taft and his group that America's defense posture could not be sacrificed for an unobtainable budget. Although Eisenhower was committed to a balanced budget, he was not going to just slash budgets at the expense of national security. Eisenhower tried to explain to Taft that NSC 149/2 was the first step towards the goal of providing a strong defense within a strong economy. Taft suggested that a complete reevaluation of national security be made in order to achieve more cuts for the FY55 budget. The next day, Eisenhower wrote in his diary that the meeting with the legislative leaders had resulted in "one of the worst days I have experienced since January 20."[43]

Political pressure was not only mounting from the right, but from the left as well. Taft and other fiscal conservatives wanted to slash the budget dangerously while many Democrats felt any budget cut was dangerous to national security, and the administration was keenly aware of such Democratic assertions.[44] By the spring of 1953, the optimism for bipartisanship in foreign policy faded. Eisenhower's Defense Reorganization message of April 30, 1953 repeated his goal of maintaining a strong defense without sacrificing a sound economy. Yet, his proposed defense budget for FY54, at $5.1 billion below Truman's, provoked loud opposition by leading Democrats in the House and Senate. Led by Stuart Symington, these Congressmen were all airpower advocates and worried that Eisenhower's proposed cuts in the Air Force budget would result in a bomber "gap" between the two superpowers.[45] Many others felt Eisenhower was not delivering on his campaign promises for a better foreign policy. One Democrat explained to C.D. Jackson that he had voted for Eisenhower because he thought, "we would get more foreign policy than under Truman and Acheson. Up to now," he continued, "I honestly feel that it is less foreign policy. How much longer should I wait?"[46] Jackson was not very sympathetic, but he understood the perception the public had of Eisenhower, which he believed to be a basic misconception. He recognized that Eisenhower rarely initiated leadership, but instead looked for his "alert, energetic staff to bat things up to him," for him to approve and lead.[47] It was time for Eisenhower's staff to bat something new up to him and find a way to reconcile political pressures over the budget and national security. In early May Eisenhower and his key national security aides did just that and formulated a way to reevaluate basic national security policy using the newly reorganized NSC and "teams of bright young fellows."[48]

A Meeting in the Solarium Room

On the afternoon of Saturday May 2, Allen Dulles, Bedell Smith, Robert Cutler, and C.D. Jackson all met at John Foster Dulles' home to discuss issues regarding national security.[49] Dulles had prepared a remarkable presentation for his guests, leaving his listeners still and silent in their chairs for over an hour. [50] Insistent that the President hear Dulles' ideas, Cutler arranged to have the same cast of characters, plus George Humphrey, meet with Eisenhower on Friday, May 8 in the Solarium room of the White House.[51]

The general purpose of this off-the-record meeting was to discuss Soviet-American relations. Dulles was not optimistic about those relations and remarked that it was "difficult to conclude that time is working in our favor."[52] He saw few exceptions in the world where Soviet influence and penetration were not formidable. West Germany might fall to communism, devastating NATO. South America, much of Africa, the Middle East, and Asia were also vulnerable. "In the world chess game," Dulles concluded, "the Reds today have the better position."

With the mere survival of Western civilization at stake, Dulles was disgusted with the attitude of the "old people" shattered from the war who were unwilling to face Soviet aggression. These leaders were "willing and glad to gamble on time bringing about a solution," so that they might live out their days in peace. Dulles believed their hope was that the "Soviets, like Ghenghes Khan [sic], will get on their little Tarter ponies and ride back whence they came." Not wishing to emulate this weak position, Dulles argued that the United States had to demonstrate to the world a different approach, an approach based on strength and defiance. The course the United States was following was "a fatal one" as it was based on a defensive position. Instead of "always worrying what the Soviets will take next," and risk losing the support of Congress and the public as the Soviets nibbled away at the world, Dulles suggested three alternative courses.

On a grand scale, the Americans might draw a line around the current Soviet sphere of influence and threaten that if one more country were to fall to communism outside that perimeter, a global war between the United States and the Soviet Union would result. On a lesser scale, that line might be limited to an area, such as Asia. If a country over the line were to fall to communism, the Americans might only threaten "measures of our own choosing," reducing the risk of global war. A third alternative was "to restore the prestige of the West by winning in one or more areas a success or successes." Some possible successes might be found in Korea, Hainan, Albania, Hungary, Bulgaria, or Czechoslovakia. All such actions would undoubtedly disturb the Kremlin, which was the goal, despite the fact American allies would likely "shudder, [and] wish to draw back." Dulles conceded that perhaps the allies were right and that there "is no other possible course than to wait and see," but he believed the Administration had a responsibility to "appraise the alternatives and see if there is not some different way."

The President agreed that these alternatives ought to be examined further, although he cautioned, "we cannot live alone" and needed the support of allies. Furthermore, any path chosen had to be accepted by the allies and Congress as right. Eisenhower also challenged Dulles to think beyond material strength in winning the Cold War and to consider the alternative of improving the standards of living throughout the world "as the way to gain true indigenous strength." Winning the hearts and minds of the people by showing them "freedom and communism in their true lights" was as important in this struggle as guns. For Eisenhower, the Cold War was truly a fight between good and evil and he saw the United States as better than the Soviets in terms beyond just military strength. This attitude was shared by George Kennan's original containment theory and it seemed that that attitude had been lost with NSC-68 and Dulles' dire scenarios. Eisenhower needed to get his team on board with that original vision.

Humphrey also agreed that American policy had to be reevaluated, because it was "sapping our strength," was leading to disaster, and turning the American people on the Administration. Eisenhower agreed that the present financial burdens being placed on national security policy could not continue. To evaluate all policy alternatives in their financial and strategic roles, Eisenhower wished to set up "some teams of bright young fellows" who would act like a debating team or a "good advocate tackling a law case." These teams were to argue one alternative "with a real belief in it" and present their case in terms of "goal, risk, cost in money and men and world relations." Eisenhower believed that with such a presentation, the NSC would be "qualified to come to a decision." Such an exercise allowed Eisenhower and his staff to reevaluate the Truman strategy of containment and the feasibility of rollback. It also provided an excellent opportunity to educate his national security staff and build them into the team players Eisenhower desired.

The end result of the exercise did not radically change previous policies, but it served a vital purpose. By giving a small committee a narrow assignment and by choosing specific members to participate, Eisenhower had an opportunity to use civilian committee members with diverse backgrounds to create an outcome he desired but which he could point to as being made by his entire team. Instead of acting alone and announcing a return to the earlier Truman-Kennan policy of containment, Eisenhower used a civilian committee to participate in the decision-making process and to educate and persuade his NSC. Therefore, the proposal made by Eisenhower was unique. It was also widely embraced by the rest of the room. Named for the room they met in, Project Solarium began immediately.

Organizing the Task Forces

A working committee made up of Cutler, Allen Dulles, and Bedell Smith worked out the details based on Eisenhower's three assignments.[53] On May 13, Cutler briefed the NSC about Solarium.[54] The Task Forces were to meet and work at the National War College under the cover that they were there to participate in the College's First National War College Round-Table Seminar on "Cold War and U.S. Foreign Policy, 1953-1963" to be held June 9-11. Security was vital to Eisenhower. He did not want to have details of the exercise leaked to the press, and, in fact, no one did find out about the project despite the fact the Task Forces worked there for over a month.[55] They were to have access to all pertinent intelligence reports, estimates, and other classified material. They were to approach their task "in the same spirit that an advocate works up a case for court presentation," and they were to play "Devil's advocate" in the plenary sessions, offering criticism to the other Task Forces.[56] Eisenhower approved the final membership selections by mid-May, and the Task Forces assembled at the War College the second week of June.[57] The final presentations needed to be completed, ready for presentation to the NSC by mid-July.

The alternatives for the Task Forces to argue stemmed from the current Truman policy of containment, Dulles' "grand and lesser scale" alternatives of drawing the line, and Eisenhower's campaign promise of rollback. To draft the exact terms of reference for each alternative, Cutler, Smith, and Dulles appointed a committee, chaired by General James Doolittle.[58] The Doolittle committee proposed a fourth Task Force to argue the desirability of a preventive war with the Soviets in light of recent nuclear weapon development and increasing U.S. vulnerability to surprise attack. Cutler's working committee postponed this Alternative "D". However, it is doubtful Eisenhower ever would have seriously considered such a policy that was, in his mind, suicidal.[59]

Task Force A's job was to defend the policy that had been in effect, with modifications, since 1948. Sticking with the NSC 149/2 fiscal requirement of bringing the Federal budget into balance as quickly as possible without sacrificing national security, Task Force A had to argue a position that maintained armed forces to defend the United States and to protect "vital areas of the free world," continuing to help build up the free world. The U.S. was to oppose continued Communist expansion by the Soviets or Chinese and "exploit the vulnerabilities of the Soviets and their satellites." Most importantly, the policy had to avoid general war. The end goal of such a policy was to eliminate the Soviet threat to the United States and, with the exception of the fiscal modifications of NSC 149/2, was the same policy outlined by previous policy papers beginning with NSC 20. It did not seek to destroy the Soviet system through war, but rather relied on the strategic thoughts put forth by Kennan in 1946 suggesting containment of Soviet power until such time when their system decayed from internal weaknesses. This policy assumed time was on the side of the free world, unlike Dulles' grim predictions.[60]

The assignment given to Task Force A mirrored the strategy Eisenhower leaned toward. Since it was reflective of Kennan's policy, it made sense to ask the former State Department member to chair the committee. Kennan, who had been Ambassador to the Soviet Union before Eisenhower's new appointee Charles Bohlen took his place, was happy to serve on the Task Force but had some concerns. Writing to Cutler on May 25, Kennan complained that he had not heard from President Eisenhower regarding his resignation from the Foreign Service, which he submitted in January. Since Bohlen was the new Ambassador, Kennan wanted some confirmation as to his present status. Furthermore, Kennan was clearly annoyed that John Foster Dulles had no position to offer Kennan in the State Department or Foreign Service. As such, Kennan was to retire that summer under a provision in the Foreign Service Act of 1946. "This is," Kennan wrote Cutler, "to my knowledge, the first instance in which this legislative stipulation, designed to enable the Government to disembarrass itself of unsatisfactory career ambassadors, has been invoked . . . Mr. Dulles must, I am sure, have had serious reasons for taking this attitude toward me."[61]

Cutler assured Kennan the next day that it was an oversight that the President had not acknowledged his resignation as Ambassador and that Eisenhower very much wanted Kennan to participate in the Solarium Project. As far as Dulles was concerned, he believed that Kennan's retirement had been agreed to by both of them since Kennan had told Dulles in January that he "did not consider [himself] available for reassignment in the Foreign Service and requested that [he] be permitted to retire as soon as the necessary arrangements could be made."[62] Dulles had told Kennan that he was happy to have Kennan remain available to the Government as a consultant as his "special talents, particularly in relation to Russian matters," would most certainly be called upon by the Administration.[63] Regardless of the misunderstanding between Dulles and Kennan, Kennan was ready and eager to chair the task force.[64] Interestingly, the Doolittle committee also suggested Nitze for membership on Task Force A. Nitze declined to participate, citing prior commitments and enjoying a month of relaxation before assuming what he expected to be a permanent job in the Pentagon.[65] Robert Cutler, however, told Kennan that Nitze would be available from time to time should Kennan need him.[66] Not surprisingly, Kennan never did.

Since each Task Force was arguing a unique line, the knowledge and experience of the individual members was just as important as the classified reports and departmental briefings they would receive, and members with specific qualifications were selected since their specific insights were extensively relied upon.[67] For example, with Task Force A arguing containment, the Doolittle committee recommended that the members have an "intimate understanding of the past policies and actions of the United States, the rest of the free world, and of the U.S.S.R, and broad gauge political, military, economic, and psychological planning for the future."[68] Task Force A accomplished that.

Under Kennan's leadership were men Kennan considered fortunate to have around him.[69] Colonel George Abe Lincoln, a long-time friend of Eisenhower who had retired to a life of academia, was asked to join Task Force A for his experience as a military planner and economist.[70] Rear Admiral H.P. Smith provided military planning experience and expertise in foreign military matters. The economist and Congressional relations expert C. Tyler Wood participated on Task Force A, and rounding out the group were Colonel C. H. Bonesteel and War College students John Maury and Captain H. S. Sears.[71]

The policy line assigned to Task Force B was a synthesis of Dulles' grand- and lesser-scale alternatives in which the Task Force had to "determine the areas of the world which the United States will not permit to become Communist, whether by overt or covert aggression, by subversion of indigenous peoples, or otherwise." Whether the "line drawn" was to be on a grand scale which risked global war, or the line drawn was to be on a lesser scale, which might only risk a regional war, was to be worked out by the Task Force. Although both alternatives risked war, the response of the United States to Soviet aggression across the line was stated only as "measures of our own choosing," which included the option of an offensive war.[72]

To head Task Force B, Air Force Major General James McCormack was selected over the Doolittle committee's recommendation of Admiral Leslie Stevens. McCormack had extensive experience as a military and political planner, as well as being an expert on atomic and new weapons. Russian expert and military planner Major General John Deane was recruited for Task Force B, and Foreign Service political planner James Penfield was called back from London to serve because of his experience in the Far East, Soviet sphere, and Great Britain.[73] The rest of the group consisted of Philip Mosley, the director of the Russian Institute at Columbia University, Calvin Hoover, and, from the War College, John Campbell and Colonel Elvin Ligon. These men were selected for their "sound political and military judgment" in regards to the Soviet Union and the free world, their knowledge of communist reactions and methods, their knowledge of American military capabilities to wage general war, and their "ability to evaluate the economic capability of the United States and the rest of the free world."[74]

Task Force C was also a Dulles alternative and resembled the policy enunciated during the campaign for rollback. Task Force C had to seek viable actions to "restore the prestige of the West by winning in one or more areas a success or successes." The policy did not outline a course for global war, nor did it say that global war was to be avoided. Psychological and covert warfare could be used instead of guns and tanks, but the goal of the policy was to gain a sense of victory in the West to inspire the free world and discourage the communist world.[75]

Having the difficult task of arguing for a policy of rollback, Task Force C required members who had "imaginative military, political, psychological and subversive planning experience" as well as superior experience on Soviet-Communist actions and reactions including the military situations in Korea and Soviet satellite areas, and the "ability to evaluate the economic resources required to follow such a course."[76] Although the recommended head of the Task Force was public servant James McCloy, Vice Admiral Richard Conolly was finally approved for the job. Foreign Service member and Russian expert G. Frederick Reinhardt agreed to be a member, being called back from the American Embassy in Paris.[77] Lieutenant General L. L. Lemnitzer, who had recently returned from Korea, brought to the group his vast experience in foreign affairs. Colonel Harold K. Johnston was asked along with Leslie Brady and Kilbourne Johnston from the War College. Finally, since Task Force C was to write out a plan that was to reverse the momentum of Soviet aggression, a difficult task, Eisenhower called upon his friend Andrew Goodpaster to sit on Task Force C. Described as a "brilliant military planner with extensive background in international affairs," Goodpaster was the man Eisenhower believed could thoroughly evaluate the option of rollback.[78] Since Goodpaster did not have any prior association with the policy of rollback, Cutler explained to him that Eisenhower "wanted somebody with some common sense" who would see to it the Task Force "didn't go completely off in their analysis."[79]

Starting work at eight in the morning and breaking only for lunch and dinner and the occasional exercise hour in the afternoon, the groups worked until midnight each day for the next five weeks.[80] The Task Forces were privy to all available intelligence information and were briefed, not always objectively, by key department officials. For example, Dulles visited the Task Forces while they were sequestered in the War College. He wanted to discuss with the group their shared assumptions and to discuss the "ultimate purpose of the safeguarding of our security."[81] The CIA representative briefing the group made the case for a more aggressive policy as he saw the Soviet threat in much harsher terms than the Task Forces did.[82] Ultimately, though, the Task Forces relied heavily on the individual knowledge and experience of their members to reach their conclusions.

Eisenhower had requested that the groups meet to coordinate their presentations so as to avoid excessive duplication.[83] As directed, the Task Forces met at a plenary session on June 26 to allow each chairman to summarize the main line his group was arguing. Kennan accepted the general framework of the most recent NSC policy paper on basic national security, NSC 153/1, which had just been completed on June 10. However, Kennan did promise to question the wording of NSC 153/1 in regards to the Soviet threat, as it seemed to commit the U.S. to the global containment of NSC 68. However, Kennan argued that the economy could withstand increased and prolonged military expenditures. General McCormack explained that Task Force B defined its position as a rigid and completely unilateral policy. It was also the most economical one, costing less than Alternative C and being more efficient than Alternative A since "the military forces will be conserved as being the best forces to wage general war" guaranteeing a "greater cohesion in the defense effort."[84] Admiral Conolly admitted that his Task Force was not as far ahead as the other two seemed to be. However, Task Force C was not going to present a policy of reducing Soviet strength at the cost of general war. Instead, military deterrence and political warfare were to be the tools for rolling back the communist presence in Eastern Europe. The economic cost of such a policy was not calculable. Like Kennan, Conolly accepted the general framework of NSC 153/1, but made clear that whereas Task Force A was trying to carry out the peace aims of NSC 153/1, Task Force C was carrying out the war aims of that document.[85] With the basic parameters defined by the three chairmen, the Task Forces went back to work on their final drafts. As they were working away at the War College, Cutler was making arrangements for the special NSC meeting where the final reports world be heard.

On June 25, Cutler sent a memo to Wilson instructing him that the NSC had planned to hold two special meetings, and Eisenhower wanted the newly-appointed Joint Chiefs of Staff and the Secretaries of the Army, Navy, and Air Force to attend.[86] Eisenhower felt that the Joint Chiefs, some of whom were not to be sworn in by those dates, had to attend these meetings in order to assume their responsibilities with the utmost efficiency.[87] The first meeting on July 14 covered FY55 budget concerns and U.S. military objectives. Eisenhower explained to the Joint Chiefs that he wanted them to take a tour of the major military institutions in order for them to be thoroughly educated with the entire military establishment. Eisenhower then ordered them to use that information to take a "completely new, fresh survey of our military capabilities in light of our global commitments."[88] Specifically, Eisenhower wanted the Joint Chiefs' views on how to best deploy American troops to find "the most effective employment of available national resources to ensure the defense of our country for the long pull which may lie ahead."[89] The Joint Chiefs' report was combined with the reports given at the second meeting, "an extraordinary" meeting, on the 16th, which heard the conclusions from Project Solarium. The synthesis of these reports resulted in NSC 162/2, or Eisenhower's "New Look."

The NSC meetings were an ideal way to educate everyone involved in policy making and get them on board with the administration. In addition to the Joint Chiefs and permanent members being in attendance, key cabinet members, relevant assistant secretaries, planning board members, and all military superiors were asked to join. In all, thirty-nine people, excluding Task Force members, attended the all-day meeting. Eisenhower wanted such an extensive audience that day so that they all heard the background, arguments, and conclusions to prepare them to get on board and support Eisenhower's final decisions regarding security policy. The special NSC meeting was a perfect opportunity to educate all the people who were to be involved in national security planning for the long haul.[90]

Being given two hours for their presentation and maximum time for questions, the Task Forces presented their conclusions to the President and the National Security council on July 16, 1953. With only short breaks between each presentation and time for lunch, the meeting lasted all day.[91]

Task Force A's Report

The conclusions of Task Force A understandably reflected Kennan's views. Although he was not happy about having been prescribed a specific line to argue, Kennan defended his original proposal of containment to Truman outlined in NSC 20/4.[92] Drafted in 1948, NSC 20/4 outlined Kennan's argument that

American defense spending and preparedness had to be sustainable over the long term, so as not to disrupt American economic stability. Therefore, the level of preparedness had only to be sufficient to meet "immediate military commitments."[93] Kennan's group also maintained that NSC 153/1 presented a suitable policy that provided a framework for success.[94] As such, Task Force A defined its mission as threefold: to preserve a level of preparedness to secure the United States and to assist in the defense of the free world; to continue economic and military assistance to the free world; and to continue the containment policy of political, economic, and psychological exploitation of the Soviet Union and its satellites through means which avoided war.[95] Eisenhower could have written that mission himself.

Although Kennan's group accepted the basic assumptions of NSC 153/1, improvements needed to be made for the United States to assume the strategic offensive. Regaining flexibility and achieving better integration and implementation were key areas to be improved. In assessing the Soviet threat, the group accepted that the political leaders in Moscow were dedicated to the destruction of western capitalism and had the military strength to carry out their aims. However, they rejected the idea put forth in NSC 68 that the Soviets were on the verge of waging war against the United States, and within their report, members of Task Force A described the U.S. position vis-à-vis the Soviets as sounder and more powerful. However, the Soviet control over Eastern Europe prohibited any chance of seeking the restoration of normal relations and stability in Europe as a whole. Additional countries were most likely to come under the control of communism through overt or covert Soviet action and soon the Soviets would possess enough nuclear capability to inflict serious damage on the United States. American priorities, in light of this threat, had to assure U.S. security against the Soviet military threat, prevent the expansion of communism, and if possible, reduce the area under Soviet control, particularly in China.[96]

In addition to the Soviet threat, Kennan's group saw the developing world and the rising discontent and resentment against the West as important areas to address. Although seen as separate from the Soviet threat, the instability in the Third World was being exploited for communist gains, and the United States had therefore to avoid policies that stressed only wartime objectives or that war was inevitable. To nurture a sound relationship with the Third World, the United States had to create a stable and reliable policy that stressed the positive elements of strengthening the free world through Western leadership.[97] It was vital to evaluate thoroughly each decision to aid a colonial power since the United States was being increasingly viewed, particularly in Asia, as imperialist, which played into the hands of the Communists.[98]

Kennan succeeded in getting his views on Germany incorporated into the report. Claiming, "the future of Germany is, in a large part, the determinate to the future of Europe," Kennan argued that the United States needed a more plausible negotiating stance over the question of reunification.[99] Unhappy about the current American position, which gladly accepted a Soviet withdrawal from East

Germany but refused to reciprocate in kind, Kennan believed such a position offered nothing to the Soviets, eliminating any possibility for negotiation. Kennan wanted to see a position that "would have put the onus of holding out against German unification more on the Russians and less on us."[100] The group also identified France as weak and "at the root of many of most serious problems faced by the U.S. in Europe." Indeed the United States needed to support its allies when necessary, but to improve this situation, Kennan's group recommended that the United States quietly shift responsibility back to France and cease bailing "her out of perennial crises." However, the Task Force did not recommend stepping away from Indochina. Rather, the report stated bluntly that Communist control in that area "would critically endanger U.S. and free world security interests." The United States had to regain the military initiative in the region, recognizing that defense of Indochina against communism was "a crucial front in the struggle" to contain communist advances.[101]

To contain communism in Asia, the group recommended that political and economic pressure continued to be placed on Communist China, being sure to avoid military confrontation. Such pressure included refusing to recognize China and continued trade embargoes until the two sides reached a peaceful settlement of the Korean and Indochina situations. Promising to protect Formosa [Taiwan] and its islands and securing the freedom of South Korea should also continue, as should the rebuilding of Japan as a Western ally. Kennan's group also recommended that Japan be "a main bulwark of the free world in the western Pacific."[102] To achieve that, Japan's trade had to grow with the West, and possibly with Communist China too.

In the rest of the world, stepping up economic aid to India and Pakistan was the wisest course. Continued economic aid to the Middle East via the World Bank, so as to "allay local suspicions of direct American interference," was recommended, particularly in the resettlement of the Arab refugees from Palestine. Being more impartial and objective in dealing with the Middle East ought to be coupled with a "clear willingness to assist where needed and when asked." Finally, the group suggested that establishment of the Middle East Defense Organization be held off until the area matured politically.[103]

In line with the policy of containment, Kennan's group insisted that the United States continued to develop an international order through active participation in the United Nations and continued attempts to convince the Soviets "of the fallacy of the fundamental concepts upon which their policies are based."[104] Reducing the Soviet ability and intent to use its power against the West was essential through overt or covert operations. The United States also had to begin thinking about negotiations with the Soviet Union. It was inevitable that some agreements be made between the two powers in the future and it was important that there be "an effective *stance* with the relation to the problem of negotiation," so that the United States did not appear to be the people "who *want* the

Cold War to continue."[105] Therefore, a policy had to be in place that allowed successful negotiations without sacrificing American security.

Not surprisingly, Kennan wrote most of the report's sections on political policy, history, and philosophical thoughts. Other members took the lead on issues regarding government expenditures and military preparations. But all were willing, as Kennan reflected back, to "stand by the statements made in the paper."[106]

In short, the thesis of Task Force A's report was that America was not doing badly in the Cold War vis-à-vis the Soviets. Believing that the free world held the upper hand, Kennan's group argued that the only significant danger to U.S. security was atomic war and so long as the U.S. maintained superiority in this field, the Soviets would be deterred from war.[107] The American economy was able to withstand the necessary military expenditures and, if containment were followed, eventually the Soviet system would disintegrate.

Task Force B's Report

The course prescribed to Task Force B was, in its words, "unprecedented in the history of U.S. foreign policy in that it is a clear and unmistakable commitment to wage general war under certain specific conditions."[108] Specifically, a line was to be drawn that the Communists were not to cross—the lines of containment would be visible to all. Led by McCormack, Task Force B argued for a continuous line to be drawn around the Soviet Union, extending from the current line drawn in the NATO area and the western Pacific. Then, a clear and open statement by the United States was to be made to the Soviets explaining the policy and the American commitment to uphold the policy, and, should the Soviet-Communists take aggressive action across that line, the United States would take all necessary action against the Soviets.[109] McCormack's group stressed that this policy of promised general war against further Soviet aggression actually reduced the likelihood of such a war.[110]

The policy was strictly unilateral and would be carried out only against armed aggression, not against "trifling border incidents." The framers accepted many of the tenets of Task Forces A and C, but added the new premise of threatening "general war as the primary sanction against further Soviet Bloc aggression."[111] As such, it was necessary that the United States maintain a constant military force capable of carrying out a general war. In essence, this was a simple policy of deterrence, promising to throw the full force of American military power at the Soviets in hopes of deterring further aggression. However, McCormack's group made clear that they perceived this as a support policy to existing approaches, not as a replacement. There was much flexibility, they thought, with such an approach.[112]

Contrary to Kennan's group, McCormack's group concluded that the Soviet threat was more dangerous to the free world if unchecked.[113] It also criticized previous attempts by the United States to check Soviet aggression at the periphery. The group believed a new approach was needed to ensure successful containment of the Soviet Union. If the Soviet Bloc advanced militarily beyond its present borders, general war would be assumed. If indigenous Communist forces seized power in a country outside the Soviet Bloc, the United States reserved "freedom of action" to "re-establish a situation compatible with the security interests of the United States and its allies."[114] The group argued that such a policy reduced the likelihood of war by acting as a deterrent.

There were other advantages with Alternative B. Subversion of free countries would be more difficult for the Soviets since such action would be viewed as "crossing the line drawn" and therefore risking war. Expansion of Communist China would be deterred as the policy extended beyond just the Soviet Union, to any communist state. And, with the clearly defined role of the U.S. military, the economic development and maintenance of the military would be more efficient. Military expenditures were not likely to decrease, but with Alternative B they would level out. Since the American military was not to commit to peripheral wars, expenses accrued during a Korean-like conflict would be eliminated. Most importantly, McCormack's group agreed with the other groups in that whatever the cost for national security, the American economy and American people had to bear the burden. Simply put, McCormack's group said, "whatever the evils of inflation, whatever the economic problems involved in efforts to control it, these cannot be weighed in the same scales with the great danger to our national survival."[115]

The group acknowledged that, no doubt, the Soviets' response to Alternative B would be a defensive posture. However, they concluded that it was unlikely that the Soviet economy would or could improve to a level sufficient enough to challenge a United States operating under plan B. The United States ought to have the upper hand for the foreseeable future. And since the Soviets risked destruction in a general war if they chose to expand, Alternative B seemed the most effective deterrent. Finally, McCormack's group insisted that for the deterrent to work, the United States had to announce publicly the terms of Alternative B and "drive home the point that the U.S. stands solidly behind its proclamation," perhaps through a Joint Resolution in Congress. Furthermore, the support of American allies was important, although the policy was not subject to a veto by the allies or United Nations.[116]

Task Force C's Report

Under the chairmanship of Conolly, the members of Task Force C agreed that the policy alternative described in their report offered "major returns and advantages as a basic policy."[117] Narrowing the lines of action for a rollback policy down to political pressure and covert action, the group rejected the option of any military action that might lead to war between the United States and Soviet Union.[118] This rejection of reckless military actions was likely the result of moderates like General Goodpaster on the committee. Instead, Conolly's group defined their mission as one which created the "maximum disruption and popular resistance throughout the Soviet Bloc," to accelerate the liberation of their nations.[119] Ending the Iron Curtain, destroying Communist influence in the free world, and crippling the Soviet capability for war were the prescribed aims. Reducing Soviet expansion was not enough. Alternative C prevented *any* Soviet expansion. It proposed to do so through Cold War, avoiding a general war.[120] In short, Conolly and his men rejected the willingness of McCormack's group to threaten and declare war.

Time had been working against the United States, and Conolly's group perceived a bigger Soviet threat than the other two groups.[121] Arguing that hanging on to the status quo was not enough, the U.S. had to weaken "Soviet power and militancy, before the Soviets cross the threshold of ability to inflict critical damage on the U.S."[122] As the group saw it, that threshold was about five years.[123] However, the group did reject the idea of a date of maximum danger. Instead, the members calculated when the Soviets might conceivably possess enough atomic weapons to do considerable harm to the United States, but they never labeled that a time of "maximum danger" like NSC 68.[124] Certainly they recognized an increased danger due to the nuclear age, but believed the Western values and political system was the stronger system in the long run.[125]

To strengthen the Western system, which rested on the "essential dignity and worth of the individual in a free society," a "climate of victory" had to be created through political action and paramilitary, economic and covert operations.[126] To do this, Conolly's group proposed numerous courses of action to follow. Educating the American people about the nature of the Soviet threat was important to securing public support for the necessary costs of building a stronger military establishment. Utilizing every aspect of American technological and industrial strength was vital to stay ahead of the Soviets. Exploiting favorable positions through diplomacy and negotiations improved the American political position. Limitation of long-term political commitments was needed to guarantee American initiative and freedom of action. The policy called for a disabling of the Communist apparatus in the free world, including outlawing the Communist Party in the United States. Finally, covert action was important to the disruption of the Soviet system and the United States was to seize every opportunity to discredit and confuse the enemy. Such action created a climate of victory and lured "doubting nations to our side."[127]

As American allies were most likely to oppose such aggressive action, Conolly's group suggested that the "full scope of the plan would be revealed to them only gradually as successes were won."[128] However, they fully supported present commitments to NATO and recognized that the allies were essential in consolidating the strength of the free world. In Europe, the group called for a united and rearmed Germany fully integrated into the European community. At a minimum, a rearmed West Germany loyal to the West and a neutralized East Germany would be acceptable. France had to be firmly told that delays in mutual security interests would no longer be accepted. In particular, Conolly's group urged the United States to "feel less constrained to subject its actions outside the scope of the NATO commitment to the veto of NATO partners, specifically France and the United Kingdom."[129] However, foreign aid had to continue to the American allies for as long as the Cold War continued.

Strengthening the American military posture, both offensively and defensively, was key to carrying out the objectives outlined in Alternative C. Since Conolly's group envisioned the need for a greater military establishment, a basic system of universal military training and service was suggested, as was stockpiling equipment reserves, increasing scientific and technological research and development, accelerating improvements in continental defense, and strengthening the atomic program. Deploying additional troops to sensitive areas and preparing for early mobilization of reinforcements also strengthened the military's position. Weakening that position through disarmament discussions and restrictive regional pacts had to be minimized.[130]

Elsewhere in the world, Conolly's group agreed with Kennan's group on a number of points. The policy argued for Japan was essentially the same, and both groups agreed that a communist defeat in Indochina was vital. Conolly's group sought to establish a closer US-French military collaboration in Indochina. It also sought to use Nationalist Chinese forces to retake the island of Hainan and conduct military operations against Communist China. A strict embargo was to remain against Communist China and the country was not to be seated in the United Nations "or any other international body."[131]

Just as important as military strength was propaganda and covert operations. The group maintained that there were two deficiencies preventing propaganda and covert successes. First was the "lack of a national strategy to end the Cold War by winning it."[132] Second, the U.S. lacked a central command post to oversee that resources were properly committed to winning the Cold War. Conolly's group concluded, "Containment is sterile as a continuing policy."[133] Instead of waiting for the Soviet Union to disintegrate, the group recommended actively seeking an end to the Cold War on American terms and preventing any further substantial Soviet aggression. The United States could not continue to live with the Soviet threat and had to destroy it.[134] In fact, Conolly's group predicted that by 1965 the Soviet satellites would be freed, "or in such a state of disaffection with the U.S.S.R. as to constitute a serious weakness rather than strength in the Soviet bloc."[135]

You Can't Get There from Here: Combining the Reports

At the end of their presentations, Eisenhower remarked that he had "never attended a better or more persuasively presented staff job."[136] "Beautifully presented," Eisenhower wrote in his notes; they "all seemed to believe" in their alternative.[137] C.D. Jackson called it a fascinating performance, one that demonstrated "real brains" and thoughtful execution.[138] The Task Forces had taken their assignments seriously and thoughtfully. What was so impressive was that each Task Force stayed on course within its given parameters. As Kennan had said, not all the members liked being boxed into a specific line to argue, but all did so, and with skill and eloquence. It was this kind of discipline Eisenhower looked for in such committees.

After praising the Task Forces for a job well done, Eisenhower made a few observations. He noted that the argument in Alternative B for a global war as a defense of freedom was "almost [a] contradiction in terms."[139] Global war was, as he saw it, a no win situation. "The only thing worse than losing a global war was winning one," Eisenhower told the group, because "there would be no individual freedom after the next global war."[140] Eisenhower also warned that any national security policy that asked the American people to bear more than they were willing would result in government controls, the loss of more of the individual liberty the government was trying to protect, and ultimately the creation of "a garrison state."[141] If, therefore, the U.S. adopted a national security policy that required increased expenditures and increased taxes, "there must be a vigorous campaign to educate the people . . . and our allies."[142] Kennan later remembered that Eisenhower had a total grasp on what had been presented and had a "mastery of the subject matter and a thoughtfulness and penetration that were quite remarkable," leaving him to conclude that Eisenhower was a "much more intelligent man than he was given credit for being."[143]

Eisenhower also remarked that he thought there were "many similarities in the three presentations."[144] For example, he noted that there were elements of Alternative B in Alternative C.[145] Also, the recommendations for covert operations and psychological warfare within Alternative C appealed to Eisenhower, who had had a long predisposition for such actions.[146] Believing that the United States and Western Europe were safe from Soviet attack, Eisenhower was convinced of the argument that the periphery was susceptible to subversion. As such, Eisenhower "indicated that there was still more for the Task Forces to do."[147] He ordered the three Task Forces to agree upon the best features of each report and create a unified report to be used as a basic national security policy.[148] It was not an easy task.

The Task Forces were exhausted and resisted Eisenhower's request.[149] Explaining, "the essential differences of approach between Task Forces A and C cannot be reconciled," the Task Forces did not see how a synthesis could be achieved.[150] Cutler briefed Eisenhower on the Task Forces' resistance and Eisenhower was obviously disgusted. He told Cutler to work something out that he believed was reasonable.[151] On Sunday, July 26, John F. Dulles, Allen Dulles, Jackson, Cutler, and Smith all met to decide how to start on integrating the reports into a national security policy. It was finally decided that the first step was for Cutler to write some kind of paper to present to the NSC.[152] In conjunction with Task Force members, Cutler worked on writing summaries of the three reports to be presented to the Council as a basis for discussion at the upcoming July 30 meeting.[153]

At the July 30 NSC meeting, Cutler distributed his two-page memorandum which served, in his words, "as an admirable kick-off for an hour's discussion."[154] The first page summarized the arguments of each Task Force. The second page proposed a "new basic concept" to serve as a jumping-off point for a committee to draft a new basic national security policy. This new concept was to accomplish five tasks: 1) build a strong offensive capability, continental defense capability, and mobilization capability; 2) secure loyal allies in Europe and Asia; 3) limit future foreign aid; 4) make a public statement that should the Soviets cross beyond their present borders, they risked general war with the United States; and 5) selectively reduce Soviet power and influence in its satellites and in the free world. Cutler also noted that a "climate of victory," discussed by Task Force C, should be sought in the near future to "bolster the morale and strength of the free world," part of Eisenhower's 'Great Equation.' Some of the aggressive actions suggested by Task Force C against the Soviet satellite and the subsequent increased risks of general war would be acceptable. Task Force A had placed the risk of general war extremely high if such aggressive action were taken, but Cutler's memo said that the risk of war was "less grave at the present moment than" Task Force A had surmised.[155] After the memo was distributed, Eisenhower observed that the "new concept" was, in effect, creating a Task Force D—a committee to prepare a report based on the other three reports.[156]

After much discussion, Eisenhower approved that the Planning Board, not a new Task Force, was to draft a new basic national security policy using the Solarium reports as a starting point. Using the Planning Board had the obvious advantage of allowing representatives from the other departments to be included in policy making. Those Task Force members who were able to stay on in D.C. worked with the Planning Board.[157] In addition to Planning Board members and Task Force members, Wilson insisted that the newly appointed Joint Chiefs of Staff have an opportunity to comment.[158]

However, it was clear from the meeting on the 30th that the final policy conclusions would not be easily decided. Questions arose as to the status of Greece and Turkey, and the Middle East in general, as those areas were not addressed in Cutler's memo. Secretary Humphrey immediately had problems over the implied military build-up of the memo and asked if a less expensive means of carrying out policy might be achieved. Eisenhower repeated his position that security was not going to be arbitrarily sacrificed for the economy and reminded Humphrey that, "it was part of our policy to build up our capability for action."[159] Debates as to how the new policy addressed situations like the one developing in Guatemala and in the Middle East, particularly with Iranian oil, indicated that the Planning Board had a formidable task in front of it.

The next day, Cutler modified his two-page memo to reflect the Council's discussion. The new "Points for Consideration in Drafting New Policy," now had six tasks outlined: 1) build a strong offensive capability, continental defense capability, and mobilization capability *at the "lowest feasible cost;"* 2) secure loyal allies in Europe, Asia, *and the Middle East*; 3) limit future foreign aid; 4) *determine if there was a line of no aggression* which the Soviets could not cross without risking general war with the United States; 5) selectively reduce Soviet power and influence in its satellites; and 6) *use means other than the military* to eliminate Soviet power and influence in the free world.[160] It was this memo that the Planning Board was to use to draft policy. Dulles, however, made clear to his man on the Planning Board, Robert Bowie, that the July 31st "Points for Consideration" memo was only to be used as a guideline, not as a binding position paper.[161] Regardless, the final policy paper, NSC 162/2, closely reflected the goals of Cutler's memo which, in turn, reflected the 'Great Equation' and the strategic thinking of Eisenhower—build an effective deterrent force through nuclear weapons, protect second-strike capabilities through continental defense, and rely on means other than general or limited war to win the Cold War. Rather than the grand scheme nature of NSC-68, which had the country spending billions on countless projects, Eisenhower's NSC 162/2 reflected a coherent national strategy with specific goals. Robert Bowie led the formulation of this paper.

Robert Bowie had been selected by Dulles in April to replace Paul Nitze as director of the Policy Planning Staff affective May 28.[162] Dulles thought highly of the Harvard Law professor and felt that he was well qualified for the position.[163] Cutler later commented that Bowie was "one of the best minds I had ever come in contact with."[164] Bowie, as director of the Policy Planning Staff, was also the State Department's representative on the NSC Planning Board, a combined position that Dulles called "one of the most important assignments there is."[165] Bowie went right to work coordinating the drafting of the new policy paper.

As Bowie saw it, the Planning Board did not have to devote much time to the policy suggestions of Alternative A since it argued along lines of current policy. The broad question for the Planning Board was whether or not to adopt any of the positions held by Alternatives B or C.[166] Bowie observed that the three Solarium Task Forces had reached many similar conclusions. All agreed that the United States needed allies for any long-term security objectives and should cultivate strong relations with current allies. All agreed too on the central importance of American policy toward Europe, especially Germany, France, and

Britain. They also agreed that it was vital to avoid a general war with the Soviet Union. Each Task Force stressed strengthening current continental defense systems for security and retaliation options. And, finally, it was concluded that the economy and the American people could withstand the necessary increases for defense levels.[167]

In addition, despite outward appearances, all three reports seemed to portray the threat from the Soviet Union in essentially the same way, rejecting the idea of a date of maximum danger and focusing on Soviet atomic capability. But few, according to General Goodpaster, really believed that the Soviets "would undertake an aggressive use of force against us."[168] Certainly this was a different perspective than the authors of NSC 68 had. The danger all three Task Forces perceived was in the American relationships with her allies, particularly with France, which was seen as weak, and with Germany, which the Soviets still threatened.[169] The Planning Board used these similarities as a base for its policy paper, but it also incorporated the JCS report, which Eisenhower had requested back in early July.

The Contribution from the Joint Chiefs of Staff

After intensive study on board the Navy's yacht *Sequoia* in early August, the Joint Chiefs were ready to submit their conclusions to Wilson on August 8. The August 8 memorandum, which was signed by all four Chiefs of Staff, concluded that U.S. troops were overcommitted in the peripheries. To rectify this situation, the Joint Chiefs recommended that priority be given to defending U.S. continental borders first, that American troops be withdrawn from overseas, and that "a clear, positive policy" regarding nuclear weapons be put forth.[170] Admiral Radford discussed the report at the NSC meeting on August 27. Making clear that the report was unanimous and only based on the Joint Chiefs' individual experience, not on staff supported research, Radford explained to the Council that a redeployment of troops was needed. Acknowledging that such a concept required the full cooperation of American allies, he explained that Congressional cooperation was needed too, since deficit spending would continue for the estimated two years it would take to implement.[171] However, the Joint Chiefs estimated that their policy would be less expensive than current policy once the initial changes were made. Humphrey called the report "terrific" and said it was "the most important thing that had happened in this country since January 20."[172] Naturally Humphrey was enthusiastic over the report's financial conclusions, but others, less concerned about budgetary reductions, questioned the report.

Dulles and Nixon were both concerned about the maintenance of overseas bases. Dulles assumed that the Joint Chiefs advocated a foreign policy that protected those bases, but worried about redeployment of troops. Radford assured the group that although it was desired that large numbers of U.S. personnel be brought home, the bases would continue to operate in a state of effective readiness with indigenous personnel taking over many tasks American personnel currently performed. Available trained reserves were almost used up, Radford explained, and it was time for the American allies "to supply more men for the task of common defense." Radford agreed with C.D. Jackson's belief that such a large redeployment of American troops was going to be interpreted abroad as America retreating back to her fortress. However, Radford said that the problem of America's present deployment of troops was just as serious a problem and that it was a question of balancing "one evil against another." Regardless, Dulles had grave concerns about public opinion overseas and cautioned against rapid implementation of the policy without first consulting the NATO allies.[173]

Since the biggest impact of withdrawing troops would be felt in Korea, Japan, and Central Europe, Dulles stressed the need for a strong deterrent in atomic and air power to ensure the security of these areas. Radford agreed, stating that tactical and strategic use of atomic weapons should be used in the event of a major conflict. America was spending vast sums of money on these weapons and it was high time that the public taboo on using them be removed. General Twining agreed fully with everything Radford had outlined. Admiral Carney seemed uncertain about many issues and General Ridgway was completely opposed to replacing American troops with allied forces. "If NATO got any inkling of the content of this new concept," Ridgway warned, "the NATO powers would almost certainly construe it as abandonment, and the consequences would be terrifying." By the end of the meeting, despite the fact that the report had been signed by all four Chiefs, it seemed clear that the Joint Chiefs' report was not accepted unanimously and further work had to be done, particularly by the Psychological Strategy Board in terms of public relations and the Planning Board in terms of the Solarium project.[174]

NSC 162/2: "The New Look"

As the Planning Board worked on drafting the new national security policy, it became evident that there were three major areas of disagreement among the participants: the budget, redeployment of troops, and the use of atomic weapons. In the final policy paper, all three were the subjects of compromise.

The budget dispute was reduced to two sides, defined by Cutler as Side A and Side B. Side A recognized the Soviet threat as the primary threat to the United States and insisted security needs must prevail over concerns about the economy, in a continuation of the Truman policies. Side B identified a dual threat to the United States—an external threat from the Soviets and an internal threat from a weak economy. A balance between meeting both threats was called for by Side B. Humphrey and Dodge enthusiastically supported Side B while Wilson criticized their position. Dulles, too, rejected any policy that called for a balanced budget at whatever cost, which he believed Humphrey and Dodge advocated. Furthermore, Dulles wanted to know why defense was always the target of budget cuts and questioned why $2 billion continued to be spent annually on agricultural price supports. Conversely, the Joint Chiefs of Staff advocated a policy that called for a strong military posture at whatever cost. Eisenhower was not sympathetic to that policy; he said, "we could lick the world if we were willing to adopt the system of Adolf Hitler."[175] In the end, the final policy paper, NSC 162/2, reflected the 'Great Equation.' It included a weak economy as a threat to national security stating that a "strong, healthy and expanding U.S. economy is essential to the security and stability of the free world."[176] But, it also included elements of Side A, stating that America must "meet the necessary costs of the policies essential for its security."[177]

The issue of redeploying troops was also defined by Side A and Side B. Side A was a reflection of the Planning Board's position and rejected a major redeployment from Europe and Asia, but considered a study on partial redeployment. Side B believed that, with Allied understanding and support, redeployment of American personnel ought to be carried out within the next few years.[178] Side B reflected the policy set forth by Admiral Radford and the Joint Chiefs in their earlier report—a report that Eisenhower had remarked was "a crystallized and clarified statement of this Administration's understanding of our national security objectives since World War II."[179] For Eisenhower, whose strategic thinking renounced the policy of limited war, there was no need for a large deployment of American servicemen in Europe or Asia. Radford reiterated his support for Side B, and Dulles agreed that the position seemed sound. But as before, he still worried about public opinion abroad and the reaction of NATO allies if they were to learn of this policy too soon. Eisenhower agreed that the key phrase in Side B was "with the understanding of our Allies."[180] Humphrey argued for immediate redeployment to save costs, but Eisenhower, Dulles, and Radford cautioned against hasty actions that could seriously undermine the European coalition. Again, Eisenhower placed greater emphasis on all sides of the 'Great Equation,' rather than on just the budgetary side. In the end, the issue of redeployment of troops went unresolved in the final NSC 162/2 policy paper. There was unanimous agreement that the U.S. was overcommitted and needed a redeployment of troops. However, the policy also stated, "any major withdrawal of U.S. troops from Europe or the Far East would be interpreted as a diminution of U.S. interest in the defense of these areas and would seriously undermine the strength and cohesion of the coalition."[181] So although troops ought to be redeployed, the authors of NSC 162/2 left the timing vague of when the troops would be called home.

The issue of atomic weapons had been debated at length in early 1953 in a Korean context, but no resolution was ever finalized. Dulles and Nixon inquired into their use at the NSC meeting with the Joint Chiefs on August 27, and Admiral Radford had taken a strong position for their tactical and strategic use. The issue arose again during NSC 162 discussions. Wilson suggested in mid-October that the Council decide upon what kind of shift in emphasis from conventional weapons to atomic weapons they were willing to make before the Joint Chiefs came up with a "new look" for American military strategy. Humphrey argued for a settlement on the issue, saying that "only their [atomic weapons] use on a broad scale could really change the program of the Defense Department and cut the costs of the military budget."[182] Wilson put it more bluntly when he asked, "Do we intend to use weapons on which we are spending such great sums, or do we not?"[183] Eisenhower and Dulles were rather quiet on the issue, but American nuclear capability was a key part of the President's strategic thinking. Eisenhower did not intend to use the weapons he was spending such great sums on, but he did want the symbolic power they held. Historian Richard Immerman explained that nuclear weapons held for Eisenhower a deterrent value through Massive Retaliation, but that the President was aware that that deterrent was unsuitable for combating subversion. Instead, Eisenhower used "nuclear saber rattling" as a way "to get and keep Moscow's attention."[184] Therefore, building a nuclear offensive was the key to deterrence, but that nuclear offensive was not something Eisenhower intended to use.

The previous draft to NSC 162/2 stated that the United States required "a strong military posture, with emphasis on the capability of inflicting massive retaliatory damage by offensive striking power." The Joint Chiefs, with the exception of Radford, wanted the phrase 'with emphasis on' replaced with 'to include.'[185] As historian Saki Dockrill pointed out, the difference between 'emphasis' and 'include' was critical. 'Include' implied a military posture that resembled NSC 68. 'Emphasis' reflected a significant break from NSC 68. Although Eisenhower saw the debate over the words as academic, he preferred 'emphasis,' which more accurately reflected his thinking.[186] Cutler suggested noting in the final draft the Joint Chiefs' dissent, but Eisenhower said no, reminding Cutler that the Joint Chiefs were merely his advisers; it was he who made the decisions.[187] In the end, the use of atomic weapons was not clearly defined, in part, because only Eisenhower could decide when to use them.[188]

With the major debates taken care of, NSC 162/2 was finally approved on October 30, 1953. The final assessment was that there was little chance the Soviets would deliberately attack the U.S., but war through mistake or miscalculation could not be ruled out. If an attack did occur, the Soviets had an ability to inflict serious damage on the United States. As such, it was estimated that an arms race would continue indefinitely between the two countries to improve power positions. Although the United States would not initiate war, in the event of hostilities, atomic weapons were available for use just like other munitions. The authors of NSC 162/2 also accepted the possibility of massive retaliation and the military force necessary for that, but also argued for flexible mobile forces to punish aggression short of massive retaliation. In addition to the massive atomic capability, continental defense and an adequate mobilization base were required for national security.[189] Increasing research and development was crucial as was the development of an intelligence system.[190] The Killian Committee further pursued these recommendations a year later.

A theme repeated in Cutler's memo and the Solarium Task Force reports for strong allies capable of defending the continent was also repeated in NSC 162/2. America was not capable of meeting the cost of defense without allied help, and the report stated bluntly that "in the interest of its own security, the United States must have the support of allies."[191] The policy called for building a "strong, united stable Germany," but in the end, Kennan did not see any of his German recommendations implemented.[192] Yet, his Task Force's suggestions on negotiation were used. The policy recommended keeping open all possibilities of negotiating with both the Soviet Union and China on whatever issues may be possible.[193]

Insightfully, the men predicted that even though the Soviet-China alliance was firm, in the future China might go off on its own and strain its relationship with the Soviets. Elsewhere in Asia, the policy towards Japan outlined in Alternative A was included as was the promise to protect the security of the offshore islands and Korea. Bilateral and multilateral agreements had to be maintained until Japan could assume a leadership role.[194] Furthermore, the final NSC 162/2 report reflected the Task Forces' assertion that Indochina was of great strategic importance and would be protected.[195]

Looking towards the "uncommitted areas of the world," the authors of NSC 162/2 recognized that many Third World nations were antagonistic to the West, but nevertheless aid had to be dispersed to attempt to help them in political and economic growth. "Although largely undeveloped," the report stated, "their vast manpower, their essential raw materials and their potential for growth are such that their absorption within the Soviet system would greatly, perhaps decisively, alter the world balance of power to our detriment."[196] Committing aid to these areas was therefore essential, as Task Force A had recommended. Along the same line, in a passage practically straight out of Alternative A, NSC 162/2 stated that in the face of the Soviet threat, the United States and its allies had to "always seek to create and sustain the hope and confidence of the free world in the ability of its basic ideas and institutions not merely to oppose the communist threat, but to provide a way of life superior to Communism."[197] In other words, talking about liberty just might stop people from becoming communists after all.

Foreign aid was another area that assisted in the fight against Soviet Communism without using the military. In his policy memo, Cutler had recommended limiting foreign aid, and the question was debated in Council meetings. Foreign aid was always an area where Congress looked to make budget cuts, but Eisenhower believed that with foreign aid, "the United States is getting more for its money than in any other" area.[198] In the end, it was agreed to limit foreign aid, but continue it "according to the calculated advantage of such aid to the U.S. world position."[199]

Finally, recognition of the fact that American nuclear superiority would not last and that, when it eroded, the world situation would change was made within the NSC 162/2 policy. As the last paragraph said, "The foregoing conclusions are valid only so long as the United States maintains a retaliatory capability that cannot be neutralized by a surprise Soviet attack. Therefore, there must be continuing examination and periodic report to the NSC in regard to the likelihood of such neutralization of U.S. retaliatory capability."[200] National security needs continued to be reevaluated through Eisenhower's tenure and NSC 162/2 was not the last basic national security policy. NSC 162/2 was a blueprint for the kind of national security policy that Eisenhower desired, accurately reflecting the three sides of the 'Great Equation:' building a spiritual resolve while meeting the Soviet threat without severely undermining the economy.[201]

Yet the document did not end Eisenhower's battles over the budget. After Eisenhower's Defense Reorganization message of April 30, Stuart Symington and other Democrats criticized the Eisenhower budget for its substantial cuts in the Air Force budget. Now, with NSC 162/2, Democrats were unable to criticize the role of the Air Force as the "New Look" gave primary emphasis to that branch. However, although airpower was given a greater piece of the budget pie, overall defense allocations were reduced, concerning many Democrats. As historian Gary Reichard explained, the New Look appeared to Democrats such as Albert Gore, Hubert Humphrey, Herbert Lehman, Mike Mansfield, and A.S. Mike Monroney to "represent an unsafe overemphasis on air-atomic power and a penny-pinching approach in general."[202] The battle would continue as Eisenhower sought a way to achieve a "bigger bang for the buck," looking to the Technological Capabilities Panel in early 1954.

NSC 162/2 did not look all that different from what was in existence before the Solarium project. What made it different was that it had what Kennan called a "greater stamp of presidential approval" than before.[203] NSC 162/2 reflected the views held by Kennan and his containment policy. The flexibility offered in Kennan's conclusions fit well with Eisenhower's desire for a policy that was not "frozen to certain positions in advance of events."[204] Even though it seemed like Eisenhower favored a more Kennan-like approach from the May 8 Solarium Room discussion with Dulles, the subsequent Solarium Exercise allowed Eisenhower to get respected civilian outsiders, as well as his national security staff, to participate in the development of the administration's first basic National Security paper and be part of the decision-making process. By stacking the deck through membership selection and narrow assignments, Eisenhower was able to re-examine containment, bury rollback, and build a team consensus for his 'New Look.'

Eisenhower supported the general aims of containment, but felt like NSC 68 had clouded them. The Solarium Exercise allowed for a general reexamination of policy that was important. Eisenhower needed to take a close look at the Truman policies, which had been established to deal with the Soviet threat. As Kennan said, Eisenhower could not just say because "Truman and Acheson thought that this was the way things ought to be . . . I accept all of this automatically."[205] Since Eisenhower had a responsibility to evaluate the old Democratic system to find its strengths and weak points, Solarium allowed him to do that and bring it to the American people as his own.

In addition to making containment his own, the Solarium Exercise allowed Eisenhower to bury the campaign pledge for a rollback policy. NSC 162/2 did use some of the rhetoric from Task Force C to enhance political containment by adding covert action. Since the Soviets had firm control over their satellites, which would be difficult to break, the authors of NSC 162/2 called for "overt and covert measures to discredit Soviet prestige and ideology."[206] Overall, the primary goal of rollback, given as Alternative C, had been buried as a policy option even though Alternative C never advocated military action. General Goodpaster and Bowie both agreed that burying rollback was one of the goals Eisenhower had for the Solarium Project.[207]

Finally, the Solarium Project clarified the general outlook of the new administration and, as Kennan said, prodded "a lot of people in the Washington bureaucracy, military, and civilian, into taking a new look at things we had been trying to do, and see whether they could not improve on our previous performance."[208] For example, the conclusions of Task Force C, which did not advocate the use of force, were helpful for Dulles in combating some of the talk and proposals coming out of the Pentagon, and the absence of radical ideas involving the dangerous use of force allowed Eisenhower to avoid force for eight years.[209] Ultimately, the Solarium Project was characteristic of Eisenhower, who liked to have, in the words of Goodpaster, "very thorough, comprehensive evaluations made, targeted ultimately on specific options and specific lines of policy."[210] By having experts evaluate a specific question and report back on it to the NSC, Eisenhower was able to have his top policymakers hear the key arguments, recommendations, and background. This approach allowed everyone around Eisenhower to understand the policy line and get behind him when he said this is the way it is going to be.[211]

Eisenhower reflected back on his military service and immediately went to work reorganizing the National Security Council into an efficient advising body. Using that forum, he established an ad hoc committee of brilliant men to act as a debating team to reevaluate national security policy. The committee took its tasks seriously and stayed within the parameters of its assignment. The result was a remarkable and unique exercise in American national security history, giving Eisenhower his "new look" in foreign policy. However, as the authors of NSC 162/2 accurately predicted, the nature of the Soviet threat continued to change. With nuclear weapon development and the increasing possibility of surprise attack, Eisenhower turned to another committee of bright young fellows to evaluate how American superiority in science and technology could be harnessed for the enhancement of national security.

Notes

1. Memo on Solarium Project, 5/8/53, EL, WHO NSCS, Executive Secretary Subject File, Box 15, "Project Solarium (3)," 1-3.

2. Letter Cutler to Eisenhower, 12/27/52, EL, AWF, Administrative Series, Box 10, "Cutler, General Robert 1952-53 (5)."

3. Draft memorandum by Kennan to Secretary of State Acheson, 2/17/50, *FRUS*, 1950, 1:160-161.

4. Dwight Eisenhower, *Mandate for Change, 1953-1956*, (New York: Double Day and Co., 1963), 114.

5. Anna Kasten Nelson, "The 'Top of Policy Hill': President Eisenhower and the National Security Council," *Diplomatic History*, 7 (Fall 1983), 308.

6. Letter to Admiral Gallery, 1/28/58, EL, Evan Aurand Papers, Box 3, "Cutler, Robert [limited war]."

7. Letter Cutler to Eisenhower, 12/27/52, EL, AWF, Administrative Series, Box 10, "Cutler, General Robert 1952-53 (5)," 3; Robert Cutler, *No Time For Rest*, (New York: Little Brown, 1965), 67.

8. Letter Cutler to Eisenhower, 12/27/52, EL, AWF, Administrative Series, Box 10, "Cutler, General Robert 1952-53 (5)," 1.

9. Nelson, "The 'Top of Policy Hill,'" 309.

10. Memorandum Lay to Acheson, 4/19/50 and Memorandum Nitze to Acheson, 1/19/51, NA RG 59, OCB/NSC 1947-63, Box 105, "NSC-Admin 1950-54."

11. Memorandum of NSC Discussion, 2/17/54, *FRUS*, 1952-54, 2:631.

12. Quoted in Robert Bowie and Richard Immerman, *Waging Peace: How Eisenhower Shaped an Enduring Cold War Strategy*, (New York: Oxford University Press, 1998), 83.

13. Eisenhower, *Mandate for Change,* 114.

14. Bowie and Immerman, *Waging Peace*, 85-88. For example, Paul Nitze, Director of the Policy Planning Staff, recommended that the PPS continue, as it was an "important element in the State Department contribution to the formulation of national policy." Memorandum Nitze to Smith, 2/12/53, NA RG 59, OCB/NSC 1947-63, Box 105, "NSC-Admin 1950-1954," 4.

15. Cutler, *No Time for Rest*, 295.

16. Memorandum for the President, 3/16/53, NA RG 59 OCB/NSC 1947-63, Box 105, "NSC-Admin 1950-1954," ii.

17. Marshall said that Truman was "not a leader, a force at the table to bring out discussion." Quoted in Bowie and Immerman, *Waging Peace*, 87.

18. Robert Ferrell, ed., *The Eisenhower Diaries,* (New York: Norton, 1981), June 1, 1953 entry, 242.

19. In all, those who were to regularly attend Council meetings were: President, VP, Secretaries of State, Defense, Treasury, Director of Defense Mobilization and the Director for Mutual Security. Report by the Special Assistant for National Security Affairs, 3/16/53, NA RG 59, OCB/NSC 1947-63, Box 105, "NSC-Admin 1950-1954," 5, 7.

20. Humphrey and Eisenhower became close friends. Eisenhower biographer Stephen Ambrose wrote of their relationship: "They were almost exactly the same age, had the same horror of deficit financing, and shared a love for hunting and fishing. At their first meeting, Eisenhower grinned at the balding Humphrey, stuck out his hand, and said, 'Well, George, I see you part your hair the same way I do.'" Ambrose, *Eisenhower: Soldier and President,* (New York, Simon and Schuster, 1990), 290.

21. Cutler, *No Time For Rest*, 295.

22. Report by the Special Assistant for National Security Affairs, 3/16/53, 6.

23. Letter Cutler to Eisenhower, 12/27/52, 2.

24. See Chapter One for discussion on this committee.

25. Cutler, *No Time for Rest,* 298.

26. Cutler Address at the Compton Memorial Dinner, MIT, 1/4/56, EL, AWF, Administrative Series, Box 11, "Cutler, Robert 1956-57 (4)," 6.

27. Ibid., 6-7.

28. Report by the Special Assistant for National Security Affairs, 3/16/53, 7. Eisenhower's NSC met every Thursday morning.

29. Quoted in Bowie and Immerman, *Waging Peace*, 87.

30. Report by the Special Assistant for National Security Affairs, 3/16/53, 10.

31. Bowie and Immerman, *Waging Peace*, 87.; ibid., 10.

32. Report by the Special Assistant for National Security Affairs, 3/16/53, 12.

33. Ibid., 19.

34. In 1953 alone, Cutler presided over 120 meetings of the Planning Board.

35. Letter Eisenhower to Cutler, 3/17/53, NA, RG 59, OCB/NSC 1947-63, Box 105, "NSC-Admin 1950-54."

36. Memorandum of 137th Meeting of the NSC, 3/19/53, EL, AWF, NSC Series, Box 4, "137th Meeting of the NSC 3/18/53," 6.

37. Ibid.

38. Memorandum of Conversation with the President at Fitzsimmons Hospital, Denver, 10/11/55, EL, JFD Papers, WH Memorandum Series, Box 3, "Meetings with the President, 1955 (2)."

39. See Chapter One for a discussion on drafting NSC 149/2.

40. Glen H. Snyder, "The 'New Look' of 1953," in *Strategy, Politics, and Defense Budgets,* (New York: Columbia University Press, 1962), 389-90.

41. Robert Taft to Edmund Lincoln, 2/26/53, Box 1145, Robert Taft Papers, quoted in James Patterson, *Mr. Republican: A Biography of Robert A. Taft,* (Boston: Houghton Mifflin, 1972), 590.

42. Ibid., 600.

43. Ferrell, ed. *The Eisenhower Diaries,* May 1, 1953 entry, 235-236.

44. Douglas Foyle, *Counting the Public In: Presidents, Public Opinion, and Foreign Policy,* (New York: Columbia University Press, 1999), 157.

45. Gary W. Reichard, "Divisions and Dissent: Democrats and Foreign Policy, 1952-1956," *Political Science Quarterly*, 93 (Spring 1978), 53-55. (51-72) Reichard cites the Yalta Resolution and the Charles Bohlen nomination as two examples of early bipartisanship. The other Congressmen joining Symington in his criticism of Eisenhower's budget were: Henry Jackson (WA), Richard Russell (GA), and John Stennis (MS) in the Senate, and John McCormack (MA), George Mahan (TX), and Melvin Price (IL) in the House.

46. July 8, 1953 entry, EL, C.D. Jackson Papers, Box 68, "Log-1953 (3)."

47. Ibid.

48. Memo on Solarium Project, 5/8/53, EL, WHO NSCS, Executive Secretary Subject File, Box 15, "Project Solarium (3)," 1-3.

49. Allen Dulles was the Director of the CIA; Walter Bedell Smith was the Under Secretary of State.

50. 5/2/53 entry, EL, C.D. Jackson Papers, Box 68, "Log-1953 (1);" Cutler, *No Time For Rest*, 308.

51. 5/8/53 entry, EL, C.D. Jackson Papers, Box 68, "Log-1953 (1);" ibid.

52. Memorandum on Solarium Project, 5/8/53. The following discussion is from this document.

53. Memorandum for the Record, 5/9/53, *FRUS*, 1952-54, 2:323.

54. Memorandum of the 144th Meeting of NSC, 5/14/53, EL, AWF, NSC Series, Box 4, "144th Meeting of NSC, 5/13/53."

55. "Project Solarium: A Collective Oral History with General Andrew Goodpaster, Robert Bowie, and Ambassador George Kennan," 2/27/88, Princeton University, Mudd Library, Woodrow Wilson School, Box 93, folder 10, 3.

56. Administrative Instructions, Task Force Operations, Project Solarium, n.d., EL, WHO NSCS, Executive Secretary Subject File, Box 15, "Project Solarium (3)."

57. Memorandum to Secretaries of Defense, State and the Director of Mutual Security, 5/22/53, EL, WHO NSCS, Executive Secretary Subject File, Box 11, "General Papers (Col. Bonesteel);" Letter Cutler to Kennan, 5/26/53, EL, JFD Papers, Subject Series, Box 6, "Kennan, George 1-0-1." For a complete membership list for the Solarium Exercise see Appendix A.

58. Memorandum for the Record by Cutler, 5/15/53, *FRUS*, 1952-54, 2:325. Also on the committee were Robert Amory, Jr., Lt. General L. L. Lemnitzer, Dean Rusk, and Admiral Leslie Stevens.

59. Memorandum Armory to Bowie, 7/8/53, NA, RG 59, OCB/NSC 1947-63, Box 122, "Solarium Project."

60. Attachment to Memorandum for the Record by Cutler, 5/15/53, *FRUS*, 1952-54, 2:325.

61. Letter Kennan to Cutler, 5/25/53, EL, JFD Papers, Subject Series, Box 6, "Kennan, George 1-0-1."

62. Letter Dulles to Cutler, 6/1/53; Letter Dulles to Kennan, 4/6/53, EL, JFD Papers, Subject Series, Box 6, "Kennan, George 1-0-1."

63. Ibid.

64. Letter Kennan to Cutler, 5/25/53.

65. After Nitze was replaced by Robert Bowie on the Policy Planning Staff, Nitze ran into Charles Wilson in April and accepted a position in ISA but asked for a month's vacation before work in early June. This may explain why Nitze declined to be on the

task force when asked in May. For a further account of Nitze's joining the Pentagon see David Callahan, *Dangerous Capabilities: Paul Nitze and the Cold War*, (New York: Harper Collins, 1990), 150-152. Nitze cited prior commitments to Cutler in Letter Cutler to Kennan, 5/26/53, EL, JFD Papers, Subject Series, Box 6, "Kennan, George 1-0-1."

66. Letter Cutler to Kennan, 5/26/53, EL, JFD Papers, Subject Series, Box 6, "Kennan, George 1-0-1."

67. Report to the National Security Council by Task Force A, 7/16/53, NA, RG 59, State Department Participation in OCB/NSC, 1947-63, Box 129, "Solarium Project," i.

68. Personnel Recommendations for Task Force "A," EL, WHO NSCS, Executive Secretary Subject File, Box 11, "General Papers (Col. Bonesteel)."

69. "Project Solarium: A Collective Oral History," 3.

70. For more biographical information on Abe Linclon, see Chapter 6.

71. Personnel Recommendations for Task Force "A;" Minutes of the 155th Meeting of the NSC, 7/16/53, *FRUS*, 1952-54, 2:395.

72. ibid., 326.

73. Personnel Recommendations for Task Force "B," EL, WHO NSCS, Executive Secretary Subject File, Box 11, "General Papers (Col. Bonesteel);" Minutes of the 155th Meeting, 395-396; Telegram to Embassy in London, 6/2/53, NA, RG 59, OCB/NSC, 1947-63, Box 122, "Solarium Project."

74. Personnel Recommendations for Task Force "B," EL, WHO NSCS, Executive Secretary Subject File, Box 11, "General Papers (Col. Bonesteel);" Minutes of the 155th Meeting, 395-396.

75. Ibid.

76. Personnel Recommendations for Task Force "C," EL, WHO NSCS, Executive Secretary Subject File, Box 11, "General Papers (Col. Bonesteel)."

77. Ibid.; Letter Reinhardt to Smith, 5/28/53, NA, RG 59, OCB/NSC, 1947-63, Box 122, "Solarium Project."

78. Ibid., Minutes of the 155th Meeting, 395-396.

79. "Project Solarium: A Collective Oral History," 10. Eisenhower's respect for Goodpaster was summed up when he told Sherman Adams that he "would ask nothing more than for my son to grow up to be as good a man as [Goodpaster] is." See Sherman Adams, *First Hand Report*, (New York: Harper & Brothers, 1961), 53.

80. "Project Solarium: A Collective Oral History," 13.

81. Ibid., 11.

82. Ibid., 17.

83. Memorandum for the Record, 6/23/53, El, WHO NSCS, Executive Secretary Subject File, Box 11, "General Papers (Col. Bonesteel)."

84. Notes Taken at the First Plenary Session of Project Solarium, 6/26/53, *FRUS*, 1952-54, 2:388-393.

85. Ibid.

86. Telephone call Eisenhower to Wilson, 5/11/53, EL, AWF, DDE Diary, Box 4, "Phone calls- February-June 1953 (1)." On May 12, Eisenhower appointed an entirely new group to the JCS to take effect on June 30 and August 15. His appointments were: General Matthew Ridgeway, Chief of Staff for Army; Admiral Robert Carney, Chief Naval Operations; General Nathan Twining, Chief of Staff for Air Force; Admiral Arthur Radford, Chairman of the JCS. See *FRUS*, 1952-54, 2:326-327.

87. Memorandum Cutler to Wilson, 6/25/53, EL, AWF, Administrative Series, Box 10, "Cutler, General Robert 1952-53 (5)."

88. Editorial Note, *FRUS*, 1952-54, 2:394.

89. Memorandum to the Secretary of Defense, 8/8/53, EL, WHO NSCS, Disaster File, Box 11, "NSC 162/2 (1)."

90. "Project Solarium: A Collective Oral History," 19-21.

91. Memorandum for the Record, 6/23/53, El, WHO NSCS, Executive Secretary Subject File, Box 11, "General Papers (Col. Bonesteel)."

92. "Project Solarium: A Collective Oral History," 4.

93. NSC 20/4, 11/23/48, *FRUS*, 1948, 1:663-69.

94. Notes Taken at the First Plenary Session of Project Solarium, 6/26/53, *FRUS*, 1952-54, 2:388.

95. Summaries Prepared by the NSC Staff of Project Solarium Presentations and Written reports, n.d., *FRUS*, 1952-54, 2:399.

96. Ibid., 400-401.

97. Ibid., 401-402.

98. Ibid., 408.

99. Ibid., 406.

100. "Project Solarium: A Collective Oral History," 6-7.

101. Summaries, *FRUS*, 1952-54, 2:407-409.

102. Ibid., 408-409. This position was taken up by Eisenhower. In June 1954 he gave an address stating that the US "either help Japan get on her feet or the Communists would use her to turn the Pacific into a Communist Sea." Eisenhower Calls Free Japan Vital For US Security, *New York Times*, 23 June 1954.

103. Ibid., 409-410.

104. Ibid., 410.

105. Ibid., 411. Italics in original.

106. "Project Solarium: A Collective Oral History," 4-5.

107. Report to the National Security Council by Task Force A, 7/16/53, NA, RG 59, State Department Participation in OCB/NSC, 1947-63, Box 129, "Solarium Project," 15; 145-146.

108. Report to the National Security Council by Task Force B, 7/16/53, NA, RG 59, State Department Participation in OCB/NSC, 1947-63, Box 129, "Solarium Project," 90.

109. Summaries, *FRUS*, 1952-54, 2:412.

110. Report to the National Security Council by Task Force B, 7/16/53, NA, RG 59, State Department Participation in OCB/NSC, 1947-63, Box 129, "Solarium Project," 19.

111. Summaries, *FRUS*, 1952-54, 2:412-413.

112. Ibid., 413.

113. Ibid., 434.

114. Ibid., 414.

115. Ibid., 415.

116. Ibid., 415-416.

117. Report to the National Security Council by Task Force C, 7/16/53, NA, RG 59, State Department Participation in OCB/NSC, 1947-63, Box 129, "Solarium Project," i.

118. "Project Solarium: A Collective Oral History," 13.

119. Summaries, *FRUS*, 1952-54, 2:416.

120. Ibid., 417.

121. Ibid.

122. Report to the National Security Council by Task Force C, 7/16/53, NA, RG 59, State Department Participation in OCB/NSC, 1947-63, Box 129, "Solarium Project," 80.

123. Summaries, *FRUS*, 1952-54, 2:416.

124. "Project Solarium: A Collective Oral History," 11.

125. Ibid., 18.

126. Summaries, *FRUS*, 1952-54, 2:417; Report to the National Security Council by Task Force C, 77.

127. Summaries, 418.

128. Ibid.

129. Ibid., 423.

130. Ibid., 419-420.

131. Ibid., 421.

132. Ibid., 422.

133. Report to the National Security Council by Task Force C, 77. Kennan of course disagreed that containment had no place. He explained that the advantage of Alternative A over B and C was that containment provided "the freedom of action to adjust to, to counter, and in certain cases to exploit, whatever line of action the Kremlin may pursue. If the U.S. adopts Course A, we can always move on to embrace some or all of the elements of Courses B or C if circumstances require." Eisenhower saw that above all else, Alternative C required the support of public opinion at home and abroad. Report to the National Security Council by Task Force A., 144; Hand notes by Eisenhower at NSC meeting, 7/16/53, AWF, DDE Diaries, Box 3, "December 1952-July 1953 (1)."

134. Summaries, *FRUS*, 1952-54, 2:434.

135. Ibid., 431.

136. Memorandum by the Special Assistant to the President for National Security Affairs (Cutler), 7/16/53, *FRUS*, 1952-54, 2:397.

137. Hand notes by Eisenhower at NSC meeting, 7/16/53, AWF, DDE Diaries, Box 3, "December 1952-July 1953 (1)."

138. July 16, 1953 entry, EL, C.D. Jackson Papers, Box 68, "Log-1953 (3)."

139. Hand notes by Eisenhower at NSC meeting, 7/16/53, AWF, DDE Diaries, Box 3, "December 1952-July 1953 (1)."

140. Memorandum by the Special Assistant to the President for National Security Affairs (Cutler), 7/16/53, *FRUS*, 1952-54, 2:397.

141. Ibid.

142. Ibid.

143. Project Solarium: A Collective Oral History," 7.

144. Memorandum by the Special Assistant to the President for National Security Affairs (Cutler), 7/16/53, *FRUS*, 1952-54, 2:397.

145. Hand notes by Eisenhower at NSC meeting, 7/16/53, AWF, DDE Diaries, Box 3, "December 1952-July 1953 (1)."

146. Historian Richard Immerman explained that: "Prior to becoming president Eisenhower was actively involved in promoting unconventional methods of prosecuting the Cold War. Soon after entering the White House he established a committee to improve America's psychological warfare capabilities and a commission to enhance the CIA's effectiveness." See Immerman, "Confessions of an Eisenhower Revisionist," 339.

147. Memorandum by the Special Assistant to the President for National Security Affairs (Cutler), 7/16/53, *FRUS*, 1952-54, 2:397.

148. Ibid., 2:397-398.

149. Memorandum by the Special Assistant for National Security Affairs, 7/16/53, *FRUS*, 1952-54, 2:397-398; "Project Solarium: A Collective Oral History," 13.

150. Summaries, 434.

151. Memorandum by Cutler, 7/16/53, *FRUS*, 1952-54, 2:397-398.

152. July 26, 1953 entry, EL, C.D. Jackson Papers, Box 68, "Log- 1953 (3)."

153. Memorandum by Lay, 7/22/53, *FRUS*, 1952-54, 2:399.

154. Memorandum for General Smith, 7/31/53, EL, WHO NSCS, Executive Secretary's Subject File, Box 17, "Special Assistant (Cutler), Memoranda, 1953 (4)."

155. Project Solarium Memo by Cutler, 7/30/53, NA, RG 59, OCB/NSC, 1947-63, Box 122, "Solarium Project."

156. Memorandum of Discussion at the 157th Meeting of the NSC, 7/30/53, *FRUS*, 1952-54, 2:435-440.

157. Not all of the task force members were able to stay on in Washington to participate on the Planning Board committee. Those who did participate included Lt. General Lemnitzer (Task Force C), Colonel Bonesteel (Task Force A), General McCormack (Task Force B), and Mr. Campbell. See memorandum for Gleason, 8/18/53, NA, RG 59, Records of the PPS, 1935-62, Box 43, "Solarium;" Overall Comment on Policy Paper, 9/18/53, EL, WHO NSCS, Executive Secretary Subject File, Box 17, "Special Assistant (Cutler), Memoranda, 1953 (5)."

158. Memorandum of Discussion at the 157th Meeting of the NSC, 7/30/53, *FRUS*, 1952-54, 2:435-440.

159. Ibid., 436-437.

160. Points for Consideration in Drafting New Policy, 7/31/53, NA, RG 59, OCB/NSC 1947-63, Box 122, "Solarium Project."

161. Memorandum Dulles to Bowie, 8/1/53, NA, RG 59, Box 65, "Review of US Basic National Policy, NSC 152-162, Sept-Dec. 1953."

162. Letter Nitze to Byrnes, 5/15/53, NA, RG 59, records of the PPS 1947-63, Box 50, "Nitze, Paul (speeches and articles) 1945-53."

163. Letter Dulles to Griswald, 4/7/53, EL, JFD Papers, JFD Chronological Series, Box 2, "April 1-31, 1953 (4)."

164. Memorandum for Bowie from Cutler, 7/9/54, NA, RG 59, Box 87, "National Security Council."

165. Letter Dulles to Griswald, 4/7/53, EL, JFD Papers, JFD Chronological Series, Box 2, "April 1-31, 1953 (4)."

166. Procedure for NSC Handling of "Solarium" Project, Bowie to Dulles, 7/29/53, NA, RG 59, OCB/NSC, 1947-63, Box 122, "Solarium Project."

167. Memorandum from Bowie, 7/18/53, RG 59, Records of the PPS, 1947-53, Working Papers, Box 66, "Review of Basic National Policy, NSC 153-162, June-Aug 1953."

168. "Project Solarium: A Collective Oral History," 16.

169. Ibid.

170. Memorandum to Wilson, 8/8/53, EL, WHO NSCS, Disaster File, Box 11, "NSC 162/2 (1)."

171. August 27/53 NSC Meeting and Memo to Wilson, 8/8/53, both in EL, WHO NSCS, Disaster File, Box 11, "NSC 162/2 (1)."

172. Memorandum of Discussion at the 160th Meeting of the NSC, 8/27/53, *FRUS*, 1952-54, 2:447.

173. Ibid., 445-450.

174. Ibid., 446-454.

175. Memorandum of Meeting at the 165th Meeting of the NSC, 10/7/53, *FRUS*, 1952-54, 2:514-519.

176. Report to the NSC, 162/2, 10/30/53, *FRUS*, 1952-54, 2:593-594.

177. Ibid.

178. Memorandum of Meeting at the 165th Meeting of the NSC, 10/7/53, *FRUS*, 1952-54, 2:526.

179. Eisenhower was in Denver during the NSC meeting with the JCS on August 27 and was briefed by Cutler. See: Memorandum by Cutler, 9/3/53, *FRUS*, 1952-54, 2:456.

180. Memorandum of Meeting at the 165th Meeting of the NSC, 10/7/53, *FRUS*, 1952-54, 2:526.

181. Report to the NSC, 162/2, 10/30/53, *FRUS*, 1952-54, 2:593.

182. Memorandum of Discussion at the 166th Meeting of the NSC, 10/13/53, *FRUS*, 1952-54, 2:547.

183. Memorandum of Meeting at the 165th Meeting of the NSC, 10/7/53, *FRUS*, 1952-54, 2:533.

184. Immerman, "Confessions of an Eisenhower Revisionist," 340. For a discussion on Massive retaliation, see Chapter 5.

185. Memorandum by the JCS to Wilson, 10/27/53, 563.

186. Saki Dockrill, *Eisenhower's New Look National Security Policy, 1953-61*, (New York: St. Martin's, 1996), 41.

187. Memorandum of Discussion at the 168th Meeting of the NSC, 10/29/53, *FRUS*, 1952-54, 2:573-574.

188. Beedle Smith explained that the purpose of the paragraph in NSC 162/2 concerning atomic weapon use was primarily to give the military the go ahead to make plans based on availability of atomic weapons, but that the paragraph did not imply atomic weapons would be used in the case of any hostilities. Only the President was to decide on what action to take against hostilities. See Memorandum Smith to Eisenhower, 12/22/53, EL, WHO NSCS, Executive Secretary Subject File, Box 5, "#19 Policy re: Use of nuclear weapons (file #1) (1)."

189. Report to the NSC, 162/2, 10/30/53, *FRUS*, 1952-54, 2:590-591.

190. Ibid., 582.

191. Ibid., 591, 583.

192. Ibid., 592.

193. Ibid., 594.

194. Ibid., 592.

195. Ibid., 584.

196. Ibid., 587-588.

197. Ibid., 595.

198. Letter Eisenhower to Gruenther, 5/4/53, EL, AWF, DDE Diaries, Box 3, "December 1952- July 1953 (3)."

199. Report to the NSC, 162/2, 10/30/53, *FRUS*, 1952-54, 2:593.

200. Ibid., 596.

201. Ibid., 590.

202. Reichard, "Divisions and Dissent," 55.

203. "Project Solarium: A Collective Oral History," 5.

204. Memorandum Discussion at 149th Meeting of the NSC, 6/11/53, EL AWF, NSC Series, Box 4, "149th Meeting of NSC 6/9/53."

205. "Project Solarium: A Collective Oral History," 19.

206. Report to the NSC, 162/2, 10/30/53, *FRUS*, 1952-54, 2:595.

207. "Project Solarium: A Collective Oral History," 13-14, 22.

208. Ibid., 8.

209. Ibid., 14.

210. Ibid., 10-11.

211. Ibid., 22.

PART TWO

Urgency Without Despair:
The Killian Report (1955)

CHAPTER THREE

"Gone are the Days When Madness Was Confined": Continental Defense and the Threat of Surprise Attack

Protected by two vast oceans on either side, the United States had little fear of surprise attack throughout its history; then on December 7, 1941 the Japanese delivered a devastating blow on Pearl Harbor. The attack on Pearl Harbor left a vivid imprint that the shores of America were vulnerable. The dawning of the Cold War and atomic age only added to the feeling of vulnerability.[1] As weapon technology advanced, concern over the threat of surprise attack grew. Once the Soviet Union had long-range bombing capabilities, surprise attack was not limited to American shores. Rather, any city could be the next Pearl Harbor, and therefore, a continental defense system was needed. An early warning system, anti-aircraft guns, interceptors, and data-processing facilities were the new necessities for defending the homeland. In addition, with the successful testing of a Soviet hydrogen bomb just one month after completion of the Solarium an enemy weapon stockpile that had recently seemed modest was now, as one presidential advisor observed, "potentially devastating."[2] By 1953, with the thermonuclear revolution, the consequence of war was terrifying—rather than face just defeat and surrender, a nation now faced extinction.[3]

In part to prevent another surprise attack on American soil, the Truman administration established the CIA, which was intended to provide information about impending attacks in time for the United States to react. The Truman administration spent little effort on securing a strong continental defense program, believing that American nuclear superiority was a strong enough deterrent. The result was that by 1953, the Policy Planning Staff of the NSC concluded that American continental defenses were totally inadequate.[4] So Truman left office without a clear national security policy and an inadequate continental defense program. Faced with growing concern over the thermonuclear revolution, surprise attack, and a deficient continental defense, Eisenhower had to balance the needs for a strong defense with his Great Equation. As he saw it, the American people faced a terrible threat, for which there was no response without imposing ever-greater controls on the economy and American freedom. "We had been trying," explained the President, "to have our cake and eat it at the same time."[5] Devising methods to meet the Soviet threat without adopting controls that transformed America into a garrison state proved challenging in light of the devastating implications of the nuclear age. By 1953 it certainly seemed to many that the words of poet Martyn Skinner rang true:

> Gone are the days when madness was confined
> By seas or hills from spreading through Mankind.[6]

Strategy and Surprise in the Nuclear Age

The advent of the nuclear age brought with it changes in strategic thinking and concerns over deterrence, surprise attack, preventive war, and continental defense. Truman was the first president who had to think about atomic strategy. He initially learned a few details about the atomic bomb at a meeting with Secretary of War Henry Stimson and the director of the Manhattan Project, General Leslie Groves, on April 25, 1945. During the meeting Stimson raised a number of notable points about the atomic bomb. First, Stimson conveyed to Truman the power the bomb had to destroy a city in a single blow and theorized that this weapon might destroy modern civilization. He also conceded that the United States would not be able to hold on to an atomic monopoly indefinitely and that it was up to America to demonstrate moral responsibility and leadership to prevent world disaster. Stimson was also aware of the potential the bomb had in a surprise attack, explaining to Truman that in the future, an adversary could employ the bomb "suddenly and with devastating power."[7] Finally, the bomb might also end the current war. Taking this all into account, Truman authorized its use.

August 6, 1945 signaled the end of World War II as the Japanese city of Hiroshima fell victim to the world's first atomic weapon. A war that began with Polish cavalry fighting valiantly against the German blitzkrieg ended with the technological revolution of atomic power. While the advent of the nuclear age left the world in awe, it left policymakers searching for answers to a seemingly deadly riddle. Once the United States lost its atomic monopoly in 1949, the question arose whether any employment of nuclear weapons could be sufficiently controlled to ensure the success of political objectives. Was a nuclear strategy even possible or merely a contradiction in terms?[8] As the Cold War and nuclear weapons escalated throughout the decades, both U.S. and Soviet policymakers continually had to evaluate and reformulate their respective nuclear strategies. The United States proceeded on a course largely determined by pragmatic considerations of each administration and the dicta of a legal, commercial, and democratic society. The Soviet Union relied on its more formulaic military doctrine to guide strategy, which was shaped by its imperial, bureaucratic, and autocratic traditions.[9] Although influenced by different criteria and values, both powers' primary aim was to establish some strategic nuclear balance to successfully prevent a nuclear world war but be sufficient enough to win a general war if war was not prevented. That meant developing a reliable military force capable of both deterring war and delivering a massive retaliatory blow if war occurred.

Although the United States and Soviet Union formulated and implemented strategy differently, 'strategy' may be defined in universal terms. General von Clausewitz was the first to define strategy, as it related to war, in the early nineteenth century. He saw war as a violent extension of politics that had to be constantly conducted with sensitivity to the political objectives at stake.[10] Strategy, to Clausewitz, was merely the use of battles to forward the aim of policy. Although this definition served many of the generals of World War II well, it was not appropriate to a nuclear age. Strategist Basil Liddell Hart offered a more meaningful definition when he defined strategy as "the art of distributing and applying military means to fulfill ends of policy."[11] In essence very Clausewitzian, this definition was useful in that it recognized the role of the political sphere in deriving strategic objectives while using military means to fulfill those objectives. Throughout the Cold War, both the United States and Soviet Union broadly defined strategy in this way, as can be seen with Eisenhower's various NSC policies. Eisenhower used military power, primarily in terms of nuclear superiority, in order to carry out the political aims of containment set forth in NSC 162/2.

Although Hart's definition spoke of "distributing and applying military means," many strategists worked from the premise that the very nature of the modern military force had made it increasingly difficult to employ the military to secure political objectives forcibly. In other words, the destructiveness of nuclear weapons made it difficult to actually use them to ensure political objectives. Instead, knowing how to use military force persuasively and how to manipulate the influence of nuclear arms on nations during peace became vital. Thomas Schelling, a strategist associated with the RAND Corporation, associated this manipulation with putting the fear of God into one's opponent. However, Schelling warned of the dangers of such a strategy since within it there existed a level of uncertainty.[12] Although it seemed that there was no foreseeable route by which the Soviet Union and United States would become engaged in a nuclear war, that in itself did not negate the possibility of war. As a result, Schelling reasoned, if war did occur, it would "result from a process that [was] not entirely foreseen."[13] In other words, deterrence might not work.

Another contemporary strategist at RAND, Bernard Brodie pointed out that deterrence as a strategy, which tries to create in the opponent's mind "a feeling compounded of respect and fear," could "overshoot the mark."[14] For the United States, the situation was particularly perilous. Brodie argued that deterrence could potentially make the opponent fear its aggressor too much. The opponent, the Soviet Union, could interpret American over-readiness to react as aggressive intent.[15] Such was the case when Stalin viewed the American atomic monopoly as reason enough to push ahead with a Soviet atomic program and, in 1954, when the Soviets viewed the decision by NATO to authorize nuclear weapons as Western aggression in Europe.[16] To people like Soviet Defense Minister Nikolai Bulganin, such measures were proof of the West's plan for surprise attack. "We cannot assume that the imperialists are spending enormous material resources and vast sums of money on armaments merely to frighten us," he reasoned. "Nor can we reckon on the humaneness of the imperialists who, as life has shown, are capable of using any weapons of mass destruction."[17]

Bulganin was only partially right. Although the United States was the only country to use the ultimate weapon of mass destruction on another country, the large atomic stockpile was meant only to frighten, or deter, the Soviets. Although both the United States and Soviets agreed that the definition of deterrence was that of restraining hostile action by the threat of severe punishment, deterrence became for America the only meaningful objective of strategic nuclear forces; therefore, Truman concentrated efforts on atomic superiority as the ultimate deterrent. Truman saw an atomic, and eventually nuclear, stockpile as the only means to deter aggression. And, if the enemy should attack despite the threat of American atomic stockpiles, retaliation was considered America's best hope of defense, and such retaliation required a large stockpile. The result was a policy of atomic superiority under President Truman.[18] Conversely, deterrence was only one of many objectives for the Soviets. They continued to be occupied by the need for survival in war should deterrence fail, concentrating efforts on continental and civil defense, for example, while the United States all but ignored such precautions.[19]

For example, Stalin knew of American plans for aerial attack on the Soviet Union, and often copies of National Intelligence Estimates (NIEs) prepared by the CIA were handed to Stalin. "It is important to understand," historian Vladislav Zubok explained, "America planned to drop atomic bombs on the Soviet Union to defend Western Europe. But Stalin saw those plans as a threat to destroy him in a surprise attack, just as Hitler had sought to do."[20] To deter such an attack, Stalin took measures to improve Soviet defenses around Moscow when he established a Third Chief Directorate of the Council Ministers in 1950 to design a defense for the capital. The group suggested two rings of radar and missile bases around the city designed to prevent even one American bomber from penetrating. Construction began in 1952.[21]

While Stalin looked at improving continental defenses as a deterrent, and Truman relied on nuclear superiority, both sides worried about surprise attack and were concerned that a massive surprise attack would be the opening shot of any war.[22] Calling upon recent history, many believed that war would start with another Pearl Harbor and that once the Soviets got the bomb they would use it without warning.[23] Paul Nitze for one believed that the Soviets were planning a surprise attack on the United States. In a February 1950 Policy Planning Staff meeting with Secretary of State Dean Acheson, Nitze concluded that the threat of Soviet aggression was high and "considerably greater than last fall."[24] It was also the Joint Chiefs' opinion that the Soviet army was capable of starting a major attack from a standstill, thereby not giving the West any warning time to mobilize.[25]

A March 1950 State Department draft statement of possible courses of action in regards to the world crisis stated that "the advantages of the initiative and of surprise are so great that a continuation of present trends may lead either the USSR or the U.S. to seriously consider the advisability of a preventive attack," and if the Soviets beat the U.S. in obtaining hydrogen weapons, "the risks of decisive pressure or an attack against the U.S. will be greatly increased."[26] These themes carried over into NSC 68 when Nitze wrote, "when it [the Soviet Union] calculates that it has sufficient atomic capability to make a surprise attack on us, nullifying our atomic superiority and creating a military situation decisively in its favor, the Kremlin might be tempted to strike swiftly and with stealth."[27] Concern over surprise attack continued into the 1950s. According to a 1953 report by a Special Subcommittee on the Soviet Union's net capability to inflict harm on the United States, the element of surprise was believed to be "the strongest weapon in the Soviet arsenal."[28]

Stalin disagreed, although he too had concerns about an American attack on the Soviet Union. Stalin did not believe the element of surprise determined the victor in war, or that it was the strongest weapon in his arsenal.[29] He did fear an American strike on Soviet soil, as shown by the defense ring around Moscow. However, discussion about surprise attack as part of military doctrine was not allowed under Stalin's reign. It was, however, taken up with great passion after his death.

Stalin had been hailed as the "greatest military genius of modern times," but his critics claimed that his policy "hindered the development of military-theoretical thought."[30] With his death in March 1953, Soviet military development was cut free from the rigid autocracy of Stalin's dictatorship.[31] Debate on nuclear weapons and the likelihood of war erupted after Stalin's death in March 1953.[32] By the mid-1950s, discussion rising from the decisiveness of the nuclear blow reintroduced surprise as a determining factor in war.[33] Soviet theorists believed a decisive advantage might be obtained by an initial attack that could destroy the opponent's armed forces, industry, and urban centers, which put an unprecedented emphasis on the importance of surprise.[34] Likewise, the Soviets believed, just as many Americans had, that the advantage could be had if they could detect a planned surprise attack early enough to mobilize their defenses. So, as strategist Herbert Dinerstein pointed out, "from a defensive as well as from an offensive standpoint, the importance of the factor of surprise had grown greatly in Soviet eyes."[35]

By the mid-1950s, Soviet leaders warned the Soviet people that they must not be caught unaware in a surprise attack. Gone were the Stalinist ideas that strategic surprise was an unreliable, transitory factor that would not ultimately affect the outcome of war. Instead, a new military doctrine emerged based on the premise that a future war would take the form of a sudden, brief nuclear exchange between the United States and Soviet Union. This doctrine stated that the advent of nuclear weapons and jet aviation enhanced the role of surprise in war, making surprise attack a real and dangerous possibility.[36]

Of course, Soviet military doctrine, particularly when discussed in the public arena, emphasized not a Soviet first strike, but a surprise nuclear strike by the imperialists against which they had to defend.[37] However, if the Soviets were fortunate enough to discover surprise attack plans from the imperialists, then the Soviets would have to respond with "pre-emptive blows at all levels—strategic, operational, and tactical."[38] Such talk of preventive war measures was not limited to the Soviet Union.

Proposals for a preventive war against the Soviet Union were common among some circles in America.[39] The JCS recommended to Truman in September 1945 a first strike against the Soviets if deterrence were to fail, and the Strategic Air Commander, General Curtis LeMay, confided to government advisors in 1957 that he was going to "knock the shit out of them," as soon as his intelligence told him the Soviets were preparing for war.[40] Eisenhower too gave a "fleeting thought" towards preventive war after the Soviets tested a hydrogen bomb in 1953. Writing to Dulles, he asked whether or not "our duty to future generations did not require us to initiate war at the most propitious moment that we could designate."[41]

However, improved Soviet retaliatory capabilities by the early 1950s limited any advantages to be gained by a preventive war, and preventive war was officially eliminated as a policy option in 1954 with NSC 5440, "Basic National Security Policy," which stated, "the United States and its allies must reject the concept of preventive war or acts intended to provoke war."[42] Yet, preventive war was never really a viable option for the United States because the American national psychology and system of values prohibited it from engaging in any form of preventive war.[43] Truman himself said "we do not believe in aggression or preventive war. Such a war is the weapon of dictators, not of free democratic countries like the United States."[44] Unable to strike first, the United States' strategy had to rely on cutting down any advantage the enemy might derive from a first strike and attempt deterrence against a first strike without "overshooting the mark."[45] In other words, a strong continental and civil defense program had to be coupled with a strong offensive capability. To complicate the situation, policymakers were continually faced with new technology, changing the basic conditions of war month to month.[46]

For example, before 1953 doubt resided over whether or not nuclear warheads could ever be miniaturized enough to be placed atop of long-range missiles. By early 1954 American scientists had solved the problem. The NSC was informed that the Soviets were probably not far behind and some intelligence reports indicated that they were even ahead of U.S. technology.[47] Intercontinental ballistic missile (ICBM) technology multiplied the fears of surprise attack. The renowned mathematician John Von Neumann of the Atomic Energy Commission explained to the NSC exactly what ICBM technology implied: a reduction in warning time of an incoming Soviet missile attack to fifteen minutes with almost no possibility of interception. Furthermore, the missiles were relatively cheap at about one million dollars each, and Von Neumann believed the Soviets could produce many of them.[48] Although Von Neumann could not say when the Soviets would have ICBMs, CIA estimates predicted a Soviet Union with ICBM capabilities by the early 1960s.[49] It was clear that the nuclear age, with its rapid technological advances, threats of surprise attack, and promise of world devastation had unleashed a certain sense of madness. With the madness no longer confined, American policymakers had to focus attention on a continental defense program that could protect America from nuclear annihilation.

A Slow Start

Despite concern about Soviet attack during the Truman Administration, little was done to strengthen continental defense. When the Department of Defense was organized in 1947, it began preparing for a continental air defense system. Even though the Department of Defense recognized the need for a continental defense system of interceptors, early warning radar, and anti-aircraft artillery, appropriations were not made to meet the development demands of such a system.[50] Interservice rivalries played a large part in prohibiting the development of a cohesive continental defense program. The army wanted to see deterrence through a universal military training program that would dramatically increase manpower. The air force saw technological advances in aircraft design as most important to continental defense, and the navy wished to play a pivotal role in protecting America's shores and offering mobility in the seas.[51] With such different views on how best to defend America, development of a continental defense program got off to a slow start.

The authors of NSC 68 did recognize in 1950 that the defense of U.S. borders against air attack was important, but they did not outline steps to improve such defense. By the end of Truman's term the NSC adopted NSC 139 and agreed that an early warning system providing three to six hours of warning should be developed "as a matter of high urgency."[52] Without such warning times, the Strategic Air Command could be crippled, and any defense measures in place could be paralyzed. If Strategic Air Command had even just two hours of warning, it could deploy 65 percent of its forces. Therefore, detection of Soviet intentions was vital, and improved intelligence and early warning systems were needed.[53]

Despite the rhetoric in NSC 68 and NSC 139, it was clear that the Truman Administration was preoccupied with offensive stockpiling of atomic weapons while ignoring continental and civil defenses.[54] While it was recognized that early warning and air defense systems were sparse and inadequate, steps were not made to improve continental defense under Truman.[55] However, a number of studies on continental defense initiated during Truman's tenure were left for Eisenhower to take resume.

As Eisenhower took office, three documents were presented to him which, taken together, identified continental defense as what one State Department staffer called "the Achilles heel of American national security."[56] Those three documents were NSC 141, the Project East River report, and the Panel of Consultants on Disarmament report. The authors of NSC 141 (a special study for the NSC) warned about American vulnerability against a Soviet attack. The men presented NSC 141 on January 19, 1953 and declared that in light of Soviet atomic capabilities, additional resources had to be committed to American continental and civil defenses. They estimated that current continental defenses provided only 15 percent effectiveness against Soviet attack, possibly allowing 85 percent of the atomic bombs in a Soviet air attack to reach their target. In their report, the men concluded that to continue continental defense measures on the present course involved critical risks, particularly in light of projected Soviet nuclear capabilities to deliver a critical blow to the United States.[57]

Project East River had been established by the government two years earlier to study civil defense. Sponsored by the Department of Defense, the National Security Resources Board, and the Federal Civil Defense Administration, the project's objective was to "determine the optimum combination of non-military measures which may be taken to minimize the effects of attack by atomic, biological, chemical, and other weapons on the population and industry of the United States."[58] Nearly one hundred civilian experts including scientists, educators, businessmen, and government representatives conducted the study. In their final report they stressed the need for military measures to help in civil defense, specifically with an early warning system that would detect an attack at least 2,000 miles off the continental borders. The experts estimated that, without some warning, 25,000,000 casualties would result from a Soviet air attack. In addition to an early warning system, interception systems were imperative as local civil defense measures could not deal with a 100 percent penetration. In their report, they explained that local civil defense was set up to only handle "leakage through the defensive net." In all, the experts had given 246 recommendations on how to improve continental defense.[59]

The Panel of Consultants on Disarmament, chaired by Robert Oppenheimer, consisted of scientists, educators, and the director of the Central Intelligence Agency.[60] It too concluded that current levels of continental defense loomed as the most important problem of national security, stating that "no problem has forced itself upon us more insistently and regularly, in the course of our work, than that of the defense of the continental United States."[61] It criticized the current "preoccupation" with building a stockpile of atomic weapons and neglecting to give equal balance to continental defense measures. The Panel concluded that "there is every reason to proceed with greatly intensified efforts of continental defense," in part because not only can strengthened continental defense protect the United States against attack, it can also act as a deterrent from attack.[62]

In early February, Carlton Savage of the Policy Planning Staff reflected that these three reports pointed to the urgency of the matter, particularly in light of future Soviet nuclear weapon development and ICBM technology.[63] Taking into account the conclusions of NSC 141, Project East River, and the Panel of Consultants, Nitze and Savage of the Policy Planning Staff concluded, "continental defense has become imperative for the United States as a consequence of the threat posed by the Soviet development of atomic weapons."[64] Critical of the lack of preparation taken towards continental defense, the two identified four reasons for such neglect: Americans underestimated Soviet technological abilities to enter the atomic age sooner than expected; Congress and the Executive did not fully appreciate the danger the Soviets posed, and therefore did not allocate the appropriate funds for continental defense; Americans relied too heavily on a massive offensive capability to protect the United States; and Americans were reluctant to divert resources away from an offensive capability to a defense at home which might not protect as promised. To rectify the situation, Nitze and Savage looked to the recommendations outlined in the most recent policy statement on the subject, NSC 149/2, suggesting that continental defense receive "an increased emphasis." Agreeing with the authors of NSC 149/2, Nitze and Savage said the main problem was "how to do this under the budgetary limitations laid down in NSC 149/2, limitations which include among other points a reduction in manpower and resources for the air force," limitations which Eisenhower wanted to uphold.[65]

Shedding some more light on the problems of continental defense for Eisenhower to consider early in his administration was the Edwards Committee. Created by an NSC directive on January 19, 1953 to look into Soviet capabilities to "inflict direct injury on the United States up to July 1955," the committee was chaired by retired Lt. General Idwal Edwards.[66] The Edwards Committee studied Soviet capabilities to harm the U.S. through direct military means, as well as through sabotage or clandestine military means. Studying the initial phase of

war, or when it was assumed the Soviets' atomic or nuclear stockpile was likely
to be unleashed, the Committee utilized reports from each of the agencies represented by its members and had full access to relevant classified reports.[67] The
committee reported its conclusions to the NSC on May 18th.[68]

The Committee assumed that the Soviet Union had the ability to launch an
air attack without warning and stated that the element of surprise was its strongest weapon against the United States. A decisive Soviet surprise air attack, the
committee estimated, would paralyze industry, destroy between 24-30 percent of
U.S. bombers with atomic delivery capability, and cause between 9 and 12.5
million civilian casualties. If, however, the United States was able to detect the
slightest evidence of an impending attack, damage figures might be cut in half.
An early warning system was therefore vital to counter a Soviet attack, and the
report concluded that Strategic Air Command needed at least a two-hour warning to be effective in countering a Soviet attack.[69] The Edwards Committee also
listed a number of deficiencies in regards to continental defense, and Edwards
came back to the NSC on June 4th to discuss them further.

At that meeting Eisenhower commented that it seemed, based on Edwards'
report, that the likely bases the Soviets might use for an attack were those on the
Chukotski Peninsula, across the Bering Straits from Alaska. Therefore, Eisenhower suggested that air defense and warning systems be set up specifically in
Alaska. Edwards agreed, but reminded him that low-flying Soviet planes could
break any radar net. Eisenhower then suggested flight radar and reengineered
Strategic Air Command to improve radar efficiency, but Edwards believed to
achieve those results SAC would have to be on 24-hour alert—a costly operation. At this, Eisenhower suggested that perhaps the report gave too much credit
to Soviet pilots' abilities to navigate long distances and actually make it to their
target. "Anyone who had ever ridden with Soviet pilots could vouch for this in-
competence," Eisenhower told the group.[70] Edwards had no reply, but it was
clear Eisenhower viewed Soviet technical capabilities differently from their actual capabilities.

Poor Soviet navigation and radar nets aside, the most obvious way to guard
against attack was to use intelligence to predetermine an impending attack, giving U.S. forces time to react. Allen Dulles, however, saw little that could be done
to foresee a Soviet attack, despite his brother's insistence that an impending attack simply could not be hidden. The Edwards Committee had not made specific
recommendations for improved intelligence, but Edwards, and everyone else in
the room, concluded that should the Soviets attack the United States, it would be
out of desperation and "not an exercise of military judgment."[71]

Whether the Soviets attacked out of desperation or not, the stark fact was
that the United States had no sound continental defense program. In fact, that
month Acting Secretary of Defense Roger Kyes worried about a NSC paper or-
dering the "acceleration" of an early warning system since the Department of

Defense had not definitively decided such a system was feasible.[72] Considering too that a recent report had indicated "difficulties and delays in the creation of such a system," the Council decided to substitute "emphasize" for "accelerate" in regards to an early warning system.[73] The end result was that the authors of NSC 153/1 *emphasized* the "development of a continental defense system, including early warning, adequate to prevent disaster and to make secure the mobilization base necessary to achieve U.S. victory in the event of general war."[74] Of course the Department of Defense favored a warning system; Kyes merely wished for the Joint Chiefs of Staff to review the whole problem of continental defense before accelerating a specific program.[75] Eisenhower thought the whole situation required a review by an adhoc committee to take up the deficiencies laid out by the various reports so that a continental defense program could be defined and accelerated. Also, such a group might suggest concrete ways to implement an improved continental defense without breaking the bank, a theme Eisenhower always kept in sight. The subsequent Continental Defense Committee, established in June, gave its report in mid-July.[76]

The Continental Defense Committee and NSC 159/4

Responding to the various reports and memos outlining the inadequacies of continental defense during the Truman Administration, Eisenhower took action and the first official policy paper on continental defense by the Eisenhower Administration was NSC 159/4, approved on September 25, 1953. It was a synthesis of three separate reports on continental defense, the first being the 80-page report from the Continental Defense Committee.[77]

Chaired by the retired Lt. General Harold Bull, the Continental Defense Committee consisted of one representative each from the Department of Defense, the Office of Defense Mobilization, the Federal Civil Defense Administration, the Interdepartmental Committee on Internal Security, and one scientific consultant.[78] Convening in early June, the committee reviewed all previous studies that had been conducted on continental defense. It issued an 80-page report to the NSC, recorded as NSC 159, on July 22, 1953. The report cited the American stockpile of atomic weapons as the most effective deterrent against a devastating Soviet attack, just as Truman had maintained. The committee stressed that the stockpile had to be maintained for both its defensive and offensive value. However, should deterrence by atomic superiority fail, the committee concluded that present continental defense systems were not adequate to "prevent, neutralize or seriously deter the military or covert attacks" by the Soviet Union.[79] In particular, there were no assurances that the current continental defense program could protect industry or the federal government from failing—unacceptable risks, in the committee's eyes, for national survival. However, their report conceded that a totally impenetrable continental defense system was unrealistic in light of current technology and recommended that long-term, fixed programs not be adopted. Rather, short-term solutions offered the most flexibility and security.[80] Continental defense had to remain modern. Although the report offered the same observation as the previous reports had offered—that continental defense was inadequate—the Continental Defense Committee recognized that a total defense shield was unrealistic both technically and financially, that technology was changing too fast to implement long-term defense programs, and that American nuclear technology offered the best defense if coupled with an improved continental defense able to protect industry and the federal government.

The Joint Chiefs of Staff also had concerns about the current continental defense program and submitted a report to Secretary Wilson at about the same time. In it, the Joint Chiefs of Staff concluded, "Soviet long range objectives remain unchanged and are aimed at the overthrow of democracy. The Soviet [sic] now has the capability of an atomic attack against Continental United States of serious though intermediate magnitude and this capability can be expected to increase."[81] Responding to the various inadequacies laid out in previous reports, in August the Joint Chiefs submitted a coordinated plan for the defense of the continental United States. The Joint Chiefs stated that "in order to prevent a disastrous surprise attack in force prior to the formal declaration of war, the armed forces must be prepared to engage and defeat the enemy by establishing and maintaining effective defense forces."[82] They recommended a coordinated effort by the services and an Early Warning System to be completed by December 1955. It seemed that the interservice rivalries were abating and an Early Warning System might proceed. They also warned that while there was a great preoccupation with a Soviet air or missile attack, the Soviets were also capable of launching a surprise attack on the United States via submarines or by concealing an atomic device in the hold of a cargo ship.[83] What shape that Early Warning System was to take, however, remained unclear.

In order to get some objective thinking from people who were "not burdened with departmental responsibilities," Eisenhower again asked for the assistance of a civilian committee in July. The group, headed by James Phinney Baxter III, was asked to review a report on Continental Defense programs being prepared by the NSC. The committee met in August, but had held their report until after the Joint Chiefs of Staff had taken office and the Bull Committee report had been given adequate review. Eisenhower called their comments to the NSC "fresh and objective." Cutler echoed Eisenhower's remarks, saying that the consultants' conclusions helped identify key points at just the right time, and both agreed that undoubtedly the NSC would use civilian consultants again.[84]

Armed with their report and the reports of the Joint Chiefs and the Continental Defense Committee, the NSC Planning Board wrote the first comprehensive policy paper on continental defense. The question of structure of an early warning system was discussed, particularly in light of the recent Soviet demonstration of nuclear capabilities. The August 12 detonation of a thermonuclear device in the Soviet Union created new concerns and made many of the observations recorded in previous continental defense reports obsolete. NSC 159/4 was the first report presented in light of the Soviet explosion.

The policy paper indicated that Soviet thermonuclear capabilities had placed a premium on determent of war, improvement of U.S. intelligence, a ready offensive force, a reliable inceptor force, improved civil defense measures, and an early warning system.[85] For an early warning system, the Planning Board looked to strengthen the defense lines in Canada by recommending seaward extensions of the southern Canadian defense line. However, Admiral Radford, speaking for the Joint Chiefs, had serious concerns about such an extension and worried that programs were going to be approved by the NSC that might tie the hands of the JCS and prevent the formulation of an overall military program. Specifically, Radford complained that a seaward extension required a perfect performance by the men who operated the defense line 24 hours per day, 365 days of the year, indefinitely. Such performance was unrealistic. Furthermore, the military simply did not have the manpower to support such an endeavor. Radford further feared that efficiency deteriorated as radar operators became bored with doing the same repetitive job "in some such dreary waste as northern Canada."[86]

Arthur Flemming, Director of the Office of Defense Mobilization, made the radical suggestion of using women to solve the manpower problem. C.D. Jackson suggested lowering the restrictions to join the military. "A soldier with flat feet or dandruff," Jackson offered, "might be completely competent to operate a Nike."[87] Harold Stassen, Director of Foreign Operations Administration, suggested improving scientific and technological study in high schools and developing more automated devices to help the military. Eisenhower reminded his audience that the main goal was a *minimum* military establishment, not a larger one. Defense had to be adjusted to survive, and increasing manpower to develop a perfectly impenetrable defense was not realistic.[88] In the final report, both the seaward extensions and the Southern Canadian early warning line were approved and were to be "completed with all deliberate speed."[89] The southern seaward extensions were to extend to Hawaii and the Azores and use the "minimum number of ships and aircraft determined by the Joint Chiefs of Staff to be necessary to meet the threat and enemy capabilities at any given time."[90] A Northern Canadian early warning line was to be developed if future committees recommended the program. At the very least, an early warning line that provided a two-hour warning was to be in service immediately.

In addition to an early warning system, the recent Soviet thermonuclear test placed a higher premium on an interceptor system that prohibited Soviet bombers and submarines from ever reaching their targets. Eisenhower agreed that the two most important elements in continental defense were the seaward extension of the Southern Canadian line and a fighter interceptor program.[91] To address the issue, members of the Planning Board submitted a final report in which they agreed with the conclusions of the Continental Defense Committee that fighter inceptor forces had to be "kept effective in ensuing years in phase with the other military programs . . . and with developing Soviet capabilities."[92] The Board recommended keeping fighter interceptor and anti-aircraft forces in high readiness and implementing a semiautomatic air control center and low-frequency detection system for submarines as soon as possible.

In other areas, the authors of NSC 159/4 again agreed with the Continental Defense Committee that continuity of the federal government was vital for national survival. In light of Soviet thermonuclear capabilities, measures were adopted to develop new emergency dispersal plans that had a wider dispersal of government facilities and improved communication links. For the rest of the public, civil defense measures were largely left to local communities with the Federal government looking into more research and public education programs. The best help for civil defense was early warning—an area the government was actively involved in improving.[93] The best help for overall continental defense was improved intelligence, but the authors of NSC 159/4 offered no suggestions except to say that knowing Soviet intentions and capabilities was "essential."[94]

Finally, the Planning Board emphasized economy in the report. It opened by saying that "the survival of the free world" depended upon the United States maintaining not only a strong military and non-military forces to deter war or win one should deterrence fail, but also a "sound, strong economy, capable of supporting such strength over the long pull."[95] Eisenhower reiterated the point in a NSC meeting discussing the report when he said the defense program had to be adjusted "to something with which we can live for a long time."[96] He did not want to burden the American people with high military costs that would destroy the American way of life. Certainly it was true America faced a terrible threat. In NSC 159/4, the Planning Board concurred with the JCS assessment that, despite overtures towards peace coming out of the Soviet Union, there was no reason to believe the Soviets had altered their basic hostility towards the free world.[97] Yet, because of the costs involved in security, Eisenhower stressed that this threat had to be met in a way that did not create a garrison state through government controls.[98] In addition, Eisenhower felt that too often these reports overestimated the ability of the Soviets to launch an attack upon the United States. The reports took into account the estimates of Soviet capabilities, but not the obstacles and difficulties the Soviets would encounter in such an attempt. With that said, it was vital to find an appropriate continental defense system that upheld the Great Equation.[99]

NSC 159/4 received final approval on September 25, 1953 and signified, as the many reports before it had, that America had an inadequate continental defense program in place to defend against an air attack from the Soviet Union.

However, NSC 159/4 also served as a catalyst for improved programs. Its purpose was to fix the timing and guidelines to govern continental defense programs. At the very least, it gave greater emphasis to the problem. Even NSC 162/2, the overall statement on basic national security, adopted at the end of October, reflected this concern, calling for a strong posture with an effective continental defense.[100]

One area governing continental defense development that the Planning Board stressed in NSC 159/4 was a cooperative relationship with Canada. No continental defense system could be successful without Canadian help. The Planning Board acknowledged that agreements with Canada had been initiated, but stated that there had to be established a "common appreciation of the urgency and character of the threat to U.S.-Canadian security."[101] Furthermore, the Board recommended exploring means to induce Canada to take up a leadership and financial role in continental defense. To help move things along, Eisenhower talked to a Joint Session of the Canadian Parliament on November 14, 1953. He promised his audience that the United States and Canada "can and will devise ways to protect our North America from any surprise attack."[102] Acknowledging that the "basic threat of communist purpose still exists," Eisenhower explained that security plans now had to take into account the Soviet capability to employ atomic attack. In suggesting that the United States and Canada were equal partners, he said, "defense of our soil presents a challenge to both our peoples. It is a common task." Eisenhower complimented the permanent Joint Board on Defense for working "assiduously and effectively on mutual problems" and stated that now was the time for action "on all agreed measures."[103]

Calling upon a greater sense of duty in this Cold War, Eisenhower told the Canadian audience, "In common with others of the free world, the United States does not rely on military strength alone to win the peace. Our primary reliance is a unity among us forged of common adherence to moral principles. This reliance binds together in fellowship all those who believe in the spiritual nature of man, as the Child of God."[104] And giving a head nod to recent Soviet thermonuclear capabilities, Eisenhower poured on the rhetoric telling the people that, "Beyond the shadow of the atomic cloud, the horizon is bright with promise. No shadow can halt our advance together. For we, Canada and the United States, shall use carefully and wisely the God-given graces of faith and reason as we march together toward it—toward the horizon of a world where each man, each family, each nation lives at peace in a climate of freedom."[105] It was up to Eisenhower to see to it that the problems outlined in NSC 159/4 were addressed so that each nation might live in peace.

Evaluating Continental Defense Again: NSC 5408

In his annual budget message to the Congress in January 1954, Eisenhower addressed the problem of continental defense. He explained that expenditures for continental defense were expected to be "greater than ever before in our history" and that the funds available in the Department of Defense budget to expand the system of continental defense "will provide improved early warning of enemy attack and the men and equipment to resist any such attack."[106] This greater emphasis on continental defense was, of course, reflected in the recent NSC 159/4 policy paper. However, NSC 159/4 was written only a month after the Soviet thermonuclear detonation, and it was important to keep continental defense up-to-date in light of changing Soviet capabilities. Therefore, the Planning Board improved upon the fine work done in NSC 159/4 with a continued review of continental defense based on the latest intelligence estimates; this review led to a second policy paper on continental defense, NSC 5408.

Submitted to the NSC on February 11, 1954, NSC 5408 was intended to supersede NSC 159/4.[107] It bluntly stated the recurring mantra that current continental defenses were completely inadequate and that such defense was a necessary element of national security.[108] It also repeated the two basic tenets stressed in NSC 159/4 and NSC 162/2: the need for a strong military posture balanced with a sound and strong economy that could withstand the long haul. But in its most recent report, the Planning Board emphasized that in financing continental defense, "full-weight" had to be given to the facts of the thermonuclear revolution and the increased capabilities of the Soviet Union. Noting the importance of overall military strength, the authors of NSC 5408 warned that too much attention had been given to "peripheral defense, offensive capabilities, and mobilization bases," and not enough attention to the element of continental defense.[109]

Agreeing with previous conclusions that the Soviet Union still sought world domination, the authors of NSC 5408 placed a great emphasis on technological research and development and improved intelligence capabilities. Again citing Soviet thermonuclear capabilities, the authors of NSC 5408, unlike the writers of NSC 159/4, necessitated that adequate support for basic and applied research and development be given to weapons' development, particularly ICBM development, because "technological superiority" was "essential" in light of Soviet developments.[110] In the same vein, means of improved intelligence to determine Soviet intentions and capabilities were equally essential. However, NSC 5408 did not provide specific recommendations on either front. Developing the necessary technological systems would be a task handled later by an ad-hoc civilian committee.[111]

As with NSC 159/4, the authors of NSC 5408 made clear that early warning lines and interceptor systems were the key components to continental defense. "The recent Soviet thermonuclear test," the policy paper explained, "brings home that it is essential with all practicable speed substantially to augment the capability to destroy attacking aircraft and submarines before reaching their targets."[112] Consequently, fighter interceptors and anti-aircraft forces were elevated from "being in a high state of readiness in two years" as stated in NSC 159/4, to "being in a high state of readiness *with all practicable speed*" in NSC 5408.[113] It was also essential that these systems be kept modern and flexible enough to "keep pace with anticipated increases in Soviet capabilities." In addition to quickly improving flight interceptor and anti-aircraft forces, continuation of the Southern Canadian early warning line and seaward extensions was recommended. Noting the obvious, the authors stated that "the longer an effective advance warning of enemy attack on the continental United States, the more successfully can many military and non-military measures be carried out."[114]

In regards to the Southern Canadian early warning line, Dr. Lee DuBridge, chairman of the Science Advisory Committee of the Office of Defense Mobilization, recommended that it be installed immediately, as the technology was ready. He said there was no reason to fear that the technology would become obsolete due to technological advances and there should be no further delays. Although Eisenhower still expressed concerns over the technology becoming obsolete, he decided that indeed the Southern line should be installed immediately and was impressed by DuBridge's comments.[115] A Northern Canadian early warning line was still to be given attention pending further review.

In other matters, civil defense continued to be placed in the hands of local and state governments, offering only public education and further research. As recommended in NSC 159/4, plans to ensure a functioning federal government during war were to be kept current and industry was to be protected. The continuity of industry was seen as important because of the lesson learned during World War II: a strong industrial force capable of maintaining high output during war was vital for victory. Incorporating all of the recommendations made by the Planning Board, NSC 5408 was indeed what Arthur Flemming called "a fine document."[116] NSC 5408 gained further approval that summer when the Council stated that American military and non-military continental defense programs outlined in NSC 5408 should be "accelerated . . . to the fullest extent deemed feasible and operationally desirable and give to these programs very high priority, having in mind that it is estimated that the Soviets will reach a high capability for strategic nuclear attacks by July, 1957."[117]

The work done by the NSC in the first year of the Eisenhower Administration was impressive. NSC 159/4 and 5408 both placed continental defense as a priority when the Truman Administration had failed to do so. But, as required by the changing nature of continental defense needs, the NSC continued its work. As was often the case, the NSC relied on outsiders to keep the Council abreast of changing needs. One individual proved enormously helpful to the NSC in regards to continental defense throughout the 1950s. He was Robert Sprague.

A Lone Civilian Takes up the Cause: Robert Sprague

Robert Sprague, an electronics manufacturer and owner of Sprague Electric Company of North Adams, Massachusetts, worked closely with the Eisenhower Administration on continental defense. Eisenhower even considered Sprague for undersecretary of the Air Force in 1953, but Sprague had declined.[118] In October 1953, Massachusetts Senator and Chair of the Armed Forces Committee, Leverett Saltonstall, asked Sprague to work as the special consultant on Continental Defense. Sprague visited Strategic Air Command and was personally briefed by General LeMay. He gained access to more classified material on the subject than any civilian or government official. Admiral Radford reminded Sprague during a briefing on weapons systems that, "while a limited number of officers and officials of the government have had segments of this information in connection with their official duties, few have had it in its entirety," and, as such, Sprague had a "great responsibility."[119] Sprague was well aware and served dutifully. He reported to the Senate Armed Services Committee on March 18, 1954, and subsequently Cutler sent the report to the chief of each agency having an interest in continental defense. Eisenhower told Saltonstall afterward that the country "was fortunate" to have citizens like Sprague who worked with such thoroughness and effectiveness. As Eisenhower saw it, Sprague "rendered a real service to his country."[120]

Sprague's report on continental defense reiterated the fact that the atomic age had made American security more vulnerable. He reasoned that even if the Soviets planned a general war in Europe, the Soviets had to plan to cripple American retaliatory abilities by destroying the planes and bases of Strategic Air Command and urban-industrial areas to prohibit quick recovery. The principal problem facing Strategic Air Command was enough warning to get the bombers airborne. Therefore, Sprague recommended expanding early warning radar, strengthening anti-aircraft defenses around Strategic Air Command bases, and increasing the number and quality of flight interceptors.[121] But, on the whole, Sprague concluded that current continental defense systems represented "a reasonable although minimum effort."[122] Acting Secretary of Defense Kyes remarked that Sprague's conclusions were a "welcome endorsement [of the Administration's continental defense system] by an intelligent outsider competent to make a judgment."[123] The report contained twenty-four recommendations of which only two were found by the NSC to be invalid—a direct warning to key executive Federal personnel and an increase in the number of daytime fighters. Five recommendations had "qualified validity," and the remaining seventeen were all valid.[124] Certainly Sprague's report served a useful purpose, but Sprague himself modified his conclusions just three months later.

Alarmed by the recent Soviet thermonuclear tests of devices with one-megaton forces, Sprague felt it necessary to brief members of the Senate Armed Services Committee to amend his previous conclusions. Meeting with Senators Saltonstall, Robert Byrd, and Styles Bridges, as well as Admiral Radford, Sprague explained that although he previously reported that continental defenses were reasonable, he now believed that the entire matter needed to be reevaluated to see that there was a "speed up in completion of present and proposed continental defense programs and an increase in the quantity and quality of defense weapons."[125] Sprague estimated that by mid-1957, the Soviets would have the ability to cause "unacceptable damage" to the United States and that the United States had three options: build an impenetrable defense system, deliver a first strike, or live in mutual fear of atomic attack. Admiral Radford was skeptical of Sprague's report, commenting that his conclusions were as black as could be and were based on evaluations that were likely to change. Furthermore, Radford insisted that America could not afford to adopt a "maginot line" concept.[126] Radford reported his concerns to Wilson while Sprague continued to work on continental defense.

As a result of Sprague's work for the Senate, the NSC called upon him in June 1954 to serve as a consultant to the Council on continental defense. Sprague was appointed as a NSC consultant on June 18, 1954, and his main responsibility was to deliver progress reports twice a year to the NSC on the state of continental defense.[127] He gave his first report on July 1, 1954. In it he recommended that several programs outlined in NSC 5408 be accelerated and he requested the Net Capabilities Evaluation Subcommittee estimate the overall damage the Soviets might inflict on the United States during a surprise attack in three years. Specifically, after evaluating the Department of Defense comments on continental defense, Sprague recommended that the Canadian early warning line, the Hawaiian end of the Pacific seaward extension, and the gap-filler programs be accelerated to be complete by July 1957. Synchronizing the simultaneous completion of these three systems, instead of prolonging some to 1958 or 1959 as originally planned, would greatly strengthen continental defense.[128] In early November the Net Capabilities Evaluation Subcommittee reported on Soviet capabilities and indicated many gaps in continental defense, including American vulnerability to low-altitude attack.[129] With that information, Sprague delivered his second progress report to the NSC on November 24.

Again, he saw the threat from the Soviet Union as greater than ever before because of the thermonuclear revolution. Seeing that the Soviets would likely have a significant stockpile of bombs and long-range bombers in a few years, Sprague worried about American defense capabilities being adequate. In addition, harmful radioactive fallout was a new element introduced by megaton thermonuclear weapons that threatened civilian populations. These new factors, Sprague said, "enormously increase the threat to our national survival in the event of a Soviet surprise attack."[130] Eisenhower was grateful for Sprague's excellent services and told Sprague that his report reflected "how deeply and painstakingly" he had delved into his subject; Eisenhower also complimented Sprague on his "remarkable comprehensive knowledge" in the vital area of continental defense.[131]

Sprague continued his reviews of continental defense, reporting to the NSC as a consultant. Yet, while Sprague was conducting his reviews, the continental defense program was still hindered by what Admiral Radford identified as technical developments and limited manpower.[132] The country still needed specific programs that could take advantage of its superior science and technology as well as work within Eisenhower's Great Equation and New Look. No one could deny by 1954 that continental defenses needed to be improved. The question now was how.

A year after the Solarium exercise, the United States faced the growing possibility that the Soviet Union could launch a decisive surprise attack. The thermonuclear age had begun and rapid technological changes such as warhead miniaturization and ICBM systems made the world a dangerous place. Even though general thermonuclear war was by and large considered insane, most agreed with the State Department's assertion that "a situation of war by miscalculation or otherwise cannot be excluded."[133] The thermonuclear revolution, the full significance of which was only now beginning to be comprehended, necessitated an examination of security policy. As Eisenhower explained, "due to the destructiveness of modern weapons and the increasing efficiency of long-range bombing aircraft, the U.S. has reason, for the first time in its history, to be deeply concerned over the serious effects which a sudden attack could conceivably inflict upon our country." Therefore, priority had to be concentrated on maintaining the "capability to deter an enemy from attack and to blunt that attack if it comes—by a combination of effective retaliatory power and a continental defense system of steadily increasing effectiveness."[134] Certainly the programs outlined in NSC 5408 improved continental defenses, but the programs did not prevent an attack. Private consultants like Robert Sprague ultimately shared these views. What was needed now was a comprehensive examination of how science and technology might be used to advance continental defenses. To take up such a study, Eisenhower turned to the Science Advisory Committee.

Notes

1. In reference to a meeting which set up the Technological Capabilities Panel in 1954, CIA member Richard Bissell said that "this was at a time when the Pearl Harbor surprise attack was still very much on everyone's mind." Quote from an interview with Bissell by Burrows in William Burrows, *Deep Black: Space Espionage and National Security*, (New York: Random House, 1986), 69.

2. Letter DuBridge to Flemming, 5/24/54, EL, WH Central Files, Confidential File, Subject Series, Box 104, "World War III (1)," 1.

3. H.W. Brands, "The Age of Vulnerability: Eisenhower and the National Security State," *American Historical Review* Vol. 94 No. 4, (October 1989), 964.

4. In February 1954 the NSC concurred, particularly in light of recent Soviet thermonuclear capabilities. See *FRUS*, 1952-54, 2:231-234; 611-624.

5. Memorandum of Discussion at the 163rd Meeting of the NSC, 9/24/53, *FRUS*, 1952-54, 2:469.

6. Martyn Skinner, *Letters to Malaya*, Vol. II (London: Putnam, 1941). Quoted in James Killian, *Sputnik, Scientists, and Eisenhower*, (Cambridge: MIT Press, 1977), 52.

7. S. David Broscious, "Longing for International Control, Banking on American Superiority: Harry S Truman's Approach to Nuclear Weapons," in John L. Gaddis, Philip Gordon, Ernest May, Jonathon Rosenberg eds., *Cold War Statesmen Confront the Bomb: Nuclear Diplomacy since 1945*, (New York: Oxford University Press, 1999),16.

8. Lawrence Freedman, *The Evolution of Nuclear Strategy*, (New York: St. Martin's Press, 1983), xviii.

9. Fritz Ermath, "Contrasts in American and Soviet Strategic Thought," in Derek Leebaert, ed., *Soviet Military Thinking*, (Boston: George Allen & Unwin, 1981), 68.

10. Benjamin Lambeth, "How to Think About Soviet Military Doctrine," Rand Corporation, February 1978, 5-6.

11. B.H. Liddell Hart, *Strategy: The Indirect Approach*, (London: 1968), 334 quoted in Freedman, *Evolution*, xvii.

12. The Soviets, recognizing both the dangers and advantages of uncertainty, managed to manipulate the uncertainty of the U.S. to their great advantage between 1957-1962.

13. Thomas Schelling, *Arms and Influence*, (New Haven: Yale University Press, 1966).

14. Bernard Brodie, *Strategy in the Missile Age*, (Princeton: Princeton University Press, 1965), 392-397. Brodie, Schelling and Albert Wohlstetter were three men associated with RAND who dominated the newly emerging field of "strategy" which historian Marc Trachtenberg called "a new field [in the 1950s] with a distinct intellectual personality." Trachtenberg credits these men, and a handful of others, with creating "enormously influential" ideas and styles of analysis that "became the sophisticated way of approaching nuclear issues in the United States." See Marc Trachtenberg, *History and Strategy*, (Princeton: Princeton University Press, 1991), 3.

15. Brodie, *Strategy*, 392-397. This was John Foster Dulles' fear if the federal government sponsored a massive civil defense shelter program.

16. See Chapter One and Vladislav M. Zubok, "Stalin and the Nuclear Age," in John L. Gaddis et. al., *Cold War Statesmen.*

17. Roman Kolkowicz, *The Soviet Military and the Communist Party*, (Princeton: Princeton University Press, 1967), 19-25.

18. Freedman, *Evolution*, 33-34; 40-42.

19. Ermath, "Contrasts in Strategic Thought," 55-58. For a history of civil defense in the U.S. see chapter 6.

20. Vladislav M. Zubok, "Stalin and the Nuclear Age," in John L. Gaddis et. al., *Cold War Statesmen*, 58. Even though the United States did not have the air power in

1950 to strike the Soviet Union with its B-36 bombers, the next generation of bombers, the B-47, had a range to strike their perimeter.

21. Zubok, 58.

22. Not everyone was convinced that the atom bomb would give an overwhelming advantage to the surprise attack in the debate during the late 1940's. Strategist Bernard Brodie noted: "The element of surprise may be less important than is generally assumed. If retaliation has to be accepted no victory is worth it." Brodie suggested that it was more likely, if both sides had bombs in quantity, that a non-atomic war would be fought. Brodie, *Absolute Weapon,* 74, Brodie quoted in Freedman, *Evolution,* 43.

23. Buhite and Hamel, "War for Peace," 370.

24. Record of the Eighth Meeting (1950) of the PPS, 2/2/50, *FRUS,* 1950, 1:142-143.

25. Ibid.

26. Terms of Reference, 3/1/50, NA, RG 59, Deputy Assistant Secretary for Politico-Military Affairs, Subject Files of the Special Assistant for Atomic Energy and Aerospace, 1950-66, Box 1.

27. A Report to the NSC by the Executive Secretary, 4/14/50, NSC 68, *FRUS,* 1950, 1:234-292.

28. Report of the Special Evaluation Subcommittee of the NSC, 5/18/53, *FRUS,* 1952-54, 2:337.

29. Stalin believed war's outcome could only be determined by "permanently operating factors" which were: the stability of the rear, the morale of the army, the quantity and quality of divisions, the armament of the army, and the organizational ability of the commanders. Transitory factors like surprise or technological advances in weaponry (the atomic bomb) could not change the essence of war. As Stalin saw it, despite Germany's surprise attack on the Soviet Union in 1941, Hitler still succumbed to defeat because of inferior permanently operating factors. For more on Stalin and Soviet military doctrine see Herbert Dinerstein, *War and the Soviet Union: Nuclear Weapons and the Revolution in Soviet Military and Political Thinking,* (New York: Praeger, 1962), 6-10; Raymond Garthoff, *Soviet Strategy in the Nuclear Age,* (New York: Praeger, 1958), 60-65.

30. Major General Pukhovsky, *O sovetskoi voennoi nauke* (On Soviet Military Science), Voenizdat, Moscow, (Nov. 16, 1953), 84-85 quoted in Garthoff, *Soviet Strategy,* 61.

31. For a discussion on the philosophies and uses of the dialectic in Soviet doctrine see Harriet Fast Scott and William Scott, *Soviet Military Doctrine: Continuity, Formation, and Dissemination,* (Boulder, CO: Westview Press, 1988), 28. For discussion on the legacy of Stalinist stagnation see Garthoff, *Soviet Strategy,* 61-63.

32. David Holloway, *The Soviet Union and the Arms Race,* (New Haven: Yale University Press, 1984), 36-38. At the end of that year, the Ministry of Defense ordered that "nuclear weapons and the particular features of preparing, conducting and securing an operation and combat in conditions of the use of such weapons" should be studied. As a result, the General Staff Academy revised its research and teaching program radically. *Red Star,* the newspaper of the Ministry of Defense, began publishing articles on the subject of nuclear weapons. Exercises were held to study possible anti-nuclear defense procedures. In early 1955, Marshall Zhukov, the new Minister of Defense, gave a speech

calling for a more thorough study on the effects of nuclear weapons on the conduct of war.

33. Scholars Harriet and William Scott affirmed that "the possible consequences of a surprise nuclear strike were a major motivating factor for developing a new military doctrine" after Stalin's death. See Scott, *Soviet Military Doctrine*, 55.

34. Dinerstein, *War and the Soviet Union*, 11.

35. Ibid.

36. Kolkowicz, *The Soviet Military and the Communist Party*, 21-25.

37. Scott, *Soviet Military Doctrine*, 55.

38. Joseph Nogee and Robert Donaldson, *Soviet Foreign Policy Since World War II*, Fourth ed., (New York: Macmillan Publishing, 1992), 125.

39. JCS recommendations in *FRUS*, 1946, 1:1160-65, found in Buhite and Hamel, "War for Peace," 372-373. Some military officers, politicians, journalists, and political scientists advocated preventive war through 1945-1955. For example, General Leslie Groves, Senator Stuart Symington, the Alsop brothers and political scientist George Eliot all recommended preventive war at one point. Even Truman contemplated it during the Berlin and Korean crises. Bernard Brodie said that preventive war thinking was the "prevailing philosophy" during the late 1940s and early 1950s at RAND and the Air War College. For more on preventive war see, Russell Buhite and William Christopher Hamel, "War for Peace: The Question of an American Preventive War against the Soviet Union, 1945-1955," *Diplomatic History*, 14 (1990), 367-384 and Marc Tractenberg, *History and Strategy*, (Princeton: Princeton University Press, 1991), 21.

40. LeMay was speaking to Robert Sprague and Jerome Weisner of the President's Commission on Civil Defense. Interviews with Jerome Weisner and Robert Sprague, "War and Peace in the Nuclear Age," Program #3, Public Broadcasting System, Winter 1989, quoted in Buhite and Hamel, "War for Peace," 374n. David Rosenberg also documents LeMay advocating preventive war. See David Alan Rosenberg, "A Smoking Radiating Ruin at the End of Two Hours:" Documents on American Plans for Nuclear War with the Soviet Union, 1954-55," *International Security*, Vol. 6 (Winter 1982), 13.

41. Memorandum Eisenhower to Dulles, 9/8/53, EL, Eisenhower Diary, August-September 1953, folder 2, Box, 3, quoted in Buhite and Hamel, "War for Peace," 381. Even scientist Isidor I. Rabi spoke of preventive war and said "we should be prepared to follow through" with it. MIT, AC4, Cambridge-New York Meeting of the Science Advisory Committee, 3/10/54, Box 195, "Science Advisory Committee, 1954."

42. Draft Statement of Policy Prepared by the NSC Planning Board, NSC 5440, 12/13/54, *FRUS*, 1952-54, 2:806-844.

43. Bernard Brodie, *Strategy in the Missile Age*, (Princeton: Princeton University Press, 1965), 392-397. Not only does American national psychology and values prohibit the U.S. from launching a surprise attack against its enemies, but so does the "form of Government and [its] constitutional processes" as Freedman noted in *Evolution*, 36.

44. Harry S Truman, *Memoirs*, vol. 1, *Years of Trial and Hope*, (Garden City, NJ: DoubleDay, 1956), quoted in Buhite and Hamel, "War for Peace," 382.

45. Brodie, *Strategy in the Missile Age*, 392-397.

46. Ibid., 17.

47. Brands, "Age of Vulnerability," 975. See also John Prados, *The Soviet Estimate: U.S. Intelligence Analysis and Soviet Strategic Forces,* (Princeton: Princeton University Press, 1986), 57-63.

48. Memorandum of discussion at 258th NSC meeting, 9/8/55, EL, NSC Series, taken from Brands, "The Age of Vulnerability," 975.

49. General Considerations for NSC, n.d., EL, WHO NSCS, Special Staff File Series, Box 1, "Basic National Security Policy 1953-54 (1)."

50. Memorandum by Paul Nitze and Carlton Savage of the Policy Planning Staff, 5/6/53, *FRUS,* 1952-54, 2:318.

51. Buhite and Hamel, "War for Peace," 371-372.

52. Report to the NSC by the NSC Planning Board, NSC 5408, 2/11/54, *FRUS,* 1952-54, 2:615.

53. Report of the Special Evaluation Subcommittee of the NSC, 5/18/53, *FRUS,* 1952-54, 2:332-349.

54. Report by the Panel of Consultants of the Department of State to the Secretary of State, January 1953, *FRUS,* 1952-54, 2:1083.

55. Memorandum by the Executive Security of the NSC to the President, 11/5/52, *FRUS,* 1952-54, 2:165.

56. Memorandum by Carlton Savage of the Policy Planning Staff, 2/10/53, *FRUS,* 1952-54, 2:231-232.

57. Report to the NSC by the Secretaries of State and Defense and the Director for Mutual Security, NSC 141, 1/19/53, *FRUS,* 1952-54, 2:209-222.

58. Letter E.T. Dickinson and James Wadsworth to Eisenhower, 01/27/53, EL, WH Central Files, Confidential File, Box 16, "Civil Defense (1)."

59. Memorandum by Carlton Savage of the Policy Planning Staff, 2/10/53, *FRUS,* 1952-54, 2:231-232.

60. The five member panel was Vannevar Bush, John Dickey, Joseph Johnson, Robert Oppenheimer, and Allen Dulles. See Report by the Panel of Consultants of the Department of State to the Secretary of State, January 1953, *FRUS,* 1952-54, 2:1056-1058.

61. Report by the Panel of Consultants of the Department of State to the Secretary of State, January 1953, *FRUS,* 1952-54, 2:1083.

62. Ibid., 1084.

63. Memorandum by Carlton Savage of the Policy Planning Staff, 2/10/53, *FRUS,* 1952-54, 2:231-232.

64. Memorandum by Nitze and Savage of the Policy Planning Staff, 5/6/53, *FRUS,* 1952-54, 2:318-323.

65. Ibid., 320-321.

66. Memorandum by the Chairman of the Special Evaluation Subcommittee of the NSC to Lay, 5/15/53, *FRUS,* 1952-54, 2:329-330.The members of the Special Committee with their affiliation were: Lt. Gen. Idwal Edwards, Chairman; Lt. Gen. Harold Bull (CIA); W. Barrett McDonnell (ICIS); Maj. Gen. Robert Webster (JCS); Lish Whiston (IIC).

67. Draft Directive Prepared by the Director of Central Intelligence, nd, *FRUS,* 1952-54, 2:207-208.

68. The report was known as NSC 140/1.

69. Report of the Special Evaluation Subcommittee of the NSC, 5/18/53, *FRUS*, 1952-54, 2:328-349. The report said one hour was not enough time, but two hours would allow Strategic Air Command to disperse 65% of its force and six hours warning would result in an 85% dispersal.

70. Memorandum of Discussion at the 148th Meeting of the National Security Council, 6/4/53, *FRUS*, 1952-54, 2:369.

71. Ibid., 369.

72. Memorandum Discussion at the 149th Meeting of the NSC, 6/11/53, EL, AWF, NSC Series, Box 4, "149th Meeting of NSC, 6/9/53." The NSC paper was NSC 153 which was a restatement of basic national security policy which synthesized four previous policies, including NSC 149/2 which had been approved on April 29, 1953. NSC 153 was presented on June 8, 1953. See *FRUS*, 1952-54, 2:370-371.

73. Memorandum Discussion at the 149th Meeting of the NSC, 6/11/53, EL, AWF, NSC Series, Box 4, "149th Meeting of NSC, 6/9/53." The recent report was the Kelly Report, named for its chair, Mervin Kelly of Bell Laboratories.

74. Report to the NSC by the NSC Planning Board, NSC 5408, 2/11/54, *FRUS*, 1952-54, 2:615.

75. Memorandum Discussion at the 149th Meeting of the NSC, 6/11/53, EL, AWF, NSC Series, Box 4, "149th Meeting of NSC, 6/9/53."

76. Memorandum of Discussion at the 148th Meeting of the National Security Council, 6/4/53, *FRUS*, 1952-54, 2:370.

77. The Continental Defense Committee report was submitted as NSC 159 on July 22, 1953. A 33-page report by the Interdepartmental Intelligence Conference and the Interdepartmental Committee on Internal Security was submitted as NSC 159/1 on August 14. A 7 page JCS report was submitted as NSC 159/2 on September 1. The NSC Planning Board wrote NSC 159/3 based on the other three reports which was adopted, after revisions, as NSC 159/4. See *FRUS*, 1952-54, 2:465-466n.

78. Members were: Lt. General Harold Bull, Retired (chairman), Maj. General Frederic Smith, Jr. (Defense); William Elliot (ODM), Justice Chambers (FCDA), W. Barrett McDonnell (ICIS), S. Douglas Cornell (scientific consultant), and Hugh Farley (Executive secretary). Enclosure B of NSC 159 Report, 7/22/53, NA, RG 59, Policy Planning Staff, 1935-62, Box 8, "Continental Defense (NSC 159 series)(NSC Memoranda)."

79. NSC 159/4, 9/25/53, *FRUS* 1952-54, 2:478-479.

80. Ibid., 478-479.

81. Memorandum to Wilson, 8/8/53, EL, WHO NSCS, Disaster File, Box 11, "NSC 162/2 (1)."

82. JCS 1899/53, "A Coordinated Plan for the Defense of Continental United States," 8/5/53, NA, RG 218, Box 61, "381 U.S. (5-23-46) sec. 25."

83. Ibid.

84. The members were: James Phinney Baxter III, President of Williams College; James Black, President of Pacific Gas and Electric; Alan Gregg, Former V.P. of Rockefeller Foundation; David McDonald, President of United Steel Workers; Arthur Page, retired from AT&T. See, Letter Cutler to McDonald, 7/15/53, EL, WHO OSANSA, NSC Series, Administrative Sub series, Box 4, "Consultants- NSC [July-September] (3);" Memorandum for Baxter et.al., 7/22/53, Box 4, "Consultants- NSC [July-September]

(3);" Letter Eisenhower to Page, 9/25/53, Box 4, "Consultants- NSC [July-September] (3);" and Letter Cutler to Page, 9/26/53, Box 4, "Consultants- NSC [July-September] (3)."

85. NSC 159/4, "Continental Defense," 9/25/53, *FRUS*, 1952-54, 2:479.

86. Memorandum of Discussion at the 163rd Meeting of the NSC, 9/24/53, *FRUS*, 1952-54, 2:468.

87. Ibid., 470.

88. Ibid.

89. NSC 159/4, "Continental Defense," 9/25/53, *FRUS*, 1952-54, 2:483.

90. Ibid., 484.

91. Memorandum of Discussion at the 163rd Meeting of the NSC, 9/24/53, *FRUS*, 1952-54, 2:471.

92. NSC 159/4, "Continental Defense," 9/25/53, *FRUS*, 1952-54, 2:483.

93. Ibid.,486-489; Memorandum of Discussion at the 163rd Meeting of the NSC, 9/24/53, *FRUS*, 1952-54, 2:471.

94. NSC 159/4, "Continental Defense," 9/25/53, *FRUS*, 1952-54, 2:482.

95. Ibid., 477.

96. Memorandum of Discussion at the 163rd Meeting of the NSC, 9/24/53, *FRUS*, 1952-54, 2:470.

97. NSC 159/4, "Continental Defense," 9/25/53, *FRUS*, 1952-54, 2:480-481.

98. Memorandum of Discussion at the 163rd Meeting of the NSC, 9/24/53, *FRUS*, 1952-54, 2:469.

99. Ibid., 469; 471.

100. Report to the NSC by the NSC Planning Board, NSC 5408, 2/11/54, *FRUS*, 1952-54, 2:615

101. NSC 159/4, "Continental Defense," 9/25/53, *FRUS*, 1952-54, 2:482.

102. Address Before a Joint Session of the Parliament of Canada, 11/14/53, *Public Papers of the President, 1953*, 767-775.

103. Ibid.

104. Ibid.

105. Ibid.

106. "Annual Budget Message to the Congress: Fiscal Year 1955," 1/21/54, *Public Papers of the President*, 1953, 120-121. (79-192)

107. NSC 5408 was given final approval on 2/17/54. See Memorandum of Discussion at the 185th Meeting of the NSC, 2/17/54, *FRUS*, 1952-54, 2:624-633.

108. Report to the NSC by the NSC Planning Board, NSC 5408, 2/11/54, *FRUS*, 1952-54, 2:612.

109. Ibid., 612; 615.

110. Ibid., 617.

111. That committee was the Technological Capabilities Committee chaired by James Killian. See Chapter 4.

112. Report to the NSC by the NSC Planning Board, NSC 5408, 2/11/54, *FRUS*, 1952-54, 2:620.

113. Ibid., 617. Emphasis added.

114. Ibid., 619.

115. Concurrently, there was a joint American and Canadian committee surveying the Southern Canadian line and developing the military criteria to implement the line. Memorandum of Discussion at the 185th Meeting of the NSC, 2/17/54, *FRUS*, 1952-54, 2:627.

116. Ibid., 627.

117. Council decision was in NSC 5422/2, approved on August 7, 1954. Quoted in Report of Robert Sprague (NSC Consultant) to the NSC on Continental Defense, 11/24/54, EL, WHO, OSANSA, NSC Series, Subject Sub series, Box 3, "Continental Defense, Study of [Robert Sprague], 1953-54 (12)."

118. David Snead, *The Gaither Committee, Eisenhower, and the Cold War*, (Columbus: Ohio State University Press, 1999), 52-53.

119. Memorandum for the Record by Radford, 12/17/53, NA, RG 218, Box 37, "381 (Continental Defense)(1953)." Sprague was given, over the course of his service to Senator Saltonstall, numerous top secret reports and documents from the DoD, Army, Air Force, CIA, NSC, AEC, and RAND including the Kelly Report, aircraft data, weapons systems data, CIA estimates, and Strategic Air Command data.

120. Letter Eisenhower to Saltonstall, 3/30/54 and Memorandum Cutler to Eisenhower, 3/31/54, EL, AWF, Administrative Series, Box 10, "Cutler, Robert 195-55 (4)."

121. Report on Continental Defense to the Senate Armed Services Committee by Robert Sprague, 3/18/54, EL, AWF, Administrative Series, Box 33, "Sprague, Robert C. Material."

122. Memorandum for the Secretary of Defense, 6/23/54, NA, 218, Admiral Radford Files, Box 36, "381 (Continental Defense)(June-December 1954)."

123. Memorandum of Discussion at the 185th meeting of the NSC, 2/17/54, *FRUS,*1952-54, 2:627.

124. Evaluation of the Sprague Recommendations, n.d., EL, WHO OSANSA, NSC Series, Subject Sub Series, Box 2, "Study of Cont. Defense by Robert Sprague [Feb 26, 1954]."

125. Memorandum for the Secretary of Defense, 6/23/54, NA, 218, Admiral Radford Files, Box 36, "381 (Continental Defense)(June-December 1954)."

126 Ibid.

127. Editorial Note, *FRUS*, 1952-54, 2:698.

128. Report of Robert Sprague (NSC Consultant) to the NSC on Continental Defense, 11/24/54, EL, WHO, OSANSA, NSC Series, Subject Sub series, Box 3, "Continental Defense, Study of [Robert Sprague], 1953-54 (12)."

129. Their report is known as NSC 5423.

130. Report of Robert Sprague (NSC Consultant) to the NSC on Continental Defense, 11/24/54, EL, WHO, OSANSA, NSC Series, Subject Sub series, Box 3, "Continental Defense, Study of [Robert Sprague], 1953-54 (12)."

131. Memorandum of Discussion at the 225th Meeting of the NSC, 11/24/54, *FRUS,* 1952-54, 2:801; Letter Eisenhower to Sprague, 11/30/54, EL, WHO, OSANSA, NSC Series, Administrative Sub series, Box 4, "Consultants-NSC [July 1954-August 1956] (4)."

132. Memorandum for the Secretary of Defense, 6/23/54, NA, 218, Admiral Radford Files, Box 36, "381 (Continental Defense)(June-December 1954)."

133. General Considerations for NSC, n.d., EL, WHO NSCS, Special Staff File Series, Box 1, "Basic National Security Policy 1953-54 (1)."

134. Letter to the Secretary of Defense on National Security Requirements, 1/5/55, *Public Papers of the President*, 1955, 2-6.

CHAPTER FOUR

Finally a Project Worthy of its Mettle: The Science Advisory Committee Applies Technology to National Security

In March 1954, Eisenhower met with some of the nation's leading scientists serving on the Science Advisory Committee of the Office of Defense Mobilization (SAC-ODM) to discuss his concerns about the problems of surprise attack and continental defense. Dr. Lee DuBridge, chairman of the Science Advisory Committee and president of the California Institute of Technology, seized the opportunity presented to SAC-ODM by Eisenhower to undertake a study on surprise attack. As DuBridge saw it, it was the technological advances in weapon systems that had created the heightened risk of surprise attack, and policymakers needed a "scientific inventory, evaluation, and synthesis of these new developments" to make the most of the new technologies "with a minimum of delay."[1] DuBridge identified the new hydrogen bomb as the obvious example of how new technology had heightened the necessity to examine the problems of surprise attack. Believing that "the bearing of science and technology on the problems of surprise attack requires an immediate and comprehensive examination," DuBridge proposed that the Science Advisory Committee establish a short-term, but full-time group to undertake such an evaluation.[2] DuBridge was successful in convincing Eisenhower to establish an adhoc group through the Science Advisory Committee to report back to him and the NSC.

The resulting Technological Capabilities Panel continued the trend of successful civilian advising for the Eisenhower administration. Although the Technological Capabilities Panel was bigger than the Solarium exercise, under the chairmanship of James Killian the group was well organized into three manageable sub panels. The first investigated striking power and recommended the rapid development of intercontinental ballistic missiles and intermediate range ballistic missiles. The second sub panel took on continental defense and recommended extending the distance early warning line, reducing the vulnerability of Strategic Air Command, and developing an Antiballistic Missile program. The third sub panel drastically improved American intelligence through its recommendation of a high-altitude reconnaissance plane, the U-2. Presented in March 1955, the overall report made a vital contribution to national security at a moment in time when the thermonuclear revolution had introduced new dangers and problems.

Like the Solarium exercise, the Technological Capabilities Panel report exhibited all the characteristics of the Great Equation in that in its implementation, the military was strengthened through the most economically efficient way. The authors of the report even addressed the need for the American people to be spiritually centered, or as they put it, to feel a "sense of urgency without despair." The committee's recommendation also fit into Eisenhower's strategic thinking, placing a great emphasis on nuclear offensive capabilities, second strike capabilities, and a strong deterrent. Finally, the Technological Capabilities Panel also tapped into the expertise of some of the top American scientists, something the Solarium Exercise did not need to do. This opened doors for science advising that had been closed during the Truman administration.

The Science Advisory Committee: A Brief History

During the Eisenhower years, science advising to the government reached its zenith. Scientific and technological advice had been provided to the government via the Office of Scientific Research and Development during World War II under the leadership of Dr. Vannevar Bush. After the war, the office was abolished but various proposals were made to Truman regarding its replacement. It was not until the outbreak of the Korean War that Truman asked William Golden, an investment banker familiar with scientific and military affairs, to review the role science and technology should play in the government. Golden interviewed over 150 scientists and engineers and concluded that another Office of Scientific Research and Development should not be implemented. Rather, he recommended to Truman the establishment of a President's Science Advisory Committee and the appointment of a full-time Scientific Advisor to the President to provide the president with scientific information regarding military matters.

Golden had the support of other leading members in the scientific community. For example, James Killian, president of the Massachusetts Institute of Technology and chair of a committee to review the Department of Defense's Research and Development Board program, concurred with Golden's suggestion that there was a need for an executive office scientific advisor to act as a "sort of rallying point for the scientists and who would have access to the President."[3] Two other members of the Board, DuBridge and Detlev Bronk of Johns Hopkins, also supported Golden's ideas. Their support proved invaluable because they were also members of the newly formed National Science Foundation.[4] Initially, opposition to a presidential scientific advisor arose from members of the National Science Foundation who were concerned that a Science Advisory Committee or presidential advisor would limit appropriated funds to the Foundation whose mandate was to sponsor research for national defense. DuBridge and

Bronk were eventually able to convince the Foundation to drop its opposition and concentrate its efforts on basic research and fellowship pursuits.[5]

Golden took his recommendations to Truman and the president established a Science Advisory Committee in April 1951.[6] Dr. Oliver Buckley of Bell Labs, who was near retirement, was asked to serve as the President's Scientific Advisor.[7] As James Killian recalled in his memoirs, Buckley did not have the drive or decisiveness by this point in his career to build the new position into one of strength and importance. As a result, Buckley reduced the position of scientific advisor to chairman of the Science Advisory Committee. Further sabotaging the position of a President's Scientific Advisor was General Lucius Clay, who was the assistant to the director of the Office of Defense Mobilization. He recommended that the Science Advisory Committee be placed within the Office of Defense Mobilization and the presidential science advisor report to the president through the director of the Office of Defense Mobilization. Buckley's reluctance to stand firm on Golden's original proposal and Clay's insistence that the Science Advisory Committee be moved from the White House led to a weaker and less influential committee than Golden and Killian had envisioned.[8] In the face of scientific and technological advances of the late 1940s, science advising was not a priority in the Truman administration, despite the 1951 establishment of the SAC-ODM.

The purpose of the SAC-ODM was to "be available to the Director of Defense Mobilization and the President of the United States for advice in connection with the application of science to the national defense."[9] The Committee's charter did allow it to report directly to the president if the members felt it necessary; however, that option was never exercised during the Truman administration. As the members understood it, SAC-ODM was created largely to study the problem of mobilization of scientists for defense work. The committee members were to "stand by" and have a plan ready in case complete mobilization was needed, but had little other direction.[10] To feel useful, the Committee occasionally occupied itself with discussions about problems confronting the United States that had some scientific content. Sometimes other governmental groups sought the advice of the Committee.[11] Although SAC-ODM had tried to take the initiative when it could, the work of the Science Advisory Committee went mostly unused and, as Killian remarked, the Committee "languished in desuetude."[12]

In May 1952, Dr. Buckley resigned as chairman of the Science Advisory Committee upon the advice of his doctors. His replacement, Dr. Lee DuBridge, tried gallantly—but to no avail—to elevate the function and influence of the Committee during the last months of the Truman Administration.[13] DuBridge strongly believed that, "the true situation regarding atomic weapons, radar networks, the technical capabilities of air force weapons and other similar matters, [could] no longer be treated as merely technical details for they come in the very heart of the decisions on national strategy which we make."[14] Frustrated by Truman's lack of interest in SAC-ODM and worried that "the mechanisms for providing scientific advice at the highest levels in the government [had] been inadequate," DuBridge organized a meeting to discuss the future of the Committee.[15]

Hosted by Dr. Robert Oppenheimer at Princeton's Institute for Advanced Study, the Science Advisory Committee met for three days in early November 1952.[16] The agenda included improving the effectiveness of applying science to defense and improving the use of science and technology in policy making.[17] It was felt that the Committee was called upon only to dispense advice to other advisors, not policy makers, and that the National Security Council would benefit from a deliberative body such as the Science Advisory Committee.[18] Specifically, the Committee agreed that both the Secretary of Defense and the National Security Council should be provided with better scientific advice. It also recommended an advisor to the Secretary of Defense and a full-time staff member on the NSC who was a scientist or engineer.[19] In light of the ongoing Korean War and the need for scientific advice for defense, the Committee members decided that rather than disbanding, they would try to be more useful as a committee.[20] They also adopted a wait-and-see attitude towards the new administration. As early as June, the Committee had held out hope that the fall election might bring about more opportunities for active service.[21] The decision to remain intact was, in Killian's words, "prophetically wise, for ultimately great responsibilities were in store for the committee."[22]

Dr. Lee DuBridge was clearly excited about the new Eisenhower administration. In particular, DuBridge hoped that science advising might receive a higher place as a result of Eisenhower's efforts to reorganize the NSC and executive branch. DuBridge immediately set out to improve the function of SAC-ODM by contacting the newly appointed President's Advisory Commission for Government Organization.[23] DuBridge and Oppenheimer met with Nelson Rockefeller of the President's Advisory Commission for Government Organization who was genuinely interested in their recommendations and passed their ideas on to Eisenhower.[24] DuBridge then wrote to Cutler as he was reorganizing the NSC. He outlined for Cutler some of the proposals resulting from the SAC-ODM November Princeton meeting. Telling Cutler that the Science Advisory Committee believed important decisions had been made in the past without "adequate consideration given to the technological situation which bore upon the decisions," DuBridge stressed the need for better scientific advising within the new administration.[25] He rejoiced in the fact that Cutler's ideas for the NSC reflected a greater need for a deliberative process, something SAC-ODM also believed was necessary. DuBridge also saw hope in Cutler's inclusion of a member of the Science Advisory Committee, Dr. Charles Thomas, on the recent Civilian Consultants Board chaired by Dillion Anderson.[26] After complimenting Cutler on the appointment, DuBridge wrote to Thomas hoping to influence the direction of the reorganization of the NSC to incorporate more importance on scientific advising.[27]

DuBridge worked hard to ensure scientific advising played a substantial role in government policy, and he saw to it that his efforts did not go unnoticed. Cutler followed up on DuBridge's suggestions, knowing that the new administration had to deal with problems relating to atomic attack, chemical and biological warfare, continental defense, and other problems that could benefit from scientific advice.[28] Exploring how science advising might help the NSC, Cutler asked Strauss to recommend some scientists who might serve on a small committee of three to advise Cutler from time to time. Strauss recommended Detlev Bronk, Karl Compton of MIT, and John von Neumann of Princeton.[29] But, in the end, no permanent committee was ever established. Cutler explained to DuBridge in a meeting with Dr. Bush and Office of Defense Mobilization director Arthur Flemming, that the NSC did not need a permanent scientist on staff because most NSC problems were not "technical."[30] Flemming disagreed and believed a scientific advisor was still necessary, but was unable to convince Cutler or Eisenhower.

Despite DuBridge's tremendous effort, SAC-ODM still languished. This was due in part because, as historian Richard Damms explained, Eisenhower initially preferred to seek scientific advice from "practical-minded businessmen," like Strauss, rather than from scientists like DuBridge, James Conant, or Oppenheimer, all of who advocated arms control and dissented on the building of the hydrogen bomb.[31] Eisenhower also had concerns about Oppenheimer in general, saying to C.D. Jackson that he "just didn't feel comfortable with Oppenheimer" and worried about his "hypnotic influence over small groups."[32] In addition, there seemed to be no reason to appoint a President's Science Advisor since Atomic Energy Commission chairman Lewis Strauss had recently been named Special Assistant to the President for Atomic Energy Matters.[33] So, in matters of nuclear technology, most of the advice Eisenhower received did not originate with Oppenheimer and SAC-ODM, but with Edward Teller, filtering through the channel of the Atomic Energy Committee via Strauss.[34] This trend left many in the scientific community doubtful about the role scientific advising could play, particularly after Oppenheimer's hearing before the Atomic Energy Committee.

Oppenheimer had been accused of being a security risk with his opposition to the development of a hydrogen bomb and due to his past communist association. An Atomic Energy Committee "security hearing" was held in early 1954, which stripped Oppenheimer of all security clearances, forcing him out of any government advising or government-sponsored research. Killian remarked that "the Oppenheimer trial and its conclusions caused many scientists to have deep misgivings about the Eisenhower administration . . . . Not only was there widespread feeling that a tragic injustice had been done to a man who had served the nation loyally and brilliantly; there was also fear that elements in the lower reaches of government, especially in the military, were not averse to destroying the influence of those whose advice ran counter to their policies and views about national defense."[35] Although this left a rift between the administration and the scientific community, it also meant that Oppenheimer was no longer a member of SAC-ODM. Furthermore, Conant had stepped down from the Committee in early 1954, leaving SAC-ODM void of the two members Eisenhower was least comfortable with.[36] SAC-ODM was ready to be given a higher purpose in the summer of 1954 when Eisenhower gave it a project that Killian called "worthy of its mettle."[37]

Establishing the Technological Capabilities Panel

In July 1954, Eisenhower directed SAC-ODM to establish a committee to study how science and technology might be harnessed to guard against surprise attack. The idea grew out of DuBridge's perseverance as well as Eisenhower's own concerns about continental defense and surprise attack. DuBridge had help from Arthur Flemming. Flemming supported SAC-ODM and believed that it should remain intact. Moreover, he understood the problem of not having scientific advising at top policy levels and agreed with DuBridge's contention that SAC-ODM could provide a valuable service to the NSC and the President. Even though the suggestions of the Science Advisory Committee put forth at their Princeton meeting were not adopted fully, DuBridge felt Flemming would see to it that the Science Advisory Committee was affective.[38] DuBridge and Flemming had their first real opportunity to elevate the Science Advisory Committee in early 1954.

In early 1954, SAC-ODM met with Trevor Gardner, the Special Assistant for Research and Development to Secretary of the Air Force, Harold Talbott. Gardner was trained as an engineer and had worked on the Manhattan Project at the California Institute of Technology. He had been described as "intelligent, vigorous, somewhat volatile, and impatient to make changes quickly."[39] He was deeply concerned about the August 12, 1953 Soviet testing of a 400-kiloton thermonuclear device and the advances being made in warhead miniaturization. Aware of the work being done at RAND in California which predicted that as much as eighty-five percent of Strategic Air Command could be destroyed by a Soviet air strike, Gardner agreed that the Soviets were not far from developing weapons that could knock out Strategic Air Command with a first strike. He lobbied for an air force ICBM program and turned to his friend DuBridge for help. As one aide recalled, Gardner met with DuBridge, cocktail in hand, and told him that SAC-ODM was not worth "a good goddamn . . . . You're abnegating your responsibility to science and the country, sitting on your dead asses in fancy offices in Washington, wasting your time and the taxpayers' money getting through a lot of goddamn motions on a lot of low-level, shitty exercises—all in the name of science."[40] He suggested to DuBridge that the Committee ought to do a study on whether or not America had the "ability, or inability, to meet" a surprise attack and that the study should be "the *true* story, not that shit Washington is feeding the American people."[41] Roused by Gardner's critique, DuBridge agreed to set up a meeting of the SAC-ODM with Gardner on January 22 and 23.[42]

At that meeting, Gardner outlined his concerns over the problems posed by the thermonuclear revolution. In particular, he wanted to see the development of new weapon systems able to counter the Soviets ability to deliver a devastating first strike on the United States. He also hoped research done by SAC-ODM might be able to lift what he saw as "somewhat arbitrary budget ceilings" in the Department of Defense.[43] Gardner urged DuBridge and his committee to discuss further how science and technology might be applied to new weapon technology. To facilitate this task, DuBridge set up rump sessions of the Committee members on the east coast and on the west coast to discuss the questions raised by Gardner.[44] DuBridge worked with committee members in Pasadena while Killian worked with members in Cambridge.[45]

Gardner met with the Cambridge group on March 10th, and the committee members concluded that two further problems needed to be discussed: "how to create a proper sense of urgency of the problems posed by new weapons and how to increase the impact of scientific developments in military planning and programs."[46] Some members of the committee worried that even if such a study was formed to answer those questions, the NSC would not be interested in hearing the findings. Killian believed that it was irrelevant whether or not the NSC would be receptive. What was important was that SAC-ODM did what it felt necessary, and a study that evaluated the effects of new weapons on deterrence and vulnerability to surprise attack was vital. Killian believed it was vital because new weapons could no longer be seen as "purely military devices," but rather they were now "an essential element in the determination of national security."[47] As such, it reasoned that the NSC needed a "broad framework for making its policy determinations," a framework that SAC-ODM could provide. The group therefore decided at the end of its meeting that the recommendation for a full-time group of highly competent individuals be established for a six to twelve month study on how to apply science and technology to the problems of continental defense and surprise attack.[48]

In addition to the information they gathered from Gardner, David Beckler, the Executive Officer of SAC-ODM, had asked C. D. Jackson to talk with the committee members before their meeting with Eisenhower. Happy to oblige, Jackson briefed the group on the Soviet Union and the work of the Operations Coordinating Board. He even advised the Committee on a line they might take with Eisenhower.[49] The meetings with Gardner and Jackson allowed SAC-ODM to become more familiar with the needs of the government and to formalize their ideas on how science and technology could help national security. The meetings also gave DuBridge a solid framework from which to approach Eisenhower. The timing was perfect since Eisenhower had spent the last year hearing about the problems with guarding against surprise attack and the inadequacies of continental defense in light of the thermonuclear revolution.

SAC-ODM met with Eisenhower on March 27, 1954. Although their meeting was brief, SAC-ODM made its mark on Eisenhower. As Eisenhower expounded upon the grave dangers of a surprise attack on the United States, he "voiced a hope that ways could be found to reduce the probability and minimize the dangers of such an attack."[50] Eisenhower was also well aware that Gardner was not the only man bitter about budget ceilings and that the military services, although in agreement on the need for an early warning system, still fought for every penny for their own interests. He therefore hoped that a study by unbiased civilians, untouched by service rivalries, could objectively produce a "rational program of weapons development."[51] It was a golden opportunity. Since its inception in 1951, SAC-ODM had wanted to apply scientific and technological solutions to the problems posed by the Cold War, and DuBridge was eager to see a study group formed immediately.

DuBridge set out to convince Flemming to recommend that an evaluation of science and technology on the problem of surprise attack be made by a "short-term, but full-time group of highly competent individuals."[52] This group, as the Cambridge group had recommended, could greatly educate the President, NSC, and other interested departments. DuBridge recommended that the study group examine three specific areas: striking power, defensive power, and intelligence. He explained to Flemming that new technology could strengthen national security through striking power only through "the most advanced kind of creative technology and scientific thinking."[53] Specifically, DuBridge focused on the questions raised by the thermonuclear revolution—the effects of radioactive contamination, the protection of allies, and the implications of intercontinental missile development. The thermonuclear revolution also increased American vulnerability to attack, and new technology had to be utilized to improve continental defense. As DuBridge said, "a striking force cannot take off if it is wiped out in a surprise attack."[54] Improving the early warning systems, interceptors, tactical nuclear weapons, and protection of overseas bases could all enhance overall defensive power. In addition, the ultimate defensive power might come through improved intelligence since, as DuBridge duly noted, "an attack is no longer a surprise if we know it is coming in advance."[55] But, DuBridge estimated that the tremendous scientific resources available in America were not being properly utilized to improve the nation's information-gathering mechanisms. In short, such a study would improve military strength and policymaking, as well as efficiently harness scientific resources for national security.[56]

DuBridge's proposal impressed Flemming enough for him to meet with Eisenhower, Cutler, Sherman Adams, and Secretary of Defense Wilson on June 21st at an off-the-record meeting to discuss setting up such a study.[57] Flemming then followed up that meeting by holding discussions with key personnel. He spoke further with Wilson and the Assistant Secretary of Defense, Donald Quarles, who was an engineer himself and had what Killian called a "clear and fast mind in dealing with technical matters."[58] Flemming also shored up support for such a study group from Allen Dulles and Lewis Strauss. [59] Meanwhile, DuBridge had organized a two-day meeting of SAC-ODM to discuss developing this committee. To say that SAC-ODM was enthusiastic is not overstating their mood; they believed their study would be extremely valuable.[60] With the support of Wilson, Dulles, Strauss, and the entire Science Advisory Committee, Flemming recommended to Eisenhower on July 9th that the project be approved.[61] On July 24th, Eisenhower gave his signature of approval.[62]

Once again, Eisenhower turned to civilian experts, this time mostly scientists, to examine an aspect of national security—how the United States might take advantage of new science and technology to defend against surprise attack. In Eisenhower's opinion, "the needs of our country at this present instance require the best judgment we can mobilize for a short term examination of the problems."[63] To do that, he mobilized the top scientists in the country to take a searching review of the entire weapons development programs, and he opened all doors to clear the way for the group to get the relevant information it needed to be entirely successful. To lead such an ambitious study, the committee needed a competent, intelligent chair and DuBridge immediately suggested his friend James Killian for the position.[64]

James Killian: A Statesman of Science

By the time Eisenhower asked Killian to chair the committee which bore his name, Killian was already a master administrator of scientists and leader in the charge for the mobilization of science for national security. He was, simply put, a statesman of science. He graduated from the Massachusetts Institute of Technology in 1926 with a Bachelor of Science degree in business and engineering administration. With no other degree in hand, Killian stayed on at Massachusetts Institute of Technology, becoming its president in 1949. During World War II, Killian carried heavy burdens in the administration of Massachusetts Institute of Technology as the executive assistant to the school's president, Karl Compton. The Massachusetts Institute of Technology, like many other private institutions during the war, was transformed into one of the nation's largest centers for weapons research and development. Its Radiation Laboratory carried out one of the most impressive assignments of the war in its development of radar, a feat that Dr. Isidor I. Rabi credited as invaluable. "Had it not been for radar," Rabi remarked, "the Allies would have lost the war."[65] Massachusetts Institute of Technology's Dr. Vannevar Bush led a full assault in mobilizing science during the war through his Office of Scientific Research and Development, developing over 200 weapons and contributing greatly to advances in medicine, chemistry, and physics. Killian's experience with World War II led him to realize the importance of science to national security. He brought to Washington a belief that in these times of crisis, no modern statesman could afford to be scientifically illiterate. Science had won WWII and it could win the Cold War.

After the war, Killian continued to serve the country both at Massachusetts Institute of Technology and in Washington. He first went to Washington in 1950 as a member of both President Truman's Communications Policy Board and the

President's Advisory Committee on Management. In 1951 Killian became the chairman of the Army Scientific Advisory Panel, staying until 1956. Also in 1951, Truman appointed Killian to the President's Science Advisory Committee.[66] Yet while Killian was acclimating himself to Washington, as President of Massachusetts Institute of Technology he was calling for the universities of America to realize "the position of basic importance in our national life which our educational institutions have come to occupy."[67]

Immediately after World War II it became obvious that science was imperative to winning the Cold War. Dr. L. H. Reyerson, professor of chemistry at the University of Minnesota, summed up the vital importance of science to the winning of the Cold War when he remarked in 1957 that the United States was "engaged in a war of a new type. Instead of being fought on the battlefields it is now being fought in the laboratories."[68] Whoever won the war in science would win the Cold War. That meant that science and engineering education had to be top notch. However, one of the first declarations made by the newly established United Nations commented explicitly on the importance of liberal arts education for avoiding wars: "since wars begin in the minds of men, it is in the minds of men that the defenses of peace must be constructed"[69] To prevent wars, not only were weapons needed for deterrence, but so too were well-educated men and women in the humanities, social sciences, and hard sciences—statesmen-scholars with the tools to prevent war. This is how Killian also viewed education, science, and duty to country.

Understanding the importance of scientific education to the preservation of America, he mobilized MIT towards the cause of national security. As he explained in 1951 to the American Chemical Society, "The university as we know it in America cannot withdraw behind an ivory curtain in a time of crisis."[70] No longer could the university remain insulated from world events.

In a January 1951 speech titled *Ivory Towers and Bullets,* Killian told his audience that the need for well-educated men had never been so apparent. He said, "We live in an age in which science and technology are vastly increasing man's knowledge and the tools with which he can be effective. Each increase in knowledge makes additional demands on man's understanding."[71] He went on to explain, "scientific advance, an industrial society, an interrelated world, and a community of free men . . . are interdependent. Together they open doors to the future which reveal vistas of great promise. But whether we advance in this direction depends on education."[72] Killian believed that with the Cold War the educational work of the colleges needed to be strengthened. They needed to be strengthened in regards both to the students' general education and to "the community at large for increased opportunities for information and discussion."[73] The universities had a responsibility to educate the public, particularly in an era of rapid scientific and technological advances. But Killian's idea extended further. For him, a general education in all disciplines was vital to the advancement of American society. Scientific specialization was of course necessary, but Killian believed a more "Renaissance" education—one balanced in the sciences and the humanities—was also necessary for the scientist to contribute fully to society. Just as the diplomat could not afford to be scientifically illiterate, the scientist could not afford to be isolated from the humanities. It was this strong belief in the role the university had to play in educating able leaders in an era of Cold War that led Killian to establish several new programs at Massachusetts Institute of Technology, including the School of Humanities and Social Sciences, the Center for International Studies, the School of Industrial Management, and the Lincoln Laboratory.[74]

Killian not only required his students to be prepared for the Cold War, he required that the university support the national defense in the laboratory, or, as he put it, "to be ready to undertake urgent defense projects for which [the university has] the appropriate facilities and staff."[75] Based on his experiences at Massachusetts Institute of Technology during WWII, Killian became convinced that this was an appropriate role for the university. In December 1950, shortly after becoming president of Massachusetts Institute of Technology, Killian was confronted by a request from the Air Force to establish a major research project devoted to air defense. Killian's agreement to proceed was, as he himself wrote, "undoubtedly influenced by the knowledge that the Russians had exploded an atomic weapon (1949), by the turn of China, under Mao Tae-Tung, [sic] to Communism, and by the tensions associated with the opening of hostilities in Korea (1950)."[76] Furthermore, Louis Ridenour, head of the Air Force Scientific Advisory Board, had convinced Killian that Massachusetts Institute of Technology had a responsibility to respond to a national need. Unlike Harvard's president, who had declared that the university should not become engaged in classified research, Killian and many others at MIT felt that they should meet the needs of national security. As Massachusetts Institute of Technology physicist and associate director of the Lincoln Laboratory Jerrold Zacharias remarked some years later, Massachusetts Institute of Technology did not believe that "the safety of the country should be sloughed off on somebody else because it's dirty work . . . . There is a need for an institution such as [MIT] to come to the aid of its country when it's in trouble."[77]

One impressive end result of this commitment between the university and serving national security was the development of the Semiautomatic Ground Environment, commonly referred to as the SAGE system, a computerized form of air defense which the military was counting on to improve continental defenses. In developing SAGE, the Lincoln Laboratory worked closely with IBM. Killian remarked that the cooperative effort between the Laboratory and IBM was "an exceedingly important contribution to national welfare" and that "perhaps one of the greatest American inventions is the technique for taking concepts and discoveries of scholars in our universities and of implementing them industrially through the rapid mobilization of engineering, managerial, employee, and financial skills, all to the end that we produce some useful end result with a minimum expenditure of time."[78]

To educate the public and gain their acceptance of the idea of a continental air defense system, Killian co-authored an article with the director of the Lincoln Laboratory, Professor Albert Hill, for the November 1953 issue of the *Atlantic Monthly*. The article, entitled, "For a Continental Defense," was designed to increase awareness about the urgency created by the Soviets' explosion of nuclear weapons. Killian and Hill also hoped to encourage the National Security Council to give continental air defenses a higher priority and therefore submitted their article for review by Cutler. Killian and Hill obtained clearance for their article while at the same time convincing many in the NSC to support a continental defense system.[79] For Killian, educating the public was vital to maintaining freedom itself. As he explained:

> Adequate information today requires an organized approach whereby our knowledge of political science, sociology, education, and economics can be brought in to round out the picture of the situation we face as a result of a scientific and technological development. For instance, if the public learns about the destructive effects of the atomic bomb, and has no related information, it is not well informed about the bomb at all. And a badly informed man loses the capacity for constructive action which alone gives freedom meaning. The same is true of any new development. Only when the picture is presented as a whole, can the layman, the citizen who will make crucial decisions, feel that he can begin to deal effectively with new problems which may accompany scientific advance.[80]

For Killian, therefore, educating and gaining the support of the public was important. Eisenhower had the same opinions and he often spoke of the need to "educate our people in the fundamentals of these problems" in order to achieve the "enlightened support of Americans and the informed understanding of our friends."[81] This likeness in thinking no doubt contributed to Eisenhower's high regard for Killian in later years. In addition, observers clearly appreciated Killian's respect for the public. For example, after hearing Killian speak, one Senator commented that Killian "doesn't require one to be a graduate of MIT to understand what he means."[82] This ability of Killian's was also certainly one of the reasons he was so highly regarded as the President's main spokesman on American science and technology after Sputnik in 1957.

Before Killian rose to his position as Science Advisor in 1957, Eisenhower asked him to chair the Technological Capabilities Panel. Killian accepted with enthusiasm and rightly noted that the President's direct interest in the study gave the project an added importance and urgency that would inspire SAC-ODM members.[83] Important, too, to the success of the committee was Killian himself. By the summer of 1954 he had proved himself an efficient administrator of scientists, had formed a deep belief that the scientific community had a responsibility toward helping national security, was well informed about the research and development going on in the area of continental defense, and was part of an extensive network of scientists which he tapped to serve on his committee.

Getting to Work

One of the first things Killian set out to do was to establish a "small and highly competent" steering committee.[84] He called upon close associates to serve with him and asked his personal friend Dr. James Fisk of the Bell Laboratories to serve as the deputy chairman. Killian and Fisk then set up an impressive committee that included men that were well familiar with government advising such as Lee DuBridge, James Doolittle, historian James Phinney Baxter III, and Robert Sprague. Killian felt it "extremely important" to ask Sprague to participate because of his recent work for the NSC on continental defense. Sprague was invaluable for his intimate knowledge.[85] Cutler agreed that Sprague was one of the best informed men in America on the subject of continental defense but only gave Killian permission to ask Sprague to participate as a Consultant to the steering committee. Since Sprague's current status was as a Consultant to the NSC, Cutler did not want to jeopardize Sprague's position and felt it best if he were not an official member of the steering committee.[86] Sprague himself saw no difference whether he was a consultant or member of the committee and enthusiastically accepted Killian's offer.[87]

The steering committee met for the first time on September 13, 1954. Between September and February the steering committee visited Strategic Air Command headquarters, Tactical Air Command headquarters, Air Defense Command, and the Air Research and Development Command. The committee members met with various representatives from the White House, Office of Defense Mobilization, State Department, Central Intelligence Agency, Atomic Energy Committee, Federal Civil Defense Administration, Supreme Headquarters Allied Powers Europe, and the military services. In all, the steering committee participated in over one hundred and thirty briefings, field trips, meetings, and conferences.[88] Overall, the committee felt it had access to all relevant information and that everyone involved was extremely helpful. Even Curtis LeMay, the commander of Strategic Air Command who, as one committee member put it, was "the kind of person that you might think would be rather suspicious of a bunch of scientists probing into strategic matters," was really very "forthcoming and encouraging."[89]

Killian admitted that the committee did face some resistance from the services at first, particularly with the Air Force, because it was unusual for a weapons study with "no holds barred" to be undertaken by a group completely outside the Department of Defense.[90] However, as the study progressed, the different services "began to cooperate more fully, and in the end we had their enthusiastic participation."[91] Killian credited Eisenhower's sponsorship and firm support for the study as reasons why the services fully cooperated. In fact, Eisenhower and Cutler often got personally involved in ensuring that the group had access to all relevant information.[92] Also helpful were Donald Quarles, whom Killian called "an utterly reasonable person," and the military advisors assigned to the group who acted as consultants and helped facilitate the gathering of pertinent information.[93]

Despite some initial suspicion from the services towards the study, the Killian committee itself worked in an environment free from interservice rivalries. Eisenhower constantly dealt with interservice rivalries that hindered the development of a rational weapons program. Killian believed that one of the basic objectives Eisenhower had in establishing the Killian committee was "to try to find a group that could override these rivalries in the Department of Defense and look at the total problem objectively."[94] Killian was successful in organizing such a team of brilliant, dedicated scientists and engineers who rose to the challenge.

Killian assembled a group of men who came in with fresh points of view and an understanding of physical science and technology that was unmatched. They rapidly came to grips with weapons technology and made "original contributions to it" in a way that men with a lesser mastery of science and technology could not do.[95] Sprague later commented that it was a thrill to work with such an intelligent group that was so dedicated to the task at hand.[96]

Killian explained that the task at hand was to look for "what we called the big jumps," to match what the committee members knew about technology with what the Department of Defense needed.[97] To better manage that task, Killian divided the entire study into three broad groups. The first panel studied the overall offensive capabilities of the United States, or its striking power. The second panel studied continental defenses, and the third panel oversaw the area of intelligence. Each panel, like the steering committee, was given access to all relevant information, and each panel participated in numerous briefings, field trips, and meetings.[98] The group worked diligently and enthusiastically for six months; many of the 42 members worked full time, reviewing existing military technology and studying new opportunities.[99]

Following the mandate handed to them, the committee presented its final report on March 17, 1955. Robert Cutler said of the NSC presentation that it was one of the high points in the record of the NSC during the Eisenhower administration because the report served as a catalyst to accelerate the missile program in the United States, and to strengthen the overall strategic position of the country.[100] The report held what Cutler called "intrinsic importance," and did not preach desperation or despair.[101] It did, however, convey a sense of urgency. It concluded that the Soviets needed only two hundred bombs to severely damage the United States to the point of defeat and that those bombs would be delivered via missiles within a few years. However, America needed only to seize the initiative through superior technology to gain the upper hand.

To demonstrate to the President and NSC how it came to this conclusion, and to construct a useful framework for the study, the committee members created a timeline that compared relative U.S. and Soviet military strength via their weapons systems. Period I covered late 1954 and early 1955, and stated that the United States had an offensive advantage over the Soviets due to superior air-atomic power through Strategic Air Command and American atomic capabilities. However, the United States was also vulnerable to surprise attack because the early warning system was not reliable, air defenses were inadequate, and the Soviets seemed to be accumulating long-range bomber capabilities.[102] Neither side could mount a decisive air strike against the other, but the United States might mount an air offensive that inflicted "massive damage and would probably be conclusive in a general war."[103]

Period II reflected the period between 1956 and 1960. This phase marked the apex of American military superiority to Russia, when American military superiority may never again be so great. This was because of a continuing buildup of long-range bombers and multimegaton weapons. Although both sides would still be vulnerable to surprise attack, the American deterrent power would be greatly increased and US military power, relative to that of Russia, would be at its maximum. The conclusion was that during Period II, the United States could mount a decisive air attack whereas the Soviets could not.[104]

Period III was defined as a period of transition from Period II to Period IV, during which the Soviets would catch up to the United States in long-range bombing capabilities and the development of multimegaton weapons. The United States would still enjoy the advantage, but Period III would eventually give way to Period IV. This last phase was estimated to begin within ten years and last indefinitely. An attack by either side during Period IV would result in mutual destruction. Neither side could position an advantage because "each country will possess enough multimegaton weapons and adequate means of delivering them . . . through the defenses then existing."[105] Furthermore, the element of surprise would be irrelevant because either side would be able to retaliate and break through the other country's defenses. It was a period "so fraught with danger to the U.S.," thought the committee members, "that we should push all promising technological developments so that we may stay in Periods II and III as long as possible."[106]

To delay the onset of Period IV and maintain superiority over the Soviets, the Killian's committee outlined many aggressive defense measures using cutting-edge science and technology. Reporting on striking power, defensive power, and intelligence, the committee members provided impressive recommendations, most of which were integrated into America's national security policies. Particularly important to the delay of Period IV was the intercontinental ballistic missile. Whichever country obtained ICBM capabilities first was to enjoy considerable advantages over the other. If the U.S. achieved that technology before the Soviets, the authors estimated that Periods II and III would last longer. This urgency to develop an intercontinental missile was fully understood by the project director for striking power, Marshall Holloway of the Los Alamos Scientific Laboratory.

The Killian Report: Striking Power

Holloway's group was assigned to study striking power, analyzing the effects of new weapons developments on the power of American striking forces, and the feasibility of ballistic missiles.[107] Holloway's background had been in developing atomic and thermonuclear weapons at Los Alamos. Having graduated from Cornell University in 1942, he went to Perdue, where his work in thermonuclear physics led to an invitation to join the Manhattan Project. After the war, Holloway stayed on at Los Alamos and was in charge of testing the first thermonuclear bombs. The first test, "Mike," was exploded in 1952 at Enewetak atoll, producing a yield a 1000 times that of the Hiroshima explosion. He was an excellent choice to lead this group.

Serious questions regarding the feasibility of ballistic missiles had arisen. Nevertheless, after meeting with the Department of Defense's Ballistic Missile Committee, which was chaired by the brilliant mathematician John von Neumann of the Institute for Advanced Study at Princeton, the group members came to the positive conclusion that ballistic missiles were obtainable. The group worked closely with von Neumann's committee and was deeply impressed by its work and director.[108]

Von Neumann had worked as a consultant on the Manhattan Project and developed a computer that performed all the calculations for the hydrogen bomb project at Los Alamos. He was curious about everything. When atomic physicist Enrico Fermi needed a calculator, von Neumann did the math in his head. His abilities earned him credibility among not only scientists and engineers, but also among military officers and policymakers. He dedicated his talents to technology of weapons of mass destruction. For example, when confronted with the problems of target accuracy of the first generation ICBMs, his solution was to make bombs dirty enough so that if the missile missed its target, everything for miles would be destroyed anyway.[109] In early 1954 he testified to the NSC on the miniaturization of warheads and the possibilities of an ICBM and he explained these advancements to the members of the panel on striking power.[110] The panel members took von Neumann's conclusions, studied them, confirmed them, and recommended that development of these ICBMs be given a high priority. In addition, due to the complexities of the ICBMs, which had a range of 5,500 nautical miles, Holloway's group recommended that as an insurance measure, the smaller IRBMs also be given the same priority.

The group members also recommended the development of a ballistic missile with a range of 1,500 nautical miles that was launched from sea.[111] This emphasis on sea-based IRBMs led directly to the development of the Polaris missile, a submarine-launched missile system.

The Polaris missile was developed in response to the belief that a hardened, dispersed, and stable deterrent was needed. The navy considered various concepts including the placement of missiles on board surface vessels as well as proposals for underwater delivery vehicles. However, the navy had been unable to reach any decisions relating to the matter. In contrast, the group members looked at the evidence for each concept and came to the strong conclusion that a submarine-borne missile was the best solution.[112]

The Polaris missile system fit perfectly with Eisenhower's strategic thinking. Preserving second-strike capabilities was an essential element of that thinking. In order for a deterrent to be successful, the Soviets had to be convinced that the United States had a retaliatory force capable of both surviving a first-strike and imposing unacceptable damage by a second-strike. The Truman administration had not concentrated on this element, but it was central to Eisenhower. A submarine-launched missile was virtually invulnerable and the Polaris system assured the United States had a secure second strike capacity for the rest of the Cold War.

Eisenhower, as well as his departments of State and Defense, also agreed with the group's assessment that it was vital to achieve ICBM technology before the Soviets in order to keep the advantage.[113] He recognized that the ICBM strengthened offensive power and deterrent capabilities, fitting in with the strategic thinking of the New Look. A combination of the ICBM, the Polaris system, and B-52 bombers would make any Soviet attempt at a surprise attack impracticable. In addition, the relative low cost of the technology was appealing. As such, he viewed U.S. development of its missile systems as a matter of great urgency and ordered that research and development of the ICBM and IRBMs be given the highest priority above all other programs.[114] As Cutler later recalled, the recommendations within the report for missile development, coupled with the work done by the von Neumann Ballistic Missile Committee, resulted in the government's annual expenditures for missile research and development to increase from a rate of a million dollars a year during the Truman administration to some billions of dollars a year under Eisenhower. Cutler explained it was a matter of having to "catch up for seven lost years."[115]

Although Holloway's group concluded that the ICBM and a defense against them required vastly improved technology, they believed that their findings were "sufficiently encouraging . . . to obviate the general prevailing feeling of hopelessness in the face of the ICBM threat."[116] This was due in large part to their sound recommendations for strengthening continental defense.

The Killian Report: Defensive Power

The project director for the defensive power group was Leland Haworth, director of the Brookhaven National Laboratory. Haworth had just recently written
a five page letter to the Atomic Energy Commission outlining plans for the
world's largest particle accelerator—or "atom smasher" as it was affectionately
referred to by the public. His lab received the funding for the project, which was
completed in 1960, and he later went on to serve as commissioner of the Atomic
Energy Commission.

Haworth's group was asked to study defensive power and the technological
developments that might allow for improved defenses, such as a practical early
warning system, using nuclear missiles in air defense and moving the air battle
away from American airspace.[117] In their resulting report, the group members
recommended that the Defense Early Warning line be extended, that the US develop an air-to-air nuclear missile system, and that the outward extension of the
combat zone be extended an additional 300 miles to protect American borders.
In addition, panel members cautioned the NSC not to limit nuclear strategy simply because of the possibility for radioactive fallout in the US, an issue that was
becoming increasingly contentious within the public discourse.[118] Essentially
Haworth's group recommended a continuation of the policies outlined in the
continental defense policy paper NSC 5408. Defense power was to be strengthened by reducing the vulnerability of the Strategic Air Command and enlarging
the early warning system—two programs strengthening second-strike capabilities.

While Holloway's group emphasized missile technology, so too did Haworth's group, agreeing that nuclear weapons should be adopted as the major
armament for air defense forces.[119] However, Haworth's group did not ignore the
fact that manned bombers, and not missiles, were currently the only delivery
vehicle available to America and the Soviet Union. Therefore, the group focused
its efforts on reducing the vulnerability of Strategic Air Command. Since the
vulnerability of Strategic Air Command was a major concern, the report suggested that the present "unacceptable" ground vulnerability be reduced more
rapidly than currently planned by Department of Defense programs. Bases
should be hardened, aircraft should be dispersed, and more bombers should be
kept on continuing airborne alert. These were the top priorities.[120] Specifically,
the group members recommended that the NSC consider "three possible coun-
termeasures: (1) construction of additional bases as a top priority emergency
program; (2) institution of an emergency dispersal program, in which more airfields—including civilian ones—would be used; and (3) an increase in active
defenses by diverting anti-aircraft guns and guided missiles from defense positions around cities to SAC bases."[121]

In discussing Haworth's recommendations regarding Strategic Air Command vulnerability, Eisenhower remarked that there had not been "any Killian

Committee to tell us the Russian side of the story," and he believed that "the Russians too have major problems to meet in this whole area."[122] As such, he hesitated to spend large amounts of money on such immediate improvements that might sacrifice the budget for the long haul. This was typical of Eisenhower to look beyond the technical capabilities of the Soviets and think about their actual capabilities.[123] The Department of Defense and Joint Chiefs agreed in theory with the group's recommendation to reduce the ground vulnerability of Strategic Air Command, but, like the President, had concerns about the cost effectiveness of such measures. For example, the Defense Department explained that on the one hand, "there is the cost and effectiveness of dispersal bases and active defenses, and on the other hand there is the cost effectiveness of warning systems and alert measures which would permit Strategic Air Command to depart on offensive strike measures after initial warning of enemy attack had been received and before their home bases could be attacked."[124] Yet the question remained: Could the country afford both dispersal of Strategic Air Command bases and an early warning system? Haworth's group recommended both.

The Distant Early Warning (DEW) line and additions of long-range and gap-filler radars to the U.S. and Canadian radar nets were programs already in development that the group endorsed. The members also urged that radar nets be installed immediately, without waiting for refinements.[125] Furthermore, Haworth's group recommended new actions. Specifically, it recommended the extension of the DEW line to Greenland across the Atlantic by way of Iceland to join the NATO warning system and an extension from Hawaii to the Midway Islands.[126] The Joint Chiefs of Staff objected to the Midway extension because repair and overhaul of aircraft would still have to be completed in Hawaii, increasing the time the aircraft would not be available for duty on the barrier line. Although the Pacific extension was never adopted, the DEW was extended northward and the extension improved overall continental defense.

The group also suggested examining the feasibility of shooting down incoming missiles with a defensive missile—an antiballistic missile. The Air Force Scientific Advisory Board was exploring this topic and the Killian committee urged that a full-time technical group be established to "carry out a rapid but thorough examination" of the program.[127] As a result of this recommendation, the Air Force Scientific Advisory Board set up such a group with the approval of the Department of Defense, and, although an Anti-Ballistic Missile was never developed by the United States, it was given serious attention.[128]

Overall, Haworth's group made valuable suggestions for strengthening continental defenses, and most of the recommendations made by the group were implemented at some point. Seen as totally inadequate when Eisenhower took office, continental defenses continued to improve during his term, and the Killian report was the impetus. Progress was also being made on continental defenses through the work of the intelligence panel.

The Killian Report: Intelligence

The project director for the group on intelligence was Edwin Land of Polaroid. The most significant outcome of his group's work on intelligence was the U-2 high altitude reconnaissance plane that came under the purview of the CIA. Fitting nicely into the Great Equation, the U-2 program allowed Eisenhower to obtain vital intelligence information about the Soviet Union at a modest cost.[129] In addition, over flights of the Soviet Bison bomber bases near Leningrad confirmed that their fleet was small, which allowed Eisenhower to confidently deny the Air Force request for increased B-52 production, knowing that he was not placing American military superiority at risk. Overall, the creation of this one program alone made the work of the Killian Committee invaluable.

Eisenhower had been deeply disturbed by the failure of intelligence at Pearl Harbor. The Battle of the Bulge experience had also taught him the limits of intelligence and the dangers of being caught off guard. Although the CIA had been trying to set up a spy network inside the Soviet Union since after World War II, they had been largely unsuccessful.[130] Understanding that the best help for overall continental defense was improved intelligence, both Eisenhower and the committee members sought improved intelligence measures. Even the title of the intelligence section of the Killian report indicated its vast importance to national security: "Intelligence: Our First Defense Against Surprise."[131] Studying the application of scientific techniques to improve U.S. intelligence gathering within the Soviet Union was the group's main task.[132] The group carried out its assignment well. As Killian later recalled, the group displayed inventiveness and scientific ingenuity which "enlarged the concept of what the role of intelligence is in the world today, viewing intelligence in its most constructive and benign sense as an instrument of national policy."[133]

Killian asked MIT lecturer and Cambridge friend Edwin "Din" Land to lead the panel on intelligence. Land had dropped out of Harvard when he was a freshman to work on filters for cutting the glare in cameras and telescopes; he later established the Polaroid Corporation to sell these filters.[134] Working on various government projects while running Polaroid, Land had been involved with projects dealing with guided missiles, infrared searchlights, anti-aircraft training devices and 3-D film for aerial photography, but it was his work on the Killian committee that gave him a leading role in guiding American reconnaissance activities for the next three decades. Land was dedicated to the work being done by the committee. He described the group's commitment by saying, "We simply cannot afford to defend against all possible threats. We must know accurately where the threat is coming from and concentrate our resources in that direction. Only by doing so can we survive the Cold War."[135] Helping him was James Baker, a Harvard astronomer and optic expert who had worked with Land on the Reconnaissance Panel of the Air Force Scientific Advisory Board since 1952.[136] The two designed a camera that could be used at high altitudes to deliver photographs covering 125 miles of territory at high enough resolutions to distinguish between objects the size of a basketball.[137]

The group was aware that the Soviets had the clear advantage in intelligence gathering. Historian Michael Beschloss explains it best by pointing out that, "in any five-and-dime, they [the Soviets] could buy maps of American bridges, factories, highways, ports, air bases, missile sites, atomic testing grounds."[138] Therefore, the Soviets could accumulate vast amounts of information concerning the United States, but American intelligence knew little about the Soviet Union. In 1951, at a MIT summer study group, Land heard Air Force men like James Doolittle explain the need for aerial reconnaissance on the one hand, while expressing the belief that flying cameras deep into Soviet territory was a near impossibility on the other hand. At the very least, these men thought, it would take ten years to develop such technology. Land did not buy into that theory, and in 1954 he asked his group on intelligence to take another look at aerial reconnaissance.[139]

At the same time, the Air Force and CIA were trying to design an airplane that could fly high enough over Soviet territory to be out of Soviet anti-aircraft defenses. Since the outbreak of the Cold War, both the British and the Americans had been trying to fly reconnaissance missions over the Soviet Union. In the late 1940s, balloons were used, but more times than not they ended up in the hands of the Soviets before making it to Japan where they were to be recovered by the West. By 1950, American airplanes were flying over Soviet territory, but they could not penetrate deep enough into the interior and were prone to being shot down by Soviet aircraft.[140] Kelly Johnson, a legendary designer for Lockheed's 'Skunk Works,' had the perfect concept: a high altitude spy plane capable of flying above seventy thousand feet for as long as four thousand miles. In April 1954 Johnson briefed a Pentagon group, which included Trevor Gardner. Both Gardner and Allen Dulles loved the concept, and Gardner introduced Johnson to Land, who thought Johnson's concept was brilliant.[141]

When Land briefed Killian about the concept of a high-altitude reconnaissance plane outfitted with the latest photographic and intelligence equipment, the two men thought the idea was too important to wait until the final report was submitted to the president and scheduled a meeting with Eisenhower. They met with Eisenhower in early November and at the end of the briefing Eisenhower gave his tentative approval with one catch—the CIA would have full control of the program so uniformed servicemen of the Air Force would not be flying the missions and so that the program did not become the victim of interservice rivalries. By the end of the month, the U-2 program was on its way.[142] Construction of the first U-2 prototype took only eighty-eight days and the first flight over Moscow and Leningrad took place on July 4, 1956.[143] Killian thought that Eisenhower's responsiveness to the innovative proposal was a clear demonstration of the President's willingness to "act upon bold new ideas in the domain of technology."[144]

The U-2 provided critical information to Eisenhower, giving him the upper
hand over the Soviets. Eisenhower later recalled the significance of the U-2 in
his memoirs. "The importance of the effort at the time cannot be overempha-
sized. Our relative position in intelligence, compared to that of the Soviets, could
scarcely have been worse. The Soviets enjoy practically unimpeded access to
information of a kind in which we were almost wholly lacking."[145] Of course the
U-2 affair was an embarrassment for Eisenhower in the spring of 1960, but the
information the flights provided outweighed any political embarrassments.[146] In
fact, after the U-2 photographed the placement of missiles in Cuba, both John F.
Kennedy and his NSC advisor McGeorge Bundy said that this one piece of information from the U-2 program "fully justified all that the CIA had cost the
country in all its proceeding years."[147]

In addition to the U-2, Land's group offered other important insights. First,
they made a clear distinction between *strategic* warning and *tactical* warning.
Strategic warning was vital. It was the warning given while the attack was in its
preparation stage, before the bombers took off, and before the subs were
launched. If the United States had strategic warning, it might deny the enemy the
advantage of surprise. The tactical warning of radar nets and early warning systems discussed in the previous sections were useful after the attack had begun,
but what was needed, the group stressed, was a strategic warning system that
gave warning well in advance of an impending attack.[148]

Although the United States had enough information to "give a probably reliable picture" of Soviet strength, how could one really know if the Soviets were
planning a surprise attack? The reality was that the United States currently had
limited knowledge of Soviet capabilities and even less about their intentions.[149]
Furthermore, just as American techniques in early warning had improved, it had
to be assumed that the Soviet ability to confuse indicators had improved as well.
As the group members stated, the Soviets were "not amateurs in these techniques."[150] For these reasons it was concluded that "there is a real possibility that
a surprise attack might strike us without useful, strategic early warning."[151]

To guard against surprise attack, there were ways to improve the chances
that strategic warning would work. It was figured that a larger attack would be
easier to detect than a small assault. If the United States could convince the Soviet Union that the only way to achieve its aim was a massive assault, the success
of strategic warning would be greatly increased. Based on the theory that if the
enemy thinks we are strong, then he will need a bigger force that will be easier to
detect, denying him surprise attack, Land's group argued that keeping up a
strong retaliatory arsenal would improve the chances of the Soviets planning a
large attack.[152] But, the group members also conceded that the Soviets could be
bluffing and that the United States might be the victim of a major hoax. If the
Soviets understood American intelligence techniques, the Soviets could easily
feed false information to develop a massive deception. That theory was not entirely faulty as the Soviets did try to convince the world they had more strength
than they did.[153]

Land's group also stressed that American strategists had to be careful about assuming the only kind of attack the Soviets would launch would be a long-range air attack. To guard against a surprise in kind as well as timing, the members remarked that, "it is only realistic to be imaginative."[154] The Soviets had no "practical experience" with long-range air attacks and if the Soviets' aim was to merely neutralize America long enough to conquer Western Europe, taking out Strategic Air Command through a long-range bomber attack might not be necessary. Soviet civil and active defense measures could absorb part of an American strike, and as such, Strategic Air Command did not need to be targeted. Instead, urban and industrial centers in America would be more likely targets. So if the Soviets were not planning a long-range air attack on Strategic Air Command, the nation had to be prepared to defend against clandestine or sea attacks. However, with all that said, a long-range air attack had to be taken seriously and that with the advent of thermonuclear weapons, the Soviets' plan to absorb an assault from Strategic Air Command might change as the civil and active defense measures of the Soviet Union would be inadequate to absorb such destruction.[155]

The thermonuclear weapons also added another problem for the military and political executive: "the problem of the *total decision*." As the group members accurately concluded, "no executive can undertake the responsibility for altering the face of our world unless he has strategic and tactical information of the highest reliability."[156] A "clever enemy" would take advantage of the total decision by creating ambiguity, disrupting communications, and "tantalizing our indicator boards." It was therefore necessary not only to provide sound intelligence, but also to prepare the executive and his staff for the psychological strains of making that total decision. Psychological rehearsals were recommended to prepare for the total decision "in urgency, in conflict, and in confusion."[157]

Satellites were another significant means to improve strategic warning on a number of levels. First, sending a 5-25 pound satellite into a low orbit would provide scientists with valuable information for the development of ICBMs. The cost would be modest and it would provide great prestige for the United States while establishing the idea that space was open to all. Furthermore, such a satellite would not be a military offensive as nothing could be launched or dropped from it, and yet it could develop into a larger satellite capable of sending very high-frequency radio and radar signals to offer detailed and extensive reconnaissance coverage.[158] Ultimately, the United States had to "take the lead in the development of appropriate international agreements on the freedom of space."[159]

Finally, Land's group envisioned a greater use of the computer for sorting and categorizing intelligence information. The computer limited human error and reduced the needed manpower, allowing a bigger bang for the buck. In addition, it provided a mechanism to conduct research and analyze intelligence. The nation did not currently take advantage of its scientific resources and needed to better utilize the top scientists. They suggested establishing a new lab "where broad, fundamental research in intelligence can be conducted."[160] The group believed such a lab would better take advantage of specialists in outside laboratories that currently contributed in limited ways as consultants and contractors.

Land's group emphasized that the United States needed the best informed government in the world; the group believed that intelligence provided the information necessary to reach sound decisions and to "better cope with those occasional fantasies such as those embraced by the military and by politicians with respect to such ideas as a missile gap."[161] The scope of the entire report was impressive, and the group's recommendations were widely embraced. Although the U-2 was certainly the crown jewel of the report, the other recommendations and analyses within the report propelled American intelligence to an elevated level for the rest of the Cold War.

Legacies of the Report: Rebuilding a Bridge

The Killian report strengthened American national security within the parameters of the Great Equation. The committee's work resulted in building a nuclear deterrent force and securing second-strike capabilities, which were the heart and soul of Eisenhower's strategic thinking. The committee also gave the President one of the most indispensable pieces of intelligence equipment in the U-2. Eisenhower was clearly thrilled with the committee's work, telling Killian that he was "deeply grateful" for the contribution his men made to national security. Speaking to Killian directly, Eisenhower said, "You have once again demonstrated your willingness to respond to the nation's needs despite your heavy and continuing non-governmental responsibilities."[162] To the other members of the Killian committee Eisenhower expressed similar gratitude, thanking each of them for their intensive work and service to the nation.[163]

Eisenhower held a deep respect for the group. Like the Solarium Exercise before it, there had been no leaks and the panel members had worked without exhibiting any desire to push through their projects. Eisenhower had a preoccupation with what Killian called "the importance of keeping this classified study from leaking to the press or to Congress," and the fact that the group came through the study "without creating suspicions or new concerns" had a real impact on the President.[164] Killian himself explained that the group understood that their report was meant only to be helpful and that the members did not "express superior judgment in any sense." In fact, they were well aware of the practical difficulties of many of their recommendations and had tried to assist in recommending "the best conceivable defense."[165] It was this "passion for anonymity" exhibited by the entire group that led Eisenhower to view the entire committee as highly responsible and react so favorably to the group's findings.[166]

In fact, the only mention of the group's existence was made in an October press release from the Office of Defense Mobilization, which stated that Killian had been appointed head of a committee of scientists who were to study "methods to mobilize more effectively scientific resources in the event of an emergency."[167] The implication was that the group was studying personnel problems in the military, not weapons systems. Since the final report contained highly sensitive and classified material, Eisenhower did not want the material leaked and was impressed by the committee members' respect for the classified nature of the study.[168]

Not only did the Killian committee make an enormous contribution to national security, it also built a bridge between the scientific community and the administration that had been severely damaged by the Oppenheimer affair. After the atomic bombings on Hiroshima and Nagasaki, scientists in America enjoyed a sense of prestige in society. Historian Paul Boyer explained that atomic scientists had gone from "bomb makers to political sages," in part because the public perceived them as the masterminds behind victory. After Hiroshima, their stature "grew to gargantuan proportions," and many found themselves in the public and political limelight.[169] The scientific community enjoyed this status for a while, but the combination of the political activities by scientists for a world government and the rise of McCarthyism damaged the scientific community's relationship with the government.[170] The most serious break in confidence between the scientific community and the administration occurred over the building of the hydrogen bomb. The scientific community was split over the need for such a bomb. Teller led the charge for the project while Oppenheimer spoke for those scientists opposed to the project. Teller, and his friend in the Atomic Energy Committee, Strauss, wanted to silence Oppenheimer, and Oppenheimer was ultimately denied the renewal for his security clearance in a rather public hearing accusing him of communist associations.

After the Oppenheimer affair, clear tensions existed between scientists and the administration. There were deep misgivings within the scientific community towards the government and ambivalent feelings in the government with respect to the scientific community.[171] Repairing that damage was difficult. The success of the Killian committee and work begun by DuBridge helped to repair the divide.

In organizing the Killian committee, DuBridge had hoped the study might "provide a better relationship between government and the scientific community" while elevating the role of the Science Advisory Committee.[172] Both DuBridge and Killian hoped that they might convince Eisenhower of the valuable contribution scientists could make to national security and mend the gulf that had been created. Killian in particular wanted to "foster greater mutual understanding and trust between the administration and the scientific community and prevent any larger rift in the government-science partnership he thought so necessary for the national security and welfare."[173]

Many in the scientific community had long wanted to educate Eisenhower on points of view other than those of Strauss, whose only mantra seemed to be to build bigger and more destructive weapons. While DuBridge and SAC-ODM advocated the advancement of weapons technology, they also thought that the application of science and technology could enhance continental defense and international arms control. Eisenhower had recognized before establishing the Killian committee that science played a vital role in the nation's "security and growth," and was increasingly being felt in foreign affairs.[174] However, after the Killian report, Eisenhower had a deeper appreciation for what science and technology could do. For example, the committee began the great strides made in space technology and weapons development, and Eisenhower expressed the desire to see the military make "maximum use of science and technology in order to minimize numbers in men."[175] By early 1955, it was obvious to Killian that there was clear evidence of "eased tensions" and that relations were on the mend."[176]

Relations continued to improve; by mid-1956 Killian felt that SAC-ODM was being viewed by the administration as an appropriate advisory group in policy-planning matters in its field. "I feel," Killian told DuBridge, "that we have definitely gained in establishing good contacts with Sherman Adams and Colonel Goodpaster."[177] That success continued, more or less, throughout the decade. The establishment of a President's Science Advisory Committee and a Special Assistant to the President for Science and Technology in1957 helped strengthen that relationship. In his role as the first Special Assistant to the President for Science and Technology, Killian assisted the administration in reassuring the American public about the country's scientific and technological strength following Sputnik. By 1959, Killian thought the committee was working well and had established "good working attitudes and relationships with Defense."[178] The whole experience, Killian believed, had served to enhance the morale of the scientific community.[179]

By 1957, many in the scientific community viewed the improved relationship between science and the administration as a direct result of Eisenhower himself and the renewed sense the Science Advisory Committee felt. Writing to Eisenhower, the vice-president for research at Bell Labs said, "You must know that in these last years you have created a new spirit" and pattern of interaction of science with society and the common welfare. "Already the influence of your Science Advisory Committee is forming a new union of the finest intelligences with the best instincts for public service."[180] Even Killian noted that since the committee completed its task, Eisenhower proved to be "extraordinarily cordial to those people whom he knew in the scientific community."[181] This repair to the gulf between the administration and the scientific community was an important legacy of the Killian committee as science and technology continued to advance national security.

What resulted from the Killian committee was a comprehensive, well-managed report that helped Eisenhower better understand how science and technology could be used in national security. Killian explained that the committee demonstrated how well intensive interdisciplinary studies were to policymakers. "When properly staffed such studies bring to the policy maker objective appraisals free of departmental bias, fresh insights and innovative ideas which executive staffs find it difficult to come by under the unremitting operating pressures to which they are normally subjected."[182] The committee rose above service rivalries, politics, and personal agendas and delivered solutions that fit nicely into the Great Equation and complimented Eisenhower's strategic thinking. Many of the recommendations, like the missile development and the U-2, provided national security with programs that were economically cost efficient. The committee also secured a greater role for science advising during the rest of the Eisenhower administration as it demonstrated how science and technology could enhance American national security. In every sense, the Killian committee proved to be a success and furthered Eisenhower's confidence in civilian committees.

Notes

1. Letter DuBridge to Arthur Flemming, 5/24/54, EL, WH Central Files, Confidential File, Box 104, "World War III (1)."
2. Ibid.
3. Killian, *Sputnik, Scientists, and Eisenhower*, 62-63; Bruce Smith, *The Advisers: Scientists in the Policy Process*, (Washington: Brookings Institute, 1992), 162-163.
4. The National Science Foundation was established in 1950 by President Truman in part to strengthen American science and science education but was greatly under-funded.
5. Killian, *Sputnik, Scientists, and Eisenhower*, 63-64.
6. Membership included: Detlev Bronk, William Webster, Alan Waterman, Hugh Dryden, James Conant, Lee DuBridge, Robert Loeb, Robert Oppenheimer, Charles Thomas, and James Killian. See Killian, *Sputnik, Scientists, and Eisenhower*, 66.
7. Dr. Mervin Kelly of Bell Labs was asked first, but declined. Killian, *Sputnik, Scientists and Eisenhower*, 63.
8. Killian, *Sputnik, Scientists, and Eisenhower*, 64-65.
9. Killian, Untitled Speech, n.d, MIT, AC4, Box 194, "Science Advisory Committee, 1952."
10. Letter DuBridge to Cutler, 3/19/53, EL, WHO, OSANSA, Special Assistant Series, Subject Sub series, Box 7, "Science and Research- General (1)[March-April 1953]."
11. Rather than offer its expertise to other groups, it was Dr. Buckley's policy to wait for someone to seek the advice of the Committee. However, in 1952, SAC-ODM invited members of Project East River, who were studying the problems of civil defense, to brief them on their findings. After hearing that briefing, the committee decided that the public needed more information on possible types of attack and various aspects of civil defense and a sub-committee was appointed by SAC-ODM to draft a letter to Truman to consider the matter of public education. See Killian, *Sputnik, Scientists, and Eisenhower*, 66; Summary of Meeting No. 10 of the Science Advisory Committee, 4/12/52, MIT, AC4, Box 194, "Science Advisory Committee, 1952." The subcommittee consisted of Bronk (chair), Killian and Loeb.
12. Killian, *Sputnik, Scientists, and Eisenhower*, 66.
13. Ibid., 66.

14. Letter DuBridge to Charles Thomas, 3/19/53, EL, WHO OSANSA, Special Assistant series, Subject sub-series, Box 7, "Science and Research- General (1) [March-April 1953]," 1.

15. Letter DuBridge to Cutler, 3/19/53, EL, WHO OSANSA, Special Assistant series, Subject sub-series, Box 7, "Science and Research- General (1) [March-April 1953]," 1.

16. Meeting No. 14 Summary of the Science Advisory Committee, 11/7-9/52, MIT, AC4, Box 194, "Science Advisory Committee 1952." It was at this meeting that those who had heard rumors warned Oppenheimer he was about to come under attack. See Killian, *Sputnik, Scientists, and Eisenhower*, 104.

17. Meeting No. 13 Summary of the Science Advisory Committee, 9/12/52, MIT, AC4, Box 194, "Science Advisory Committee 1952."

18. Meeting No. 12 Summary of the Science Advisory Committee, 6/15/52, MIT, AC4, Box 194, "Science Advisory Committee 1952."

19. Letter DuBridge to Charles Thomas, 3/19/53, EL, WHO OSANSA, Special Assistant Series, Subject Sub series, Box 7, "Science and Research - General (1)[March-April 1953]."

20. Killian, *Sputnik, Scientists, and Eisenhower*, 67.

21. Meeting No. 12 Summary of the Science Advisory Committee, 6/15/52, MIT, AC4, Box 194, "Science Advisory Committee 1952."

22. Killian, *Sputnik, Scientists, and Eisenhower*, 67.

23. For more on PACGO see Chapter one.

24. Memorandum DuBridge to Members and Consultants of the Science Advisory Committee,1/5/53, MIT, AC 4, Box 195, "Science Advisory Committee 1953;" Memorandum DuBridge to Members and Consultants of the Science Advisory Committee, 4/20/53, MIT, AC 4, Box 195, "Science Advisory Committee 1953."

25. Letter DuBridge to Cutler, 3/19/53, EL, WHO OSANSA, Special Assistant Series, Subject Sub series, Box 7, "Science and Research - General (1)[March-April 1953]."

26. Letter DuBridge to Cutler, 3/19/53, EL, WHO OSANSA, Special Assistant Series, Subject Sub series, Box 7, "Science and Research - General (1)[March-April 1953]." For more on the Civilian Consultants see Chapter One.

27. Letter DuBridge to Charles Thomas, 3/19/53, EL, WHO OSANSA, Special Assistant Series, Subject Sub series, Box 7, "Science and Research - General (1)[March-April 1953]."

28. Cutler called the suggestions appropriate and useful and invited DuBridge to meet with him, Dr. Bush, Assistant Secretary of Defense Kyes, and ODM director Arthur Flemming in May. Memorandum DuBridge to Members and Consultants of the Science Advisory Committee, 4/20/53, MIT, AC 4, Box 195, "Science Advisory Committee 1953."

29. Strauss to Cutler, 4/23/53, EL, WHO OSANSA, Special Assistant Series, Subject Sub series, Box 7, "Science and Research - General (1)[March-April 1953]."

30. Memorandum to Members of the Science Advisory Committee from DuBridge, 5/20/53, MIT, AC 4, Box 195, "Science Advisory Committee 1953."

31. Richard Damms, "Eisenhower's 'Scientific-Technological Elite,'" *Diplomatic History*, 24 (Winter 2000), 62. James Conant was president of Harvard from the mid-thirties to the mid-fifties and had worked on the atomic bomb. See James Hershberg,

James Conant: Harvard to Hiroshima and the Making of the Nuclear Age, (New York: Knopf, 1993).

32. Jackson to Henry Luce, 10/12/54, CD Jackson Papers, Box 66, "Oppenheimer," quoted in Damms, 62.

33. Memorandum to Lay from Hugh Farley, 4/2/53, EL, WHO OSANSA, Special Assistant Series, Subject Sub series, Box 7, "Science and Research - General (1)[March-April 1953]." Strauss coveted his position as main science advisor to Eisenhower and resented it when Eisenhower did finally create the position of Special Assistant to the President on Science and Technology in 1957 and appointed James Killian. See Killian, *Sputnik, Scientists, and Eisenhower*, 38.

34. Killian, *Sputnik, Scientists, and Eisenhower*, 152. Edward Teller can be considered the father of the hydrogen bomb and fought hard for its development, much to the opposition and dismay of Manhattan Project director, Robert Oppenheimer. Both Teller and Strauss continued to advocate bigger bombs and opposed arms control and test bans throughout the 1950s. For more on Teller and the hydrogen bomb see Richard Rhodes, *Dark Sun: Making of the Hydrogen Bomb*, (NY: Simon & Schuster, 1995).

35. Killian, *Sputnik, Scientists, and Eisenhower*, 223. For the best account on the Oppenheimer case see Philip Stern, *The Oppenheimer Case: Security on Trial*, (NY: Harper Row, 1969). For a recent work on the scientific community during the cold war and McCarthyism see Jessica Wang, *American Science in an Age of Anxiety: Scientists, Anticommunism, and the Cold War*, (Cambridge: MIT Press, 1999).

36. Hershberg, *James Conant*, 568-569; Damms, "Eisenhower's 'Scientific-Technological Elite,'" 62.

37. Killian, *Sputnik, Scientists, and Eisenhower*, 67.

38. Memorandum to Members of the Science Advisory Committee from DuBridge, 5/20/53, MIT, AC 4, Box 195, "Science Advisory Committee 1953."

39. Herbert York, *Race to Oblivion: A Participant's View of the Arms Race*, (New York: Simon and Schuster, 1970), 84.

40. Interview with Vincent Ford by Michael Beschloss, May 1985, quoted in Michael Beschloss, *MayDay: Eisenhower, Khrushchev and the U-2 Affair*, (New York: Harper & Row, 1986), 73-74.

41. Ibid.

42. Meeting of the Cambridge-New York Group of the Science Advisory Committee, 3/10/54, MIT, AC 4, Box 195, "Science Advisory Committee, 1954."

43. Ibid.

44. Telegram DuBridge to Killian, 2/11/54, MIT, AC 4 Box 195, "Science Advisory Committee, 1954;" Letter E.R. Piore to DuBridge, 3/1/54, MIT, AC 4 Box 195, "Science Advisory Committee, 1954."

45. Telegram DuBridge to Killian, 2/11/54, MIT, AC 4 Box 195, "Science Advisory Committee, 1954."

46. Meeting of the Cambridge-New York Group of the Science Advisory Committee, 3/10/54, MIT, AC 4, Box 195, "Science Advisory Committee, 1954."

47. Ibid.; Letter David Beckler to Killian, 3/19/54, MIT, AC 4, Box 195, "Science Advisory Committee, 1954."

48. Ibid.

49. Log 3/18/54 and 3/26/54, EL, CD Jackson Papers, Box 68, "Log- 1954 (2);" Letter Beckler to Jackson, 3/18/54, EL, CD Jackson Papers, Box 95, "Speeches, Comments, Misc., 1954."

50. Letter DuBridge to Flemming, 5/24/54, EL, WH Central Files, Confidential File, Subject Series, Box 104, "World War III (1)," 1.

51. James Killian, Jr., Oral History, Columbia University Oral History Project, 1969-1970, 19.

52. Letter DuBridge to Flemming, 5/24/54, EL, WH Central Files, Confidential File, Box 104, "World War III (1)."

53. Ibid.

54. Ibid.

55. Ibid.

56. Ibid.

57. Memorandum for Eisenhower from Flemming, 7/9/54, MIT Collection, AC4, Box 195, "SAC, TCP 1954-March 1955;" The President's Appointments, 6/21/54, EL, The President's Appointments 1954 (January-June)."

58. Killian, Oral History, 240.

59. Memorandum for Eisenhower by Flemming, 7/9/54 and Memorandum for Adams by Flemming, 7/21/54, both in EL, WH Central Files, Confidential File, Box 104, "World War III (1)."

60. The two day meeting was held on July 19 and 20. Letter DuBridge to Flemming, 7/21/54, MIT Collection, AC4, Box 195, "SAC, TCP 1954-March 1955."

61. Memorandum for Eisenhower from Flemming, 7/9/54, MIT Collection, AC4, Box 195, "SAC, TCP 1954-March 1955."

62. Memorandum for Flemming by Carroll, 7/26/54, EL, WH Central Files, Confidential File, Box 104, "World War III (1)."

63. Letter Eisenhower to Killian, EL, WH Central Files, Confidential File, Box 104, "World War III (1)."

64. Letter DuBridge to Flemming, 7/21/54, MIT Collection, AC4, Box 195, "SAC, TCP 1954-March 1955."

65. James Killian, *The Education of a College President,* (Cambridge: MIT Press, 1985), 26.

66. Killian said the SAC-ODM had little to do and "was called on hardly at all by President Truman." Killian, *The Education of a College President,* 325.

67. James Killian, "The University's Responsibility to Science," *Chemical and Engineering News,* (American Chemical Society) vol.29, May 21, 1951, MIT Collection 423 (Papers of James Killian, Jr.), Box 39, file folder 21-1, 2033.

68. "Dept. of State Memo of Conversation, October 10, 1957" (Reyerson, Trytten, Herter), NA, RG59, Series 911.80-911.82, Box 5204.

69. Constitution of the United Nations Educational, Scientific and Cultural Organization, November 16, 1945 as found at the Avalon Project at the Yale Law School, wysiwyg://10/http://yale.edu/lawweb/avalon/decade.

70. Killian, "The University's Responsibility to Science," 2033.

71. James Killian, "Ivory Towers and Bullets," Speech to Rochester City Club, January 13,1951. MIT Collection 423, Box 39, file folder 21-1, 29-30.

72. Ibid., 31.

73. Ibid., 42.

74. Killian, *The Education of a College President*, 71-76; 199; 220-230.

75. Killian, "Ivory Towers and Bullets," Speech to Rochester City Club, January 13,1951. MIT Collection 423, Box 39, "21-1," 43.

76. Killian, *The Education of a College President*, 71-72.

77. Ibid., 72 and Thomas Hughes, *Rescuing Prometheus: The Story of the Mammoth Projects*, (New York: Pantheon Books, 1998), 29.

78. James Killian, "Dedication of IBM's Kingston, NY Building," November 2, 1956. MIT Collection 423, Box 40, "22-1," 2.

79. Killian, *The Education of a College President*, 74-75.

80. Killian, "Ivory Towers and Bullets," 38-39.

81. Memorandum to Dulles from Eisenhower, 9/8/53, EL, AWF, DDE Diary, Box 3, "August-September 1953 (2)."

82. Vonda Bergman, "Vermonter in Washington," *Burlington Free Press*, January 11, 1958. MIT Collection 423, Box 11, "Women's National Press Club," 1.

83. Letter Killian to Eisenhower, 8/9/54, EL, WH Central Files, Confidential Files, Box 104, "World War III (1)." Eisenhower had said to Killian that he was "keenly interested" in the project.

84. Letter Killian to Cutler, 8/19/54, MIT Collection, AC4, Box 195, "SAC, TCP 1954-March 1955."

85. Ibid.

86. Letter Cutler to Killian, 8/30/54, MIT Collection, AC4, Box 195, "SAC, TCP 1954-March 1955."

87. Letter Sprague to Killian, 9/1/54, MIT Collection, AC4, Box 195, "SAC, TCP 1954-March 1955."

88. Report by the Technological Capabilities Panel, "Meeting the Threat of Surprise Attack," 2/14/55, NA, RG 59, Sub Files of the Special Assistant for Atomic Energy and Aerospace, 1950-66, Box 1, "Killian Report," 185-186. (Hereafter TCP Report.)

89. Killian, Oral History (interview with Beckler), 263.

90. Killian, Oral History, 240.

91. Killian, Oral History, 98.

92. When Killian and Sprague wished to know how a particular weapons system would work in the event of a sneak attack, Eisenhower agreed to their request for an oral briefing and further suggested that the men be taken to a location to be shown just exactly how the system worked. See Conference in the President's Office, 12/22/54, EL, WHO, OSANSA, NSC Series, Briefing Notes Sub series, Box 17, "TCP of the Science Advisory Committee, 1954-56 (3)."

93. Killian, Oral History, 15; 240; In the final TCP report, the Panel "gratefully" thanked the military advisors who "rendered an invaluable service in arranging for briefings and inspections, in making available classified material, and generally in paving the way for a close working relationship between the Armed Services and the Technological Capabilities Panel." See TCP Report, 186.

94. Killian, Oral History, 19.

95. Ibid., 236.

96. Letter Sprague to Eisenhower, 5/19/55, EL, WH Central File, Confidential File, Box 104, "World War III (1)."

97. Killian, Oral History, 16; TCP Report, v.

98. Specifically, the numbers of briefings, field trips and meetings each panel participated in is as follows: Panel 1: 86; Panel 2: 50; Panel 3: 39. See TCP Report, 186.

99. Killian, Oral History, 98; Memorandum of Discussion at the 241st Meeting of the NSC, 3/17/55, *FRUS*, 1955-57, 19:63.

100. Cutler, *No Time For Rest*, 350.

101. Memorandum for Dr. Flemming from Cutler, 02/23/55, EL, WHO OSANSA, NSC Series, Briefing Notes Sub series, Box 17, "TCP of the Science Advisory Committee, 1954-56 (3)."

102. TCP Report, 10. It was estimated that the only Soviet long-range bomber, the TU-4 (the equivalent of the American B-29A), could only make a two-way mission from the Chukotski Peninsula in northern Siberia, threatening only an arc passing through San Diego and Lake Superior, leaving southern, eastern and central areas untouched. However, one-way missions could target most of industrial America and it was believed that the Soviets would embark on one-way missions if need be. See Decision on JCS 1924/76, "Magnitude and Imminence of Soviet Air Threat to the United States- 1957," 10/30/53, NA, RG 218, Box 65, "CCS 350.09 USSR (12-19-49) sec. 5."

103. TCP Report, 10. The report defined "decisive" as: (1) ability to strike back essentially eliminated; or (2) civil, political, or cultural life reduced to a condition of chaos; or both (1) and (2).

104. TCP Report, 11.

105. TCP Report, 12.

106. TCP Report, 12-13.

107. Study on Surprise Attack, 8/25/54, NA, RG 59, Box 87, "National Security."

108. Killian, Oral History, 17. Other prominent members of the Ballistic Missile Committee included George Kistiakovsky of Harvard, Jerome Wiesner of MIT, and Clark Millikan of Cal Tech.

109. Newhouse, *War and Peace in the Nuclear Age*, 112; York, *Race to Oblivion*, 85.

110. See chapter 3. The breakthrough that allowed ICBMs was that the nuclear warheads could be made smaller and lighter which meant that the missiles themselves could be smaller and lighter. The Soviets, conversely, did not have that technology and built big, cumbersome missiles substantial enough to launch heavier warheads. See Killian, Oral History, 17.

111. TCP Report, 38.

112. Killian Oral History, 28; 234; Killian, *Sputnik, Scientists, and Eisenhower*, 77.

113. The State Department and Defense Department concurred with the recommendations to make the ICBM program a high priority and the State Department commented that a Soviet success with ICBM technology before the U.S. would challenge the assumption of American technological superiority and embolden the Soviets. See Comments on the Report to the President by the TCP, 6/8/55, EL, WHO OSANSA, NSC Series, Policy Papers Sub Series, Box 16, "NSC 5522- TCP (1)."

114. Eisenhower approved NSC Action No. 1433-a, which gave ICBMs the highest priority, on September 13, 1955. Two months later he accorded the IRBMs the same priority. See Memorandum for the NSC, 9/16/55, EL, WHO NSC Staff, Disaster File, Box 42, "Science and Technology- Technological Capabilities (2)."

115. Cutler, *No Time For Rest*, 349.

116. TCP Report, 43.

117. Study on Surprise Attack, 8/25/54, NA, RG 59, Box 87, "National Security."

118. TCP Report, 38-39.

119. Ibid., 40.

120. Killian, Oral History, 18.

121. TCP Report, 37; Memorandum of Discussion at the 270th Meeting of the NSC, 12/8/55, *FRUS*, 1955-57, 19:171.

122. Ibid., 171-172.

123. In other words, as seen with his discussion with General Bull in Chapter 3, just because the Soviet Union had the technical ability to build a long-range bomber, that did not mean they had the actual capability of finding a qualified pilot to navigate. In this case, Eisenhower is thinking beyond the technical capabilities of the Soviet Union and considering whether or not they have the money, the manpower, or the materials to compete.

124. Comments on the Report to the President by the TCP, 6/8/55, EL, WHO OSANSA, NSC Series, Policy Papers Sub Series, Box 16, "NSC 5522- TCP (1)," A-19.

125. TCP Report, 39.

126. Ibid., 41-42.

127. TCP Report, 43. For more on the Air Force Scientific Advisory Board, see Thomas Sturm, *The USAF Scientific Advisory Board: Its First Twenty Years, 1944-1964*, (Washington, DC: GPO, 1967).

128. Comments on the Report to the President by the TCP, 6/8/55, EL, WHO OSANSA, NSC Series, Policy Papers Sub Series, Box 16, "NSC 5522- TCP (1)," A-34.

129. Each plane cost approximately one million dollars and had a total personnel assigned to the project of 500-600. See Richard Bissell, *Reflections of a Cold Warrior*, (New Haven: Yale University Press, 1996), 112.

130. Ambrose, *Eisenhower*, 377.

131. Report by the Technological Capabilities Panel, "Meeting the Threat of Surprise Attack," 2/14/55, EL, WHO, OSS, Subject Series, Alphabetical Subseries, Box 16, "Killian Report- Technological Capabilities Panel, Feb 55-May 56 (1)," 133. (The Intelligence Section of the TCP report was recently declassified by the Eisenhower Library. Pages 133-152 are from the Eisenhower Library, not the National Archives.)

132. Study on Surprise Attack, 8/25/54, NA, RG 59, Box 87, "National Security."

133. Killian, Oral History, 228.

134. Historian Michael Beschloss explained how the Polaroid camera came to be: "On a wartime trip to the Southwest, Land's three-year-old daughter Jennifer asked him why snapshots could not be produced right away. He went for a stroll and worked out the basic design of an instant camera in his head. In 1948, his first camera went on sale at the Jordan Marsh department store in Boston." Beschloss, *MayDay*, 75.

135. Quoted in Dwayne Day, John Logsdon, Brian Latell, eds., *Eye in the Sky: The Story of the Corona Spy Satellites*, (Washington: Smithsonian Institution Press, 1998), 29-30.

136. Sturm, *The USAF Scientific Advisory Board*, 151.

137. Burrows, *Deep Black*, 70-75.

138. Beschloss, *MayDay*, 75.

139. Ibid., 75.

140. For more on the beginnings of aerial reconnaissance flights over the Soviet Union see Beschloss, *MayDay*, 76-80; Burrows, *Deep Black*, 59-60; John Prados, *The So-*

viet Estimate: U.S. Intelligence Analysis and Soviet Strategic Forces, (Princeton: Princeton University Press, 1986), 29-35.

141. Beschloss, *MayDay*, 78-79.

142. Ibid., 81-83; Killian, *Sputnik, Scientists, and Eisenhower,* 82-83; Richard Bissell Oral History, Princeton, John Foster Dulles Collection, 16.

143. Beschloss, *MayDay*, 365.

144. Killian, *Sputnik, Scientists, and Eisenhower*, 83.

145. Eisenhower, *Waging Peace*, 545.

146. On May 1, 1960, a U-2 flight flown by Gary Powers went down over the Soviet Union. Eisenhower, presuming the pilot and plane had been destroyed, said publicly it was a weather plane that had gotten off course. The Eisenhower Administration was caught in an embarrassing lie when the Soviets produced the American pilot who confessed to espionage. President Eisenhower took full responsibility, but refused to apologize for the flights, citing the Soviets had known of the flights for years but had not protested. For a complete account of the U-2 affair see Michael Beschloss, *MayDay: Eisenhower, Khrushchev, and the U-2 Affair,* (New York: Harper & Row, 1986).

147. Ray Cline, *Secrets, Spies, and Scholars,* (Washington, D.C.: Acropolis Books, 1976), 197 quoted in Killian, *Sputnik, Scientists, and Eisenhower,* 83.

148. TCP Report, 135-136.

149. TCP Report, 135-136. Italics in original.

150. TCP Report, 136.

151. TCP Report, 136.

152. TCP Report, 137.

153. The Soviet Union's image of having greater nuclear power than it really did was vital to its strategy. Scholars Arnold Horelick and Myron Rush contended that "the attempt to deceive the West regarding Soviet missile capabilities had a central place in Soviet policy." They believed that despite the technological know-how of the Soviets to decrease the margin of U.S. superiority, the Soviets chose to let the U.S. speed ahead while they deceived the West as to their pace and scope with regards to the ICBM program. Khrushchev took this route because he was certain the United States would not initiate war, but the result left the Soviet Union lagging far behind the United States by the time of Khrushchev's removal in 1964. See Horelick and Rush , *Strategic Power and Soviet Foreign Policy,* 53-55, 105-106; and Holloway, *Arms Race,* 43.

154. TCP Report, 140.

155. TCP Report, 140-141.

156. TCP Report, 142. Italics in original.

157. TCP Report, 142.

158. TCP Report, 146-148.

159. TCP Report, 148.

160. TCP Report, 145.

161. Killian, Oral History, 229.

162. Letter Eisenhower to Killian, 4/5/55, EL, WH Central Files, Confidential File, Box 104, "World War III (1)."

163. Letters from Eisenhower to Fisk, Doolittle, Holloway, DuBridge, Sprague, Land, Baxter, and Haworth, 4/4/55, EL, WH Central Files, Confidential File, Box 104, "World War III (1)."

164. Killian, Oral History, 20; 35.

165. Memorandum of Discussion at the 241st Meeting of the NSC, 3/17/55, *FRUS*, 1955-57, 19:64.

166. Killian, Oral History, 36; 222.

167. Press release recorded in Killian, Oral History, 219.

168. Killian, Oral History, 220; 223.

169. Paul Boyer, *By the Bomb's Early Light: American Thought and Culture at the Dawn of the Atomic Age*, (Chapel Hill: University of North Carolina Press, 1994), 47, 59-60.

170. See Boyer, *By the Bomb's Early Light*; Jessica Wang, *American Science in an Age of Anxiety: Scientists, Anticommunism, and the Cold War*, (Cambridge: MIT Press, 1999).

171. Killian, Oral History, 98.

172. Letter DuBridge to Flemming, 5/24/54, EL, WH Central Files, Confidential File, Box 104, "World War III (1)."

173. Damms, "Eisenhower's 'Scientific-Technological Elite,'" 60.

174. Eisenhower, "Statement by the President Upon Signing Executive Order Strengthening the Scientific Programs of the Federal Government," 3/17/54, *Public Papers of the President*, 1954, 336.

175. Sherman Adams, Oral History, Columbia University Project, 201; Eisenhower, "Letter to the Secretary of Defense on National Security Requirements," 1/5/55, *Public Papers of the President*, 1955, 2.

176. Killian to Bush, 3/22/55, Library of Congress, Bush Papers, General Correspondence, Box 62, "Killian, J.R., Jr.," quoted in Damms, "Eisenhower's 'Scientific-Technological Elite,'" 73.

177. Letter Killian to DuBridge, 5/29/56, MIT, AC 4, Box 195, "SAC, 1956."

178. Memorandum Killian to Andrew Goodpaster, 07/15/59, EL, WHO OSS, Subject Series, Alphabetical Subseries, Box 16, "Dr. Kitiakowsky (1)."

179. Ibid.; Killian, Oral History, 20.

180. Letter W.O. Baker to Eisenhower, 05/10/57, EL, WHO OSS, Subject Series, Alphabetical Sub Series, Box 23, "Science Advisory Committee (1)."

181. Killian, Oral History, 20.

182. Ibid., 28.

PART THREE

Portraying a United States in the Gravest Danger in its History: The Gaither Report (1957)

CHAPTER FIVE

You Want How Much for Bomb Shelters? Civil Defense and the Fear of Fallout

The advent of the hydrogen bomb brought not only the concerns over surprise attack and continental defense discussed earlier, but it also brought concerns about civil defense and the consequences of radioactive fallout. As the decade progressed, the Eisenhower administration faced mounting pressure from Democrats, cultural critics, and the public to change national defense strategy to better protect the population from nuclear attack. The New Look and the doctrine of Massive Retaliation, seen by many as fiscally irresponsible and potentially fatal, encouraged critics to charge the administration with taking a spotty approach to the problem of civil defense. In light of increasing pressures and a Federal Civil Defense Administration (FCDA) report that recommended the Federal Government spend $32 billion on a national shelter program, Eisenhower was put into a difficult position by 1957.

The President wished to evaluate the relative merits of passive and active defenses. Passive defense measures like shelters, evacuation plans, and other civil defense programs would, in Eisenhower's opinion, take valuable monies away from active defense measures like Strategic Air Command, an early warning line, an offensive nuclear stockpile, and second-strike capabilities. Eisenhower favored active defense over passive defense because, as he saw it, there was little hope in surviving an all-out nuclear war, so passive defenses could never be adequate. The real promise for preventing nuclear war lay with active defenses. Passive defenses simply did not uphold the Great Equation.

Although logical, that kind of rhetoric was not politically wise. Telling the American public hope was futile in a nuclear war was not going to raise the morale and spiritual side of the Great Equation. People were afraid and they looked to Washington for answers. If the FCDA recommended a nationally sponsored fallout shelter program, the general public felt that the program should be implemented. Likewise, the public was becoming more educated about fallout and began pushing the government for guidance. So, whereas internal forces brought about the Solarium Project and the Killian Committee, the public discourse on civil defense and outside political pressures convinced Eisenhower to have the Science Advisory Committee create another ad hoc committee of civilians to evaluate whether Federal money should be spent on a national shelter program or whether that money would be better spent on active defenses. The resulting committee was a disappointment to Eisenhower.

Critics of the New Look

Eisenhower had to deal with criticism of his New Look from both outside and within his administration. Each of the Joint Chiefs continually fought against the defense budgets laid out by the New Look, arguing that while the budgets for the other services were adequate, the budget for his own service was completely inadequate. At one point Eisenhower sent for Wilson and the Joint Chiefs and explained his defense budget acknowledging that each member would undoubtedly find some shortcoming. He told them to understand that he had to look at the total picture, including the economy, and that the Chiefs needed "to get on the team."[1] But they continued to supply Eisenhower's critics, particularly the Democrats in Congress, with statistics proving a need for more money towards conventional forces. The Democrats did not need much persuading, as they concentrated their criticism on the "Neanderthal fiscal views" of Eisenhower and Treasury Secretary George Humphrey, which allegedly endangered the security of the country.[2] In addition to the fiscal concerns of the Democrats, many in the party were critical of the Massive Retaliation policy outlined by John Foster Dulles in 1954.

With exceptions for Strategic Air Command and nuclear weapons, the New Look emphasized slashing defense costs. As part of this strategy to cut costs, Dulles explained in January 1954 that the Administration sought "a maximum deterrent at a bearable cost."[3] No longer was the United States going to allow the Kremlin to prescribe battle conditions that suited it. Rather, Dulles made it clear that American policy was to "respond vigorously at places and with means of its own choosing."[4] That meant a massive retaliation against the Soviet Union using nuclear weapons, even if the aggression was through conventional arms and in a location outside of the Soviet Union. Democrats responded to Dulles' speech with alarm. Senator Albert Gore of Tennessee believed that the new doctrine, coupled with the defense budget cuts, made World War III all but inevitable. Dean Acheson questioned the constitutionality of the new doctrine since it was in effect proclaiming the ability to launch an instant attack without a Congressional declaration of war. Charles Bowles argued that Massive Retaliation killed any chance at meaningful arms control, and Paul Nitze complained that Dulles had a "psychopathic urge to have a new policy."[5] Furthermore, critics of massive retaliation argued that once the Soviets had enough hydrogen weapons of their own, the policy ceased to be credible, so other options had to be explored.[6]

Attempting to solidify some kind of unified foreign policy for his party, Acheson wrote in 1955 that Eisenhower's policy of massive retaliation— overemphasizing nuclear weapons—was wrong. What was needed instead was a "military establishment capable of meeting—we would hope jointly with our friends—force which might be employed against our interests, without involving the world in nuclear warfare."[7] In Acheson's mind, Dulles' policy was sure to lead to nuclear annihilation. To prevent that from happening, Acheson argued that a prepared conventional force was needed to fight limited wars.[8]

Limited war was something that Eisenhower rejected, but Democrats like Nitze embraced. NSC 68 had been based on the idea of building up conventional forces to fight globally and, by mid-decade, Nitze even believed a limited nuclear war could be fought and won.[9] Nitze outlined his "nuclear thesis" in six points:

> (1) the time is about here when massive retaliation against the USSR would involve the loss of a huge portion of the American population; (2) in such circumstances, massive retaliation makes sense only as a deterrent against the use of nuclear weapons by the USSR; (3) any other purpose for our nuclear offensive and defensive capabilities is senseless in the absence of an effective shelter program, and our intention to so use them would not be credited by the enemy; (4) therefore, the principal military support of our foreign policy must be the capability for limited military operations; (5) in time, the use of nuclear weapons in limited military operations will face the same sort of stalemate now faced in the general use of nuclear war; (6) this leaves no alternative but to build up conventional military strength.[10]

Nitze minimized the long-term success that Massive Retaliation could have and concluded that future wars with the Soviet Union would undoubtedly be limited conflicts. Not advancing American limited war capabilities seemed irresponsible to Nitze.

The idea of limited war was embraced not only by Democrats, but also by members within the Eisenhower administration. The Joint Chiefs of Staff, for example, had long argued that Eisenhower's New Look prepared the defense establishment to fight only a global nuclear war while leaving it weak to fight small-scale conflicts, which they saw as more likely to occur.[11] Many perceived that the New Look's de-emphasis on conventional arms made American defenses vulnerable. Captain Evan Aurand, Eisenhower's naval aide and Killian Committee participant, argued that "our capability for limited war has been the chief victim of the defense cuts," and that the improper balance between limited war capabilities and all-out nuclear war capabilities had to be rectified.[12] Since an all-out nuclear war was likely to end in annihilation, Aurand concluded that limited wars were "the only type of armed conflict in which net gains to the free world can occur."[13] Also, many members in the State Department believed limited war capabilities needed to be expanded. A paper for Dulles prepared by the Policy Planning Staff responding to Sputnik stated that limited war capabilities had to be developed to a greater capacity.[14] Eisenhower fervently disagreed.

To Eisenhower, adopting a limited war capability and mentality was irresponsible. Historian Campbell Craig explained that Eisenhower was adamant about not engaging in such war because he believed any war eventually led to general war.[15] Eisenhower was keenly aware that many, including even Dulles, believed a limited war could be won. Eisenhower constantly tried to push people away from this position because he believed a limited war—nuclear or conventional—could not be won before it developed into a general war.[16] Eisenhower agreed with Clausewitz, who argued that a power will not surrender until it has used its most powerful weapon; ergo a limited war would escalate into a nuclear war. "Imagine the position of a military commander in the field," Eisenhower said to his NSC. "His radar informs him that a flock of enemy bombers is on the point of attacking him. What does the military commander do in such a contingency? Does he not use every weapon at hand to defend himself and his forces?"[17] Eisenhower could not conceive of any military commander surrendering before using every last weapon available.

Another critic of Eisenhower's New Look whose views were often heard and shared by the Joint Chiefs of Staff was Albert Wohlstetter. Wohlstetter became a prominent member of RAND during the 1950s and believed that the policy of massive retaliation and the apparent complacency within the administration toward the Soviet threat was a sign of "intellectual bankruptcy."[18] At RAND, Wohlstetter demonstrated that American forces were vulnerable. Rather than assume that a Soviet attack would come as a massive air-strike, he visited the Strategic Air Command bases and studied their vulnerability in terms of small, unconventional, discrete attacks made by the Soviets. In other words, he assumed that the Soviets were intelligent enough to take advantage of American weaknesses. His conclusions beyond the vulnerability of Strategic Air Command were that a nuclear stockpile by both sides—mutual deterrence—did not make war impossible or peace stable. The nuclear balance was delicate and, as such, the current administration had to do more than it was doing to assure security.[19]

Eisenhower also faced criticism from what his Assistant to the President, Sherman Adams, called "armchair strategists" who continually harped on Eisenhower in the newspapers that he "did not really know what was going on, especially in Russia."[20] Adams recalled one day when the President was furious because a friend wrote to him in a letter that it seemed the journalists Stewart and Joseph Alsop had made "what seemed to him a sensible estimate of how Russia's military strength surpassed that of the United States."[21] Eisenhower shot back a reply that explained to his friend that a war in the thermonuclear age could no longer be won; consequently, comparative military strength was no longer the only vital issue—economic and spiritual strength were just as important. Furthermore, he reminded his friend that, as President, he had access to information "from experts, technicians, consultants and various other advisers who knew more about Russia and its military strength than the Alsops did."[22] As convincing as Eisenhower's remarks were, such private letters to friends did little to silence what the journalists published for the public to read.

Between the press, Wohlstetter, Aurand, the Joint Chiefs, and even Dulles, it seemed, at times, that the only real support Eisenhower had for the New Look was from himself.[23] To complicate matters further, the major heart attack Eisenhower suffered on September 24, 1955 while in Denver was perceived by many of his critics to have slowed him down. The result was that the Democrats went on the attack during the 1956 election.

The Democrats had nominated Adlai Stevenson again. Acheson was never impressed by Stevenson's "soft style" and had even said Stevenson had a "third-rate mind that he can't make up."[24] Although he personally liked Stevenson and admired his "unparalleled facility with words," Nitze agreed that Stevenson "lacked the toughness to deal" with the Soviets effectively.[25] However, Stevenson was their only chance to regain the White House and control foreign policy once again—something both men wanted dearly. So, they accepted an invitation to join a think-tank established in early 1956 at the suggestion of Charles Bowles to formulate a foreign policy alternative the Democrats might use in the upcoming election. Although the two men wrote the foreign policy section of the platform adopted by the Democrats in August 1956, much of what Acheson had written was edited out not because of its substance, but because of its "venomous" language.[26] Ultimately, it did not matter because Stevenson wanted to rise above the fray on foreign policy, and during the campaign he offered little criticism of Eisenhower on the subject.[27]

Stevenson lost. Within weeks of the election the Democratic Advisory Council—a "kind of cabinet in exile"—was established in an effort to launch what historian Gary Reichard called a "united offensive on foreign policy during Eisenhower's second term."[28] The cabinet was formed by Stevenson supporters hoping to offset the tendency of Democrats to work with Eisenhower in Congress formed it. Stevenson was convinced that the Democratic Congress, led by Lyndon Johnson in the Senate and Sam Rayburn in the House, had gone out of its way to "protect the Eisenhower administration from the consequences of its own folly."[29] The Democratic Advisory Council remained active throughout the rest of the decade, trying to position the Party for certain victory in 1960.[30] Both Acheson and Nitze worked as enthusiastic members of the Council. Acheson was appointed chair of the Council's committee on foreign policy, and Nitze was appointed vice chairman. Nitze biographer David Callahan wrote that "for the remainder of the 1950s, Nitze and Acheson would be co-conspirators in a common cause: to undermine the Eisenhower-Dulles regime and return the Democrats to power."[31] Their golden opportunity came in 1957, when Nitze was able to voice his concerns with current policy and influence the direction of Eisenhower's national security policy as a pseudo-member of the Gaither Committee. As an invited guest, Nitze brought to the table and subsequently to the final report, his and Acheson's viewpoints on limited war and massive retaliation.

This mid-decade criticism of the administration's New Look and Massive Retaliation policy was compounded by additional criticism towards the administration's complacency about civil defense as the fear of fallout continued to increase. Not only did Eisenhower hear criticism from those within government circles, he also heard growing concerns from the general public. The fear of fallout had placed civil defense in the public discourse.

Civil Defense: Forever Taking a Back Seat to Active Defense

Civil defense simply refers to nonmilitary activities designed to protect civilians and their property from enemy actions in time of war. Civil defense measures like blackouts were common during World War II. After the Soviet Union detonated its own atomic weapon, civil defense again took on importance in the United States. Local and state authorities oversaw civil defense measures; the federal government rarely provided anything more than literature and advice. However, with the Bravo tests of the hydrogen bomb in 1954, radioactive fallout became a significant public concern. Consequently, the debate over the federal government's role in civil defense and shelter building grew louder.

Despite the debates throughout the Cold War period, civil defense always took a back seat to the overall national security programs. No coherent national policy on civil defense ever took hold despite increasing fears about nuclear attack and radioactive fallout. Truman and Eisenhower both felt that the costs involved in passive defense measures such as blast or fallout shelters were too high. Even when John F. Kennedy became president and received $207.6 million from Congress to reinforce existing community shelters, he too quickly retreated from his proposal for a five-year shelter program designed to protect the entire population because of the prohibitive costs.[32] He instead continued Truman's and Eisenhower's policy of encouraging individual citizens to take up a shovel and build their own home shelters.

Of course shelters were not the only form of civil defense. During the Truman Administration, one focus of civil defense was on population and building dispersal. City evacuations were also an option, but Truman never seriously considered a national shelter program. Instead, civil defense during the atomic age took a rather playful tone, with school children learning to "duck and cover" from the loveable cartoon character, Bert the Turtle. The message was simple: remember to duck and cover in times of danger and you will not be harmed. An atomic blast was portrayed as a kind of inconvenience that could be dealt with easily. Civil defense posters explained to the public that "an atomic blast is something like a tornado, a fire and an explosion all rolled into one," and to survive such a blast, a family only needed to have a few first-aid items on hand.[33]

Bert the Turtle booklets and civil defense flyers were provided by the FCDA, but the daily operational responsibilities of civil defense were left to the state, as mandated by The Civil Defense Act of 1950. The FCDA was only a source for technical information and policy guidance. By vesting the power to the states, the Federal Government almost ensured that civil defense was little more than a public education program. As the authors of one 1960 report on civil defense observed, the federal monies that had been allocated to the states for civil defense purposes "have been used to purchase fire trucks, emergency water piping, and various items of equipment suitable for combating relatively minor disasters."[34] Acknowledging that nearly $10 million had been invested in studies of the feasibility of evacuation, the authors concluded that the efforts of the federal government represented "a crude and primitive approach to the highly complicated task of protecting the nation from thermonuclear weapons."[35]

The 1950s represented the "bomber age," since the Soviet Union's only means of delivering nuclear weapons was via jet bombers. Therefore, it stood to reason that there was enough response time to an impending attack that cities could be evacuated. As such, during the early Eisenhower years, evacuation became the centerpiece of civil defense. The focus shifted "from 'Duck and Cover' to 'Run Like Hell'" as the *Bulletin of the Atomic Scientists* accurately observed in 1956.[36] One benefit for the country that derived from this shift in focus was the 1956 Federal Interstate Highway Act, which built the road system needed for massive evacuation plans. It was one of the few federal programs Eisenhower supported enthusiastically.[37]

The Eisenhower administration played around with various cost-effective ideas to protect the population, industry, and government during a nuclear exchange. For example, in a June 1953 NSC meeting, Val Peterson, director of the FCDA, suggested a policy to reduce government expenditures on minimizing urban vulnerability. Rather than the government paying for the dispersal of installations, Peterson suggested that the Government insist that companies make arrangements to disperse themselves. If they failed to comply, defense contracts might be withheld. Acting Defense Secretary Roger Kyes immediately protested, saying it was wasteful and impractical for companies to scatter the components of their organization, and withholding defense contracts from those companies who, for one reason or another, could not comply was dangerous.[38] After more discussion, Eisenhower finally spoke, noting that this was a "many-sided problem" which should not be oversimplified. "What we require," Eisenhower said to the men, was to show "that in all facets of our life we are proposing to use the power of the federal Government to get people to do the sensible thing."[39] To have individual citizens and local communities take responsibility was the central theme Eisenhower stressed in regards to civil defense throughout his presidency.

In his January 1955 budget message, Eisenhower said that for civil defense to succeed, the American communities had to be willing to take civil defense planning into their own hands and that "the Federal Government will not assume the responsibilities which belong to local governments and volunteer forces."[40] The Federal Government's responsibility, explained the President, was simply to "provide warning of impending attacks, and to stockpile medical supplies."[41] Again in 1956, Eisenhower stressed that survival in an attack rested mainly with the individual and community, and that the Federal Government had to remain in partnership with states and local authorities in order to obtain more citizen participation and more vigorous efforts by state and local governments. Eisenhower firmly believed that "civil defense can never become an effective instrument for human survival if it becomes entirely dependent upon Federal action."[42]

Although Eisenhower wanted the federal government to provide leadership, assistance, and information, but little funding for civil defense, the issue of radioactive fallout was making evacuation of cities pointless. As one contemporary noted, "some rural people have been pretty smug about civil defense being a city problem, but now the radiation effects may be felt anywhere."[43] This issue of fallout, and subsequently the issue of fallout shelters, brought civil defense into the public debate and many would try to force Eisenhower into the debate.

While the Eisenhower administration was working on its New Look, the American public, cultural critics, and some scientists were growing more concerned over the threat of fallout not only from a nuclear exchange between the two superpowers, but also from atmospheric testing.[44] For example, in 1949 the public became aware of radioactivity from nuclear weapons when David Bradley, a doctor and observer of the Bikini Islands atomic testing, published *No Place to Hide* based on his experiences in the Pacific. In the book, Bradley suggested that there was no defense against the bomb because of radioactivity; there was simply no place to hide. His book remained on the *New York Times* bestseller list for ten weeks and sold over a quarter million copies.[45]

At first the public was enthusiastic about the American advances in weapon technology and approved of the testing. In fact, one test in the Nevada desert was even broadcast live in April 1952.[46] However, the public's confidence slowly eroded as accidents became more frequent and popular culture began to dramatize the dangers of fallout.[47] The first prototype hydrogen bomb was tested on November 1, 1952 at the Eniwetok Atoll, and that explosion left a crater a mile wide and 175 feet deep where the island had been. The first deliverable hydrogen bomb test was equally shocking. The March 1954 "Bravo" test in the Pacific resulted in one of the most widely publicized effects of fallout. Ninety miles away, the crew of a Japanese fishing boat called the *Lucky Dragon* felt the explosion and saw the red fire ball rising from the sky. Unable to outrun the cloud, they were coated by the radioactive fallout. The fishermen became ill by the end of the day and eventually one of the crewmembers died. The crew of the *Lucky Dragon* garnered worldwide attention and the United States apologized to Japan and compensated their fishing industry. But Lewis Strauss of the Atomic Energy Committee forever denied fallout had anything to do with the crew's illness and said the boat was probably a Russian spy boat monitoring the tests.[48]

A few years later, Australian novelist Nevil Shute published *On the Beach,* which was a best seller and two years later was made into a Hollywood movie staring Gregory Peck. *On the Beach* opens after a nuclear war with the entire population of the northern hemisphere dead because of radiation sickness from fallout. The radiation was moving towards the southern hemisphere—towards Australia where the story takes place. Eventually, Australians develop radiation sickness and begin to die. Shute's story ends with a scene in which a banner hanging in an empty town square reads "There's Still Time, Brother." The message was powerful: No one was safe and there were no winners in a nuclear war, but the public could advocate for change. Although many scientists viewed that change in terms of a nuclear test ban, some of the public viewed the change in terms of more federal involvement in a fallout shelter program.[49]

To keep the public calm, Eisenhower's Cabinet met to discuss ways to discredit the movie. They suggested telling the public it was scientifically inaccurate and fell into the genre of science fiction.[50] Throughout the decade, the administration also handed out millions of pamphlets like *Facts About Fallout,* which explained that there was no need to panic. And Eisenhower himself, when the public was still largely unaware of the facts, told Strauss in 1953 to keep the public confused as to fission and fusion.[51] The FCDA also talked nonsense. In a stock speech for general audiences to be used by FCDA officials, the public was told that, "Fallout is a new and dreaded word in our language but we should be grateful for it."[52] Exactly what the public was supposed to be grateful for was unclear.

One politician who must have been grateful to fallout for giving his political career new meaning was the guru of civil defense in the 1950s, congressman Chet Holifield (D-CA). Holifield spent the latter part of the decade pushing for increased federal involvement in civil defense, particularly for fallout shelters. In 1956 the House Military Operations Subcommittee, chaired by Holifield, heard testimonies from doctors, scientists, engineers and public officials as to the dangers of fallout and how to create a new national effort towards civil defense.[53] Included in this list was James Killian, who testified before the committee that research deficiencies in the civil defense program included, among other things, the need to analyze the national policy on shelters.[54] This emphasis on shelters corresponded nicely with Holifield's own opinions.

Holifield was extremely critical of the FCDA under Eisenhower. He was particularly critical of the FCDA's emphasis on evacuation, something Holifield called "dangerously shortsighted."[55] In January 1957, Holifield's committee submitted legislation that would have significantly changed the Civil Defense Act of 1950. Whereas the Civil Defense Act of 1950 placed the burden of civil defense upon the state, Holifield's H.R. 2125 would have made the federal government responsible for civil defense planning through the establishment of a Department of Civil Defense. The Department would orchestrate a meaningful master plan for civil defense as well as the construction of shelters throughout the country. The proposed fallout shelters, intended to save the entire American population, were estimated to cost $20 billion.[56] The legislation failed to get enough support in the House, but Holifield's findings opened the door for further scrutiny and pushed the burden of civil defense further towards Eisenhower.

However, Eisenhower did not waver on his belief that the public had to be willing and eager to learn about civil defense measures they could take on themselves so that they would be less prone to panic in the event of a war. It was not up to the federal government to build fallout shelters for all of its citizens. Talking to the Conference of the National Women's Advisory Committee on Civil Defense in 1954, Eisenhower told the attendees that they had to prepare themselves to be ready to do even just the smallest routine action necessary during a war—first aid, helping the wounded, helping to put out a fire. "There is," he said, "so much that can be done to remove the fear, the danger of panic from our lives."[57] Keeping the public calm was an important part of the Great Equation and he refused to let panic dictate massive spending on defense or a government-by-crisis mentality. However, as the dangers of fallout became more known and political pressures were mounting, Eisenhower did turn to the FCDA to propose a reasonable civil defense plan.

The Federal Civil Defense Administration Recommends Shelters

The FCDA was established in 1950 by Congress to "provide a plan for civil defense for the protection of life and property in the United States from attack."[58] The first administrator of the FCDA was Millard Caldwell, who made a plea in 1951 for improvements in shelters. Focus had been on constructing deep community shelters, but Caldwell pointed out that there were too many logistical problems involved. "In the first place," he commented, "we will probably not be able to give adequate warning to all the people who could get in [deep] shelters. In the second place, it will take too long to construct them. In the third place, they will use too much in the way of labor and critical materials, steel, and concrete."[59] His recommendation was to concentrate efforts on aboveground shelters that were relatively inexpensive. Project East River also reinforced the idea that shelters should be given serious consideration. Even Eisenhower's director of the FCDA, former Nebraska governor Val Peterson, was inclined to agree that shelters made sense.[60] In fact, one of the first reports Peterson saw as director was the 1953 Project East River report.[61] Deeply impressed by the conclusions of the report that civil defense had to be recognized as a "co-partner in the nation's total defense planning," Peterson echoed Eisenhower's belief that to maintain industry and sustain the morale of the people, civil defense had to be a joint effort between the Federal government and local communities. Peterson explained, "Operationally, the problem is almost entirely a local one in character. Logistically, and from the standpoint of leadership, it is a Federal and state problem."[62] Peterson based this belief in part on previous laws like the Civil Defense Act which stated that the "responsibility for civil defense shall be vested primarily in the several States and their political subdivisions."[63] Although all forty-eight states had enacted some kind of civil defense law by 1953, Peterson assessed that while some State directors had made definite progress, others had done very little, instead expecting the Federal Government to do their job.[64]

Before Peterson took over the FCDA in 1953, the agency had placed shelters as its top priority. Shelters made sense in an atomic age. Some Japanese living in caves near Hiroshima had escaped the bomb, which convinced some Americans that shelters were a feasible option.[65] In fact, the FCDA had proposed a shelter program that would cost approximately $1.8 billion. The costs were to be shared equally between the States and Federal government, but Congress never approved the funding. In light of the new technologies, Peterson believed the time had come to reevaluate the requirements for a shelter program. Since the financing would be immense, shelters needed to be considered for the total security needs of the country. Although Peterson understood the arguments behind shelters, when he took office in 1953 he shifted the focus of the FCDA towards evacuation because it seemed to him that the original shelter proposals were inadequate to cope with the forces of the thermonuclear revolution. No shelter designed to withstand a Hiroshima-type blast could withstand the power of a hydrogen bomb. In short, Peterson did not believe a shelter program in 1953 was necessary. Evacuation plans replaced shelter plans. New technologies were promising an early warning system that would allow enough time to evacuate an area, and Peterson urged the military to build an early warning system as a top priority. Give the country an early warning system, he said, and "there may be no need for an expensive shelter program."[66] In fact, he surmised that an early warning system would be less expensive than initiating a national shelter program. However, as the decade progressed and the dangers from radioactive fallout became a public concern, Peterson revisited the topic of shelters.

Writing to Peterson in 1956, Eisenhower said that "an effective civil defense is an important deterrent against attack on our country and thus helps preserve peace," but "the destructive capabilities of potential enemies have been outpacing our non-military defensive measures since the Federal Civil Defense Act was passed six years ago." Therefore, "our whole civil defense effort needs both strengthening and modernizing."[67] Eisenhower was asking Peterson to re-examine civil defense. However, assuring national survival after a nuclear attack was a daunting task.

Peterson had recognized by 1955 that his earlier dismissal of the need for shelters was now compromised by two factors. First, the greatly increased radiation hazard from fallout from the new, higher-yield nuclear weapons had emphasized the need for fallout shelters.[68] Second, the military had not yet provided the accurate, reliable early warning system that the FCDA needed for evacuation. Hence, shelter construction had been encouraged by the FCDA as early as February 1955. In the NSC report, "Status of United States Programs for National Security as of December 31, 1954," the FCDA said that shelters were necessary if evacuation of a city was unfeasible; the Administration recommended the construction of shelters by states and also supplied homeowners with manual and pamphlets containing instructions on how to build home shelters.[69] The need for shelters was recognized, but the organizing and building of shelters was left to the states and individual citizens. The FCDA continued to issue such recommendations until 1957, when it finally recommended that the Federal Government take on a larger role.

To protect the entire population from radioactive fallout the FCDA recommended in January 1957 that the government allocate $32 billion for the construction of fallout and blast shelters.[70] This was a shift in FCDA policy in that it asked the Federal Government to assume most of the financial burden of a national shelter program. Receiving this kind of proposal from the typically conservative Peterson took Eisenhower by surprise. Comfortable with the advisory role the Federal Government had played in the area of civil defense, Eisenhower was not eager to begin allocating large funds for shelters.

The January report was based on the assumptions that the Soviet Union had the ability to launch a nuclear attack on the United States using bombers and submarines and that a "substantial number of high-yield nuclear weapons would be successfully detonated over targets" in the United States.[71] In addition, it was assumed that within ten years the Soviet Union would have ICBM capabilities. Despite current defenses such as Strategic Air Command and diplomatic policies designed to prevent a nuclear war, a desperate enemy could still attack. Furthermore, the most recent estimates from the Net Evaluation Subcommittee predicted that an attack on the United States within the next few years "might be of such magnitude as to raise real questions of our survival as a nation."[72] Fallout, in particular, concerned the FCDA.

With a bomber attack and longer warning times, evacuation of cities was an option. But as warning times shrank to just minutes with ICBMs, evacuation would no longer be an option. Even if a city's population could be moved, the people were not safe from the radioactive fallout. Therefore, a nationwide shelter program was needed as evacuation became more meaningless and predicts of where radioactive fallout would drop were impossible. The Net Evaluation Subcommittee estimated that 80% of the casualties in a mock attack came from fallout compared to only 20% casualties from blast and heat. Therefore, shelters might save a substantial percentage of the population. Without the shelters, the Peterson predicted that less than 10% of the population in a blast area would survive under the currently inadequate civil defense program. Shelters increased that survival rate to 60%. Most important, the Peterson estimated that the millions of additional lives saved through a national shelter program "could make the difference between the survival of the nation and its disintegration."[73] In a follow-up report in March, the FCDA reinforced that notion, explaining the "very preservation of the Nation itself *demands* the protection that the [shelter] program will provide."[74]

Advocates for a national shelter program had a sense of urgency so that shelters would be completed before the Soviet Union had operational ICBMs. To complete the shelters within eight years, it was suggested that other national construction projects currently in progress had to be postponed in order to divert all resources to the shelter program. The cost for such a program was going to be high and Peterson admitted as much. During an eight-year construction period, the FCDA estimated the total cost for blast and fallout shelters to be $32.4 billion. However, there were psychological and economic advantages to these shelters if they were constructed to be useful in times of peace. Such suggestions included "underground parking garages, community recreation centers, meeting places, and overflow classrooms for schools."[75] Even new subways and tunnels could be built and used secondarily as shelters.[76] Keeping with a long tradition of downplaying the dangers of nuclear war, the government continued to paint a rosy picture, hiding shelters in the form of a community center or subway. In addition, tax breaks and federal mortgage insurance were suggested as incentives to individual homeowners to build shelters of their own which met FCDA guidelines.[77]

After reviewing the FCDA report and other related reports, the NSC Planning Board reported in late March that it was unable to make a recommendation to the Council and the President that would help them to take action on any shelter program. The Planning Board said it was "deeply troubled by a number of important considerations which apply both to the specific FCDA proposal and to the overall problem of the protection of the civil population."[78] Those considerations included determining the optimum balance between passive and active defense measures, determining how well shelters could really protect, determining the economic impact of a national shelter program on the economy, and determining the political and psychological implications of a shelter program. To find answers to these questions, the Planning Board recommended a series of studies to be undertaken by appropriate government agencies.[79]

The Planning Board's recommendations included four specific studies pertaining to shelters. One study was to be conducted by Defense, FCDA, Office of Defense Mobilization and the Atomic Energy Committee on significantly different shelter programs. Another study was to be carried out by the Council of Economic Advisers on the broad economic effects and consequences of the various shelter programs covered by the aforementioned study. The third study was to be completed by Treasury on the types of Federal financial assistance to private industry and individuals to stimulate the construction of shelters under such alternative shelter programs. The final study was to be of a general and nontechnical nature and to be based in part on the above studies. It was to be established under the Science Advisory Committee of the Office of Defense Mobilization and was to study "the relative value of various active and passive measures to protect the civil population in case of nuclear attack and its aftermath, taking into account probable new weapons systems."[80] The Gaither Committee grew directly out of that fourth study recommended by the Planning Board.

Between January and March, the merit of passive defense measures such as shelters continued to be debated; debated to the point of suggesting at a presidential luncheon that a "high level task force" of "extremely able people [be set up] to develop the facts as to the civil defense measures which [were] both possible and feasible."[81] This suggestion was from Nelson Rockefeller's committee on Government Organization for a Study of Civil Defense Measures. Cutler did not make the recommendation because he felt it duplicated the other civil defense studies suggested by the Planning Board that were already under way by the NSC. The debate continued at an April NSC meeting where the recent FCDA report was discussed. Gordon Gray, Director of the Office for Defense Mobilization, accused the administration, as well as Congress, of taking a "spotty approach" to the problem of shelters and said that his Science Advisory Committee was "very willing" to take on the study assigned to it by the Planning Board. Dulles complained about the cost of any shelter program and dismissed the idea of passive defense measures over active defense measures, which he felt were the best way to spend the country's resources. The Under Secretary of the Treasury and the Acting Secretary of Defense agreed with Dulles, and the President admitted that he too, for the moment, "leaned toward Secretary Dulles' views."[82]

Peterson understood their hesitations. He agreed that any shelter program should proceed slowly and deliberately and admitted that the total expenditures could not be known because of the many different cost components. For example, would food, bedding, water, or medical supplies be included in the costs? He also stressed the FCDA's support for dual-use shelters to offset costs. With that said, however, Peterson told the Council that "while he clearly realized the fiscal implications of a large-scale shelter program, no one could tell him that the

United States could not afford to spend $3.2 billion each year for ten years for a shelter program if securing the shelter program really meant the survival of the United States in the event of a nuclear attack."[83] To that Eisenhower commented that the traditional state of war was coming to an end and was being replaced by a contest between death and survival. Whichever side could dig in and ride out a nuclear war would win. Yet some wondered if survival was worthwhile if the post-war world was destroyed.[84]

After Eisenhower spoke, Admiral Radford added that the British had recently raised the question of passive versus active defenses. The British reasoned that the country could not afford to build both "an elaborate passive defense program" as well as a strong active deterrent program, and the British government came out strongly in support of the active deterrent program.[85] Eisenhower, admitting that the matter of shelters "was a very serious problem," might have been hoping that by giving the go-ahead to the Science Advisory Committee to study the relative merits of passive verses active defenses, the group would reach the same conclusions as the British.[86] This would allow Eisenhower to reject the FCDA's shelter program based on the recommendations of an ad hoc group of civilian consultants free from political and inter-service rivalries. Should the group come back with a different point of view, that shelters were wise and should be pursued, Eisenhower could reject their conclusions as unpersuasive while maintaining that he had had an open mind to the problem as demonstrated by his solicitation of civilian advice. Either way, his decision could be seen as one based on a comprehensive examination of the facts and not one based on what his critics called "Neanderthal fiscal views." Eisenhower went ahead and approved the Science Advisory Committee study.

Organizing the Security Resources Panel
(The Gaither Committee)

Influencing Eisenhower's decision may have been the suggestions he had recently heard from Dr. Isidor Rabi, chairman of the Science Advisory Committee. Eisenhower knew Rabi from Columbia and respected him immensely.[87] The Science Advisory Committee had not met with Eisenhower since March 27, 1954 when the Killian committee was organized. In a letter to the President, Rabi explained that the 1954 meeting was a continued source of inspiration to the Committee and that it was time to "renew" that connection with the President.[88] Eisenhower agreed that a meeting was a good idea because there were "many points of interest to explore."[89] Eisenhower met with the Science Advisory Committee on March 29th. One issue discussed was shelters. Although Eisenhower did not give outright approval to Rabi's suggestion to organize "an intensive study of the shelter program by a small group of experts drawn from the inside and outside of Government," Eisenhower did agree with Rabi that there was a need for a "broadly based study in which personnel protection is examined" in relation to various factors.[90] Those factors included strategic concepts, advances in weapon systems, active defense capabilities, the costs of shelters and the relative values of their protection, and the practicability of protecting densely populated urban areas.[91] The final committee that undertook this broad based-study, the Gaither Committee, did indeed incorporate these factors.

Although the Science Advisory Committee was instrumental in the original formation of the Gaither committee, SAC-ODM played no other role in the study except to select the project director. Killian was given the task of recommending a chair, and he called upon his friends H. Rowan Gaither, Jr. and Robert Sprague to be co-directors. Killian knew Sprague from his work as a consultant for the Killian Committee in 1954/55, and Sprague had certainly established himself as an expert consultant on continental defense throughout the decade. Killian knew Gaither from the Radiation Laboratory at MIT.

Gaither was trained as a lawyer. During WWII, while practicing law in California, he was asked by the Radiation Laboratory to serve as the associate director in charge of administration—a kind of liaison officer between the Lab and the military services. After the war, he returned to law briefly before being asked in 1947 to serve as the chairman of the board for the RAND Corporation after it reorganized into a non-profit organization.[92] With the exception of one year, Gaither served as chairman from 1948 until his death in 1961. He also became chairman of the board of the Ford Foundation in 1953.[93] Despite these high-profile positions of leadership, his reputation as an administrator was mixed. One observer from the scientific community called him an "outstanding executive and organizer," but another observer from the military said, "Mr. Gaither has certainly not had any impressive record as head of the Ford Foundation, nor as head of anything else."[94] Killian was of the mind that Gaither was the right man and, going on the recommendation from Killian, Cutler and Gray endorsed Gaither's appointment.[95]

Gaither established the committee's membership and direction, but he did not serve as the Security Resources Panel's chair for very long, having fallen ill in August. He was replaced by committee member William Foster, who had served in many positions within the Truman administration, including under secretary of commerce and administrator of the Economic Cooperation Administration. Ultimately he was appointed deputy secretary of defense in 1951. From this post, Foster formed opinions as to the weaknesses of Strategic Air Command and overall continental defenses, but, after Eisenhower took office, he resigned and did not maintain strong ties to the new administration. However, as executive vice president of the Olin Mathieson Chemical Corporation, a company with active ties to government defense agencies, Foster remained connected to developing defense needs.[96]

On May 8, 1957 Eisenhower wrote to Gaither asking for his "active participation in helping the Government come to grips with one of the most important
and perplexing problem areas affecting our future national security."[97] Gaither
accepted "with a full sense of the magnitude and urgency of this task."[98] Eisenhower assigned Cutler and Gray to brief Gaither and organize the scope of the
study. The first briefing was on June 27, and Cutler explained how the FCDA
report, the Planning Board's assessments, and Dr. Rabi's suggestions brought
this study group into existence.[99] Cutler made clear that the objective of the
committee was to form a "broad-brush opinion" of passive and active defenses in
their relative value of protecting the civil population. The committee was to also
understand that the threat to the U.S. was "in the years ahead."[100] In short, the
committee was to offer its opinion as to what active and passive defense measures were to be the most effective in relation to their costs and capability of protecting the civil population. The question was: How does a nationally financed
shelter program measure up to the Great Equation?

During the briefing, Cutler also stressed to Gaither what the committee was
not to be. He said that it should be "clearly understood that the Panel's mission
does not extend to a detailed examination of national security policies and programs for the purpose of recommending specific modifications in such policies
or programs. No such study as was made by the Technological Capabilities
Panel is intended or desired."[101] In addition, the Gaither committee was to receive the other studies called for by the Planning Board and receive numerous
briefings from the FCDA, Office of Defense Mobilization, Atomic Energy Committee, CIA, Defense, and the Net Evaluation Subcommittee of the NSC. Cutler
explicitly told Gaither that the purpose of acquiring this information was not for
suggesting detailed changes, revisions, or modifications. The information was
for assessing the relative merits of passive defense measures compared to active
defense measures and whether or not the Government ought to spend money on
shelters.[102]

The Deputy Secretary of Defense, Donald Quarles, had some concerns
about the scope of the Gaither committee's mandate. Quarles worried that it was
going to be another detailed study like the Killian committee, which the Department of Defense would have problems implementing. Cutler assured him that it
was not. The Gaither committee was to study the relative value of various active
and passive defenses designed to protect the civilian population in case of war. It
was not, Cutler said, "intended to recommend detailed corrections, changes or
modifications in what is being done or is planned to be done."[103] The committee
was not to suggest changes. "The last thing the President wants to come out of
this study," Cutler explained, "is a series of detailed recommendations for changing our defense program."[104] Quarles made sure Gaither understood this distinction.

During the June 27th briefing, Quarles told the group that the Gaither Panel would not undertake another Killian committee-type study. Furthermore, he expressed to the group that the committee was to "accept the validity of our military Continental Defense programs without getting into the 'hardware business' and without undertaking to recommend the reorganization of a Continental Defense System which takes 10 years to bring about in the first place."[105] In short, Quarles told the group that its mission was simply to provide the basis for a decision as to whether the Federal Government should provide—and tax the people for—shelter protection for the population in addition to the effective deterrent the government already provided the people. The question was, Quarles said, "whether our main effort should be to deter the attack from occurring in the first place, or whether efforts should also be made to protect the people if the attack should come."[106] Quarles ended by adding that he personally rejected the latter viewpoint because he believed passive defense measures reduced the deterrent effect.

Gaither thanked Cutler for the briefing, saying that the meeting was most helpful in providing a dimension for the study. He was appreciative of the "broad-context" set down, which allowed him "to proceed with the selection of the kind of talent to be recruited and with the organization of the Panel's work."[107] There should have been no doubt in Gaither's mind as to the assignment handed to his committee after that briefing. Cutler, Gray and Quarles all clearly outlined the scope of the study and emphasized that the final report was not to repeat the work of the Killian Committee. The group was being asked a simple question. However, as Gaither proceeded to organize his committee, he sought to expand the committee's assignment and the entire study grew like a cancer.

The thermonuclear revolution brought heightened concerns over radioactive fallout from high-yield weapons. The Federal Government traditionally took a leadership role, offering advice and information, but left the funding for civil defense up to states and local communities. In 1957, the FCDA recommended that the leadership role of the Federal Government expand to finance a national shelter program. Responding to pressures from political opponents, cultural critics, and even from members within his own administration, Eisenhower chose to use an ad hoc group of civilian advisors to divert attention away from him and grapple with a politically impossible question. Strongly opposed to federal funding for civil defense measures that he believed the individual citizen ought to be responsible for, Eisenhower's mind was made up on the issue. However, unable to avoid the issue of shelters, Eisenhower authorized the use of civilian outsiders to debate the merits of passive verses active defenses. With little stake in the outcome, Eisenhower left the running of the committee to his advisors. Expecting a report on whether or not there ought to be a nationally funded shelter program, Eisenhower was shocked when the Gaither committee members took it upon themselves to completely reevaluate Eisenhower's national security policy and report back that it was not only inadequate, but placed the United States in its gravest danger in history.

Notes

1. Ambrose, *Eisenhower: Soldier and President,* (New York: Simon and Schuster, 1990), 376. Ambrose explained that Eisenhower felt he was qualified to make slashes in the Pentagon's budget because as a military man he knew what could be cut without damaging anything. His great fear was that someday there would be a president who was not "raised in the military services," and he said "If that should happen while we still have the state of tension that now exists in the world, I shudder to think of what could happen to this country."

2. Ibid.

3. "Secretary of State John Foster Dulles Explains Massive Retaliation, 1954," in Thomas Paterson ed., *Major Problems in American Foreign Relations*, Vol. II, 4th ed., (Lexington, MA: DC Heath, 1995), 423-45.

4. Ibid.

5. Gary W. Reichard, "Divisions and Dissent: Democrats and Foreign Policy, 1952-1956," *Political Science Quarterly,* 93 (Spring 1978), 56-57.

6. Gregg Herken, *Counsels of War,* (New York: Oxford University Press, 1987),111.

7. Quoted in Reichard, "Divisions and Dissent," *Political Science Quarterly,* 93 (Spring 1978), 64.

8. For an overview of the origins of limited war thinking see Marc Trachtenberg, *History and Strategy*, (Princeton: Princeton University Press, 1991), 4-11.

9. Nitze expounded upon those ideas as a participant in a study group sponsored by the Council on Foreign Relations. See David Callahan, *Dangerous Capabilities, Paul Nitze and the Cold War,* (New York: Edward Burlingame, 1990), 165.

10. The Nitze Nuclear Thesis, 11/18/57, NA, RG 59, Records of the PPS, 1957-61, Box 181, "Draft of Papers/ Speech by PHN."

11. For an excellent account on Eisenhower's constant disagreements with the JCS, see Gerard Clarfield, *Security With Solvency: Dwight D. Eisenhower and the Shaping of the American Military Establishment*, (Westport, CT.: Praeger, 1999), xiii-xv.

12. Memorandum from Evan P. Aurand to Cutler, 08/14/57, EL, Evan Aurand Papers, Box 11, "Special Folder (1)." For a description of Aurand's duties and relationship with Eisenhower, see Dwight Eisenhower, *Mandate for Change,* (New York: Double-Day, 1963), 262-263.

13. Memorandum from Evan P. Aurand to Cutler, 08/14/57, EL, Evan Aurand Papers, Box 11, "Special Folder (1)."

14. Carlton Savage, "Some requirements for National Security," 10/18/57, NA, RG 59, Records of the Policy Planning Staff, 1957-61, Box 128, "National Security," 4.

15. Campbell Craig, *Destroying the Village: Eisenhower and Thermonuclear War,* (New York: Columbia University Press, 1998), 57.

16. Dulles made it clear as early as 1954 that he disagreed with Eisenhower's "all or nothing" approach to nuclear war. See Craig, *Destroying the Village*, 52.

17. Memorandum of February 27, 1956 NSC discussion, *FRUS* 1955-57, 19:204, quoted in Craig, *Destroying the Village*, 57.

18. Gregg Herken, *Counsels of War*, (New York: Oxford University Press, 1987), 111-112; Trachtenberg, *History and Strategy*, 17.

19. Wohlstetter published his views in a widely read article in the January 1959 issue of *Foreign Affairs* called "The Delicate Balance of Terror." See Trachtenberg, *History and Strategy*, 17-21.

20. Sherman Adams, *First Hand Report: The Story of the Eisenhower Administration*, (New York: Harper & Brothers, 1961), 413.

21. Ibid.

22. Ibid.

23. This is true particularly in regard to limited war capabilities. Marc Trachtenberg suggests that as early as the end of 1954, Dulles was retreating from Massive Retaliation and by the end of the decade the outgoing Secretary of Defense, Thomas Gates, felt America had a fine limited war capability. Trachtenberg wrote: "Reading the documents, one sometimes gets the sense that Eisenhower himself was one of the last true believers. To him, even as late as 1960, a major U.S.-Soviet limited war was an absurdity." Trachtenberg, *History and Strategy*, 40-42.

24. Douglas Brinkley, *Dean Acheson: The Cold War Years, 1953-71*, (New Haven: Yale University Press, 1992), 47.

25. Paul Nitze, *From Hiroshima to Glasnost: At the Center of Decision*, (New York: Grove Weidenfeld, 1989), 160-161.

26. Brinkley, *Dean Acheson*, 48.

27. Reichard, "Divisions and Dissent," *Political Science Quarterly*, 93 (Spring 1978), 66-68.

28. Reichard, "Divisions and Dissent," *Political Science Quarterly*, 93 (Spring 1978), 69.

29. Nitze, *From Hiroshima to Glasnost*, 161.

30. During the 1960 election, the Council charged Eisenhower's foreign policy of having collapsed. See Robert Divine, *Foreign Policy and U.S. Presidential Elections: 1952-1960*, (New York: New Viewpoints Press, 1974), 206-207.

31. Callahan, *Dangerous Capabilities*, 155.

32. Winkler, *Life Under a Cloud*, 127; "A Message to You from the President," *Life*, 09/15/61.

33. "Mummy, what happens to us if the bomb drops?" Civil defense poster in author's possession from the Eisenhower Library.

34. John Fowler, ed., *Fallout: A Study of Superbombs, Strontium 90, and Survival*, (New York: Basic Books, 1960), 125.

35. Ibid.

36. Mary Simpson, "A Long Hard Look at Civil Defense," *Bulletin of the Atomic Scientists*, 12 (Nov. 1956), 346, quoted in Winkler, *Life Under a Cloud*, 117.

37. The Federal National Highway Act was passed in 1956 and it was a program Eisenhower had been interested in since taking a cross-country trip by Army convoy in 1919. Impressed by the German *Autobahnen*, Eisenhower felt a highway system "was an

ideal program for the federal government to undertake." For more see Ambrose, *Eisenhower: Soldier and President*, 387.

38. Memorandum of Discussion at the 149th Meeting of the NSC, 6/11/53, EL, AWF, NSC Series, Box 4, "149th Meeting of the NSC, 6/9/53."

39. Ibid. In a conversation with Cutler about whether or not Eisenhower should give a speech to the American people encouraging them to take up civil defense, Eisenhower was not responsive to the idea and told Cutler "it was curious that everybody thinks the Federal Government ought to spend the money to save them from being killed. When the ordinary American citizen is in danger of being killed, he should do something about it himself . . . it was funny that everyone wanted *him* to tell them why *they* should get busy to save themselves." Italics in original. See Letter Cutler to Val Peterson, 05/06/54, EL, WHO OSANSA, NSC Series, Briefing Notes Subseries, Box 4, "[Civil Defense](3)[1953-57]."

40. Dwight Eisenhower, "Annual Budget Message to Congress: Fiscal Year 1955," 01/21/54, *Public Papers of the President*, 1954, 120-121.

41. Ibid.

42. Letter from Eisenhower to Val Peterson, 07/17/56, Attachment B of the Civil Defense Legislative Program for FY 1958, NA, RG 273, Box 44, "NSC 5709- Background Documents," 28.

43. Peterson at the Conference of Mayors, Washington DC, 12/2/54, quoted in Quotable Quotes from the FCDA Administrator Prepared by the FCDA, 04/01/55, EL, Virgil Couch Papers, Box 2, "Civil Defense Facts, Speaker Kits, 1955-56 (2)."

44. Winkler, *Life Under a Cloud*, 84-85.

45. David Bradley, *No Place To Hide*, (Boston: Little Brown, 1948); Winkler, *Life Under a Cloud*, 91.

46. Winkler, *Life Under a Cloud*, 91. Between 1951-1963, the United States conducted approximately 100 above ground tests in Nevada.

47. In May 1953, one test blanketed a small town in Utah with excessive amounts of radiation. Several residents became ill and 42 sheep died. The ranchers said fallout was the cause of their deaths, but the government won the suit on the grounds the ranchers had not provided scientific testimony to support their claim. Twenty five years later a new trial was ordered by a federal judge who said the government had deliberately withheld vital information and distorted the facts. See Winkler, *Life Under a Cloud*, 93.

48. Winkler, *Life Under a Cloud*, 94.

49. Nevil Shute, *On the Beach*, (New York: Morrow, 1957).

50. Cabinet Paper, "On the Beach," 12/7/59, EL

51. Winkler, *Life Under a Cloud,* 105.

52. Speech for General Audiences: Evacuation and Fallout, n.d., EL, Virgil Couch Papers, Box 2, "Civil Defense Facts, Speaker Kits, 1955-56 (2)."

53. House Military Operations Subcommittee of the Committee on Government Operations, *Civil Defense for National Survival, Hearings before a Subcommittee of the Committee on Government Operations,* 84th Congress, 2nd session, 1956, found in Allan Winkler, *Life Under a Cloud: American Anxiety About the Atom*, (Chicago: University of Illinois Press, 1999), 118.

54. Letter, Killian to David Beckler, 02/01/56, and Letter, Beckler to Killian, 02/02/56, MIT, AC4, Box 195, "SAC, 1956."

55. Quote found in Snead, *The Gaither Committee*, 45.

56. Ibid.

57. Eisenhower, Message to the Conference of the National Women's Advisory Committee on Civil Defense, Washington DC, 10/26/54, Quotable Quotes from President Eisenhower Prepared by the FCDA, 04/01/55, EL, Virgil Couch Papers, Box 2, "Civil Defense Facts, Speaker Kits, 1955-56 (2)."

58. Civil Defense Legislative Program for FY 1958 Submitted to NSC, 01/03/57, NA, RG 273, Box 44, "NSC- 5709- Background Documents," 2.

59. Quoted in Fowler, *Fallout*, 126.

60. Eisenhower had great respect for Peterson. He had originally tried to appoint Peterson in 1953 as ambassador to India. He found out in preliminary meetings that if he did nominate Peterson, the two Nebraska senators would state the nomination "personally objectionable," not because of Peterson's character, but because of his political standing. Eisenhower was outraged and found Peterson a position that did not need Senate confirmation. When Peterson's political enemies were gone, Eisenhower appointed him ambassador of Denmark in 1957. See Eisenhower, *Mandate for Change*, 119.

61. See chapter 3 for more on Project East River.

62. Statement of the Honorable Val Peterson, Administrator, FCDA, Before the NSC, 3/31/53, NA, RG 59, OCB/NSC 1947-63, Box 125, "The Federal Civil Defense Program," 2.

63. Public Law 920, enacted by the 81st Congress, January 12, 1951. Quoted in ibid., 3-4.

64. Ibid.

65. "Shelters" Speech, n.d., EL, Virgil Couch Papers, Box 9, "Fallout Shelters, c. 1957," 3.

66. Ibid., 7-10. For Peterson on early warning systems, see Chapter 3.

67. Ibid., 2; Letter from Eisenhower to Governor Val Peterson, 07/17/56, ibid., Attachment B, 26-28.

68. In the early years of the hydrogen bomb, the AEC continually told the public, and government officials, that there was nothing to fear from radioactive fallout. The AEC's reassurances did not hold up as more and more scientists came out about the hazards and the bombs became bigger.

69. NSC 5509, Part Five- The Civil Defense Program, 02/01/55, NA, RG 273, Box 36, "NSC 5509 (Parts 3-8)," 9.

70. Report to the NSC by the FCDA, Civil Defense Legislative Program, 1/3/57, NA, RG 273, Box 44, "NSC 5709- Background Documents," 3-4.

71. A Federal Shelter Program for Civil Defense, NSC 5709, 03/29/57, NA, RG 273, Box 44, "NSC- 5709," Annex A, 1-2.

72. Ibid.

73. Ibid., A-3.

74. Ibid., A-5, italics added.

75. Ibid., A-3-4.

76. Ibid., A-5.

77. Ibid., A-3, A-12. The report estimated that these two incentives might eventually increase the number of home shelters in existing dwellings to approximately 20%, plus an increase of 25% in new home construction by 1961. That would result in an estimated

44.5 million individuals being protected by home shelters. These measures would not be the first time the government provided incentives to individuals taking up the task of civil defense. For example, civil defense volunteer workers were also allowed by the IRS to deduct from their income taxes unreimbursed expenses incurred from their work. See Income Tax Ruling on Expenses of CD Volunteers, 11/2/55, EL, Virgil Couch Papers, Box 11, "Speeches by Virgil Couch 1955-57 (1)."

78. A Federal Shelter Program for Civil Defense, NSC 5709, 03/29/57, NA, RG 273, Box 44, "NSC- 5709," 2.

79. Ibid., 2-5.

80. Ibid., 2-5; Informal Memorandum for Use at Meeting with Mr. Gaither, 06/27/57, EL, WHO SANSA, NSC Series Briefing Notes, Box 8, "[Fallout Shelters](3) 1957-60."

81. Memoranda Rockefeller to Adams and Brundage, 4/12/57, EL, WHO OSANSA, NSC series briefing notes, Box 4, "[Civil Defense] (1) 1953-57," 1; Memorandum for the Assistant to the President from Cutler, 04/24/57, EL, WH Central Files, Confidential File, Box 17, "Civil Defense (6)."

82. Memoranda of Discussion at the 318th meeting of the NSC, 4/4/57, *FRUS*, 1955-57, 19:459-464.

83. Ibid., 461.

84. Ibid., 462-63.

85. Ibid., 463.

86. Ibid., 462.

87. Killian, Oral History, 20; 34-35. Killian wrote that Rabi was able to make suggestions and proposals to Eisenhower "that were very influential in the ultimate advisory arrangement Eisenhower created." Ibid., 35.

88. Letter Dr. I. I. Rabi to Eisenhower, 3/23/57, EL, WH Central Files, Confidential File, Box 23, "Defense Mobilization, Office of (4)."

89. Letter Eisenhower to Rabi, 3/27/57, EL, WH Central Files, Confidential File, Box 23, "Defense Mobilization, Office of (4)."

90. Informal Memorandum for Use at Meeting with Mr. Gaither, June 27, 1957, 06/25/57, EL, WHO SANSA, NC Series, Briefing Notes Subseries, Box 8, "[Fallout Shelters](3) 1957-60."

91. Ibid.

92. RAND was a research and development outfit created during the war as part of Douglas Aircraft for the Army air force. After the war, Douglas and the Air Force agreed to spin it off into a non-profit organization. For a complete history of RAND, See Bruce L. R. Smith, *The RAND Corporation: Case Study of a Nonprofit Advisory Corporation*, (Cambridge: Harvard University Press, 1966).

93. Snead, *Gaither Committee, Eisenhower, and the Cold War*, 49-51.

94. Memorandum to Andrew Goodpaster from David Beckler, 05/08/57, EL, WHO OSS, Subject Series, Alphabetical Subseries, Box 23, "Science Advisory Committee (1);" Letter, General Robert Wood to Eisenhower, 12/30/57, EL, WH Central Files, Official File, Box 676, "OF-133-R" (Gaither Report).

95. Memorandum to Andrew Goodpaster from David Beckler, 05/08/57, EL, WHO OSS, Subject Series, Alphabetical Subseries, Box 23, "Science Advisory Committee (1)."

96. Snead, *The Gaither Committee, Eisenhower, and the Cold War*, 52.

97. Letter Eisenhower to Gaither, 5/8/57, EL, WHO OSS, Subject series, Alphabetical Subseries, Box 23, "Science Advisory Committee (1)."

98. Letter Rowan Gaither to Eisenhower, 05/15/57, EL, WHO OSS, Subject series, Alphabetical Subseries, Box 23, "Science Advisory Committee (1)."

99. Also at the briefing were Deputy Secretary of Defense Donald Quarles; Gordon Gray, W.Y. Elliott, and Dave Beckler of ODM; Jerome Wiesner and Col. Vincent Ford of the Gaither Committee; two members from the NSC staff and an Admiral from the Department of Defense. Memorandum for File: Gaither Panel, 06/28/57, EL, WHO OSANSA, NSC Series, Briefing Notes Subseries, Box 8, "[Fallout Shelters](3) 1957-60."

100. Informal Memorandum for Use at Meeting with Mr. Gaither, June 27, 1957, 06/25/57, EL, WHO, OSANSA, NSC Series Briefing Notes, Box 8, "[Fallout Shelters](3) 1957-60."

101. Ibid.

102. Ibid.

103. Cutler to Donald Quarles, 06/20/57, EL, WHO, OSANSA, NSC Series Briefing Notes, Box 8, "[Fallout Shelters](3) 1957-60."

104. Ibid.

105. Memorandum for File: Gaither Panel, 06/28/57, EL, WHO OSANSA, NSC Series, Briefing Notes Subseries, Box 8, "[Fallout Shelters](3) 1957-60."

106. Ibid.

107. Ibid.

CHAPTER SIX

Questioning the Wisdom of Using Civilian Committees:
The Gaither Committee Goes Too Far

Responding to the public debate on a nationally funded shelter program, Eisenhower authorized the formation of another civilian ad hoc committee. However, the subsequent Gaither Committee was not as successful as the Solarium Exercise or Killian Committee in the eyes of Eisenhower. In fact, the experience Eisenhower had with the Gaither Committee was so poor, Eisenhower confessed that the entire exercise had proved "definitively the unwisdom of calling in outside groups."[1] As Eisenhower saw it, the Gaither Committee's recommendations did not fall within the parameters of the Great Equation. However, the reason for Eisenhower's change of heart for a process that had proved so successful in the past was not simply because of the Great Equation. Rather, Eisenhower's disappointment came from the fact that the Gaither Committee had gone beyond its mandate and had become politicized, embarrassing Eisenhower and thus threatening the balance of the Great Equation.

Eisenhower hoped to use the group as a diversion away from the problem of civil defense. Creating the Gaither committee gave the appearance to the public that the administration was seriously looking into the matter. If the Committee reported back that it was more fiscally sound to spend money on active defenses instead of passive defenses, then the president could accept the results with pleasure. If the committee reported back that there was value in spending money on passive defenses, then the president could publicly say he had consulted all sides of the matter and, after careful consideration, decided that the matter needed further investigation, thus postponing having to make a decision on a politically difficult question. This kind of passing the buck was certainly not unique to Eisenhower. What went wrong was that the Gaither Committee did not report back just on passive defense spending and, after Eisenhower disagreed with their conclusions, some committee members leaked parts of the report to the newspapers.

The Gaither committee went too far on a number of levels. First, the Committee itself was too large, having grown to over eighty participants. Unlike the earlier Killian and Solarium committees, these Committee members were not

broken down into smaller, manageable panels. Second, one of the primary authors of the final report was Paul Nitze, a man who did not support Eisenhower's
New Look and was far from being able to operate above the political fray. Third,
the Committee enlarged its original assignment into a study that evaluated the
entire defense program, even after being specifically told that was not what Eisenhower had wanted. Fourth, the Committee presented an alarmist report indicating that the United States was in grave danger. The members wished to
change Eisenhower's security strategy, and proposed substantial modifications
which did not compliment Eisenhower's New Look or Great Equation. Furthermore, even in spite of its enlarged mandate, the report did not look at the problem of defense in its entirety. Rather, as John Foster Dulles noted, it dealt only
with segments of the total problem, which led to complications.[2] Ultimately, the
report failed to shift Eisenhower's strategic thinking.

Finally, the desperate tone and criticisms towards defense programs found in
the final report were leaked to the press, which created a public outcry and led to
members of Congress demanding the report's release. Eisenhower had been
deeply impressed by the fact that both the Solarium and Killian exercises had
operated in complete secrecy. The Gaither Report leaks infuriated the President.
In addition, after the report was presented to Eisenhower and the NSC, many
Committee members actively sought the implementation of their recommendations. As Eisenhower saw it, there was no "passion for anonymity" among the
Gaither Committee members as he had witnessed with the Killian committee.
Certain members were zealous in their effort to see the Gaither Report implemented thoroughly. These members wished to make policy, but Eisenhower did
not call upon civilian ad hoc committees to make policy. He used them to advise
in policy. The result was that Eisenhower never requested the use of a civilian ad
hoc committee to advise in national security policy in the final three years of his
presidency.

Selecting a Committee and Expanding a Mandate

Selecting his committee and organizing its course of work was the next step for
H. Rowan Gaither. He worked with the Office of Defense Mobilization, which
had prepared a list of 100 prospects to draw from, pending security clearances.
Gaither thought he could organize a core group by July 15 and be ready to begin
by the first of August.[3]

To start, Gaither worked with the Office of Defense Mobilization in establishing a steering committee and advisory panel for the committee. Of the nine-
teen members that made up these two principal groups, only four had served on
either the Solarium Exercise or the Killian Committee: Robert Sprague, James
Phinney Baxter, General James Doolittle, and Jerome Wiesner.[4] The two smaller
advisory groups within the Gaither Committee—the subcommittee of the Science

Advisory Committee and the Institute for Defense Analyses—had more experienced members, such as James Killian, James Fisk, and Isidor Rabi, General James McCormack and Albert Hill.[5] Aside from these advisory committees, Gaither recruited another sixty-seven consultants to provide advice and recommendations. Of these, only three had past experience on either the Solarium Exercise or Killian Committee.[6]

The consultants who were recruited were mostly drawn from engineering firms, business institutions, and strategic think tanks like RAND and the Brookings Institute. Although the scientific community was also represented, its presence was small compared to the Killian Committee. Also, the presence of military advisors was comparably smaller than what was found on the Solarium and Killian committees. These deficiencies are an important distinction between the three committees. The presence of military minds on the Solarium task forces enabled Eisenhower to craft a national security policy that reflected military realities in terms of capabilities and practical strategies. The Killian Committee found itself in debt to its military advisors, acknowledging that their service was invaluable.[7] Without the sound advice from the military, the Gaither Committee was left to overestimate Soviet capabilities and underestimate American defenses. Likewise, without sound scientific advice, it was difficult to understand all of the technical nuances concerning nuclear attack and shelter construction.

Historian David Snead contended that the qualifications of some of the advisory and steering committee members like Killian, Rabi, Baxter, Foster, and Robert Lovett were "ample evidence of the committee's expertise" and high caliber.[8] However, Killian and Rabi played only very minor roles in the Gaither Committee and when Baxter was asked to write the final report, he found the technical aspects too daunting to bring together, despite being a Pulitzer Prize winning scientific historian, and asked another member to write the report.[9] In addition, neither Foster nor Lovett, who served as the deputy secretary and secretary of defense respectively in the last years of the Truman Administration, were strong supporters of Eisenhower, nor had they been asked to participate in an advisory role before.

The Committee was composed of experienced men, but many of those men were what historian Richard Immerman called "alarmist critics" of the Eisenhower administration.[10] And this is where the trouble arose with the Gaither Committee—it was political from the start. Eisenhower had carefully overseen the selection of committee members for the Solarium Exercise and Killian had crafted a small and politically unbiased group. However, the participants of the Gaither Committee were left to Gaither, and they came to the committee with preconceived ideas about the absurdity of massive retaliation, the vulnerabilities of Strategic Air Command, and the belief that the present administration had become complacent about national security. Those members who did not come to the table with these perceptions were quickly convinced otherwise. As a result of the members' concerns, and the very size of the committee, it was "virtually guaranteed," explained historian Gregg Herken, "that they would extend their charter to include a wholesale reassessment of the administration's military policy."[11] One member who embraced this expansion was Paul Nitze.

Nitze had been an outsider. He established himself as a well-known critic of the Eisenhower administration, working diligently with the Democratic Party to defeat Eisenhower in 1956.[12] He also had no love for Dulles. Dulles knew that Nitze had hostile feelings towards him, explaining to a friend that, "Paul Nitze felt a strong personal hostility toward me . . . because I had not kept him on as chief of the Policy Planning Division, and he blamed me . . . for his failure to get a high position in the Department of Defense."[13] So when Gaither committee member Baxter learned of the new direction the committee was to travel, and suggested that his good friend and strategy expert Paul Nitze be asked to join their group, it was not an invitation extended by the White House. It was, however, a golden opportunity for Nitze to try to shape national security policy, and he quickly became a full-time participant.

However, the fact that the Committee was composed of many members with whom Eisenhower disagreed was not necessarily a liability. As stated earlier, if the committee members should recommend that America concentrate only on active defense measures, Eisenhower could accept their report and claim that his critics were part of the decision-making process. Should the group recommend that passive defenses be emphasized, Eisenhower could claim he was open-minded about the problem and had asked diverse civilian outsiders for their advice, but found their conclusions unpersuasive. This was, after all, how Eisenhower liked to use civilian committees. What Eisenhower had not expected was that the group would take on an expanded mandate or that the report would be leaked to the public.

After his June 27th briefing with Cutler, Gray, and Quarles, Gaither asked his friends at RAND how to organize the group. Albert Wohlstetter of RAND argued to Gaither that a broader mandate needed to be pursued so as to not miss the real issue of defending U.S. bomber bases against surprise Soviet attack. U.S. defenses were vulnerable, argued Wohlstetter, because, according to RAND's alarming figures, the risk to the Soviet Union to launch a surprise attack was low and the Soviet Union would have 500 ICBMs deployed by 1960, a number which fatally compromised U.S. security within three years.[14] Convinced that a complete analysis of civil defense could not be achieved without investigating the entire American defense policy, the members of the Committee wanted to enlarge their task. In addition to being persuaded by Wohlstetter, the Committee took inspiration from the President himself.

The Advisory Panel and Steering Committee of the Gaither Panel met with Eisenhower on July 16.[15] At that meeting, Eisenhower reportedly asked the panel, "If you make the assumption that there is going to be a nuclear war, what should I do?"[16] Taking their inspiration from there, Gaither and Foster approached Cutler for permission to expand their inquiry into the overall defense program. In his memoirs Cutler explained the consequences of his approval: "The request seeming reasonable, I gave my assent without foreseeing the result.

The Committee was soon busying itself more about military than Civil defense matters . . . . I had inadvertently 'opened up' the Council procedures and processes in a way not intended."[17] Without Eisenhower's approval, the Gaither Panel began a study of the entire American defense program.

What began as a rather modest study of civil defense soon spread like a cancer. As one member recalled, the project became "a caricature of government sprawl. Some people wanted to go on a wartime footing. They worked themselves into a state of hysteria. It was the establishment gone wild."[18] To complicate matters, Gaither did not divide the multitude of consultants into manageable panels assigned to examine one aspect of the assignment. For example, panels could have been established to study the costs of shelters, the various types of shelters, and the effectiveness of shelters in light of high-yield weapons. Without a systematic way to direct the energy of these consultants, the members were left to operate without any buffers.

The members decided early on not to "try for invention," but rather work towards synthesizing the numerous reports and studies "undertaken by large and experienced groups" that were relevant to the group's assignment.[19] As such, the members of the group spent time with members of various other study groups and became well informed. Throughout July and August, the Committee was briefed extensively by all the relevant agencies.[20] One important briefing was between Sprague and the commander of Strategic Air Command, General Curtis LeMay.

Wohlstetter had already briefed Sprague and Nitze about the vulnerability of Strategic Air Command, and Wohlstetter thought that they were deeply affected by the dire portrait he had painted. However, Wohlstetter thought Sprague was ultimately convinced that there had been no improvements in Strategic Air Command since the Killian committee's recommendations over two years ago when he met with LeMay, Secretary of the Air Force James Douglas, and Wohlstetter. In discussing a recent Army study on air defense which concluded that neither Strategic Air Command nor the nation was at much danger of being caught on the ground by a Soviet attack, Sprague asked Wohlstetter about the discrepancy between the reports. Wohlstetter explained it had to do with different estimates in how long the Strategic Air Command bombers could get off the ground. Sprague then asked the group, if war were to break out today, how long it would take for the forces to become airborne. Douglas immediately said forty-five minutes. LeMay, who had not said anything up to this point, took the cigar out of his mouth and said "Nine hours."[21] Sprague was convinced that reducing the vulnerability of Strategic Air Command had to become the highest priority. The final committee report reflected this view.

In addition to the vulnerabilities of Strategic Air Command, increasing evidence supported the charge that the Soviets were surpassing the United States in military technology. In February 1955, Georgi Malenkov was ousted from the premiership in the Soviet Union and replaced by Nikolai Bulganin. With Malenkov gone, Nikita Khrushchev and Bulganin began to increase the military budget and took steps to "remedy the disadvantageous impression of the strategic balance that had been created by the intra-Party dispute."[22] One of those first steps was to update the Soviet delivery capabilities through new bombers. By the summer of 1955, Foreign Minister V.M. Molotov declared that the Soviet Union had surpassed the United States. An impressive air show on Aviation Day in July conveyed to the world a new conception of strategic balance through the flybys of numerous bomber squadrons. Although the Soviets did not actually have the bomber force displayed, but were merely flying the same squadron of bombers around in circles, the display, coupled with the Soviet acquisition of the hydrogen bomb and the rhetoric of Bulganin, Khrushchev, and Molotov, led the West to estimate a rapid buildup of Soviet nuclear capabilities. [23] In fact, the CIA had reported in the fall of 1957 that the Soviet Union was embarking on a "crash" ICBM program.[24] The U.S. response, concluded the Gaither committee, had to be a crash missile program as well. Thus the two main tenets of the Gaither report had been formed: Strategic Air Command had to be protected at all costs, and nuclear superiority had to be maintained. Added to these two priorities was a strong belief by Committee members that the U.S. needed to increase its limited war capabilities.

In a memo to Cutler regarding limited war, Evan Aurand said "Several members of [the Killian Committee] felt the need for consideration of the subject of limited war at the time, but the problem presented to the Killian Committee was, of course, restricted to that of an all-out nuclear attack on the U.S."[25] The members of the Gaither committee felt limited war was too important not to consider. Nitze strongly advocated limited war and even believed that the U.S. could fight and win a limited nuclear war.[26] However, although he and co-author of the final report, Abe Lincoln, felt strongly about it, limited war was given short attention within the final report.

To complicate matters, as the Gaither committee was wrapping up its study in the fall, the Soviets launched *Sputnik*, a 184-pound man-made satellite, on October 4th. The launching of Sputnik was a great coup over the West. Killian observed that its success "created a crisis of confidence that swept the country like a windblown forest fire."[27] The implications were frightening. It was clear that if the Soviets could launch a satellite, they were close to having an ICBM that could realistically reach the United States. Although the CIA had correctly estimated that the Soviets would launch a satellite in 1957, that information was top secret, and Western shock over the Soviets beating the U.S. into space with Sputnik gave rise to the feeling that the Soviets were indeed surpassing the U.S. in nuclear superiority.[28] From the impressive display at Aviation Day in the summer of 1955 to the launching of Sputnik in the fall of 1957, Khrushchev and his supporters were well on their way to establishing a "missile-gap" myth that lasted until the summer of 1961 and helped John F. Kennedy win the presidency in 1960.

Eisenhower was not as concerned about Sputnik as the public thought he should be. In a news conference days after the launching, he said that the satellite did not raise his "apprehensions . . . as far as security was concerned."[29] However, it raised the apprehensions of the public. For example, before the launch of Sputnik, the top three concerns of Americans were inflation, avoidance of war, and segregation. After Sputnik, the major public concerns were catching the Russians in the defense race and educating better scientists.[30] Although Eisenhower attempted to address the public's concerns over education and national security, when the Soviets sent up *Sputnik II* on November 3, his approval rating fell sharply by twenty-two points.[31] Clearly he was not successful in addressing the issues of American opinion in a serious way.[32]

While Eisenhower was not very concerned about Sputnik, the launching of Sputnik seemed to confirm the worst fears of one future Gaither committee member, Paul Nitze. Nitze saw the Soviet success as a clear indication that American foreign policy had to change. Nitze had been in Rome in early October to attend a conference on transatlantic relations. While there, the launching of Sputnik shocked the world, and he and a British official outlined a policy approach they felt the West should adopt in light of Sputnik. Over a bottle of wine, they created a plan that called for "an intensive effort on the part of the United States to increase both the capability and credibility of our strategic deterrent, to effect close collaboration between the United States and its NATO allies in the development of adequate forces in Europe."[33] Seeing as Nitze was no longer in the policy-making circles of Washington anymore, it was unlikely the plan would become policy. Yet, upon returning from Rome, Nitze learned that the Gaither committee had asked Baxter, the only historian on the committee, to write the final report. Feeling that the task of synthesizing technical and military analysis was too difficult, Baxter turned to his friend Nitze to write the final report. Here was Nitze's opportunity to submit his ideas to the President.

Nitze co-wrote the final Gaither committee report with his friend, Colonel George "Abe" Lincoln. In his memoirs, Nitze said, "Abe and I were mentioned as 'project members' at the back of the report, which masked the fact that we shared importantly in shaping the substance of the final version."[34] If Nitze was not a welcomed voice within the administration, Lincoln was. Eisenhower had great respect for Lincoln. He described Lincoln as a man "of splendid character" and as someone he admired personally.[35] In fact, Eisenhower had wanted Lincoln to take the position of Assistant Secretary for Policy Planning in August 1957. Lincoln accepted, but the Foreign Relations Committee rejected his nomination on grounds the position called for a civilian, not a military man. Eisenhower thought "many military officers had a thoroughly 'civilian' viewpoint just as many civilians had a 'military' viewpoint" and figured politics were behind the decision.[36]

Lincoln had served his country long before his participation in the Gaither Committee. In fact, he had been a member of George Kennan's Task Force A during the Solarium Exercise and participated in a 1956 government committee that examined the psychological aspects of U.S. strategy.[37] However, as much as Lincoln and Eisenhower respected one another, Lincoln did publicly express opposing views. In a 1954 publication called *Economics and National Security*, Lincoln argued that the U.S. had to prepare for war. Although he did not expect the Soviets to launch an attack, the threat of war by miscalculation could not be ignored. Since the Soviets were bent on world domination, the U.S. had no choice but to sustain an economy based on being prepared for war while ensuring that the economy stay healthy through government controls if needed. The implication here was similar to that of NSC-68 in that the nation could handle the added burdens to its economy for the sake of national security. In May 1957, Lincoln took issue with the policy of massive retaliation in an essay that advocated limited war capabilities. He believed that future wars would likely be limited wars and asked his readers, "Are we of the Western World so committed to deterrent nuclear force, and so fearful of the slightest nuclear threat that we lack the means, or wit, or both, to deal with local and limited situations?"[38] Nitze completely agreed with both of these views put forth by Lincoln, and together they got to work on writing the Gaither report.

Meanwhile, a week before their final presentation, Cutler and Gray met with the Gaither committee for two hours. Cutler recorded that he and Gray tried to impress upon the group "the necessity of their taking the same kind of broad, overall look at the problems involved which the President has to take, and not focusing their attention merely on rectifying particular deficiencies at considerably increased expenditure."[39] In Cutler's mind, it looked like the Committee was going to recommend adding some $73 billion in programs over the next five years. Worried, Cutler wrote to Eisenhower on November 4, explaining that the advisory group would meet with him that morning before presenting the final report and that he had "been working hard to get the top Advisory Group to approach this tremendous subject from a Presidential, rather than a parochial, viewpoint."[40] Apparently Cutler was fearful that the final report reflected a narrow vision that did not consider a broader context of foreign relations, foreign opinion, the economy, and overall strategy. He was right.

The Committee's Conclusions

The final report, titled "Deterrence and Survival in the Nuclear Age," was presented to Eisenhower and the NSC on November 7, 1957. The Killian committee had spoken of a steady confidence and urgency without despair, but the Gaither committee's report read like crisis with desperation. It read more like NSC-68 than anything else, but considering that those two documents had the same author, the similarity is no surprise. In fact, had the administration chosen to react to Sputnik in the same way Truman reacted to the Korean War, the Gaither report could easily have become the next NSC-68.

Advisory Panel member Lovett reportedly said after reading the report, "It was like looking into the abyss and seeing Hell at the bottom."[41] It was reported that the United States was in the gravest danger in its history, and Sputnik was proof enough for many people. The committee had concluded that active and passive defense programs in existence and those programmed for the future would not protect the civilian population against thermonuclear war. They accepted Wohlstetter's assessment that Strategic Air Command was incredibly vulnerable. The solution was to dramatically improve Strategic Air Command, while developing an early-warning radar system for an ICBM attack, and increasing production of IRBMs and ICBMs.[42] In addition to the improvements made to Strategic Air Command and the missile program, the committee also argued for increased limited war capabilities. And as far as the original question of fallout shelters was concerned, they concluded that "a nationwide fallout shelter program to protect the civil population . . . was the only feasible protection for millions of people who will be increasingly exposed to the hazards of radiation."[43] The costs were great, but well within the means of the country.

In the report, the committee claimed that the Soviet Union spent more than the United States on national defense and estimated that Soviet annual military expenditures would be twice that of America in the next ten years. In addition, the authors were greatly concerned by the rapid military advances made by the Soviets since WWII. After the war, the Soviets were left with a formidable army, but little else. Now the nation boasted a nuclear weapon program, advanced long-range bombers, long-range submarines, and an ICBM program. Of course Eisenhower was much more informed about the actual status of those Soviet programs than the committee members were, through information collected by the U-2 flights. In short, the committee concluded the Soviet military threat lay not only in their present military capabilities, but also "in the dynamic development and exploitation of their military technology."[44] As Gaither explained to the President, "the peril to the United States must be measured in megatonnage in the years ahead."[45] The economic and military threat posed by the Soviets was so large, said the report, that should the Soviets launch a nuclear attack on the United States, the current active and passive defense programs, and those programmed for the future, offered little to no protection to the civil population.[46] To remedy the situation, the committee recommended four things: building up American nuclear offensive capabilities, strengthening active defenses, building a national fallout shelter system, and introducing limited war capabilities.

First, in keeping with the tradition of relying on nuclear superiority as the first line of deterrence, the committee recommended increasing American nuclear striking power. Preventing war was the best protection for the civil population so a strong deterrent power was vital—so vital that the report assigned it the "highest relative value" in defense. Specifically, the committee members recommended increasing ICBMs (Atlas and Titan) from 80 to 600 and increasing IRBMs (Thor and Jupiter) from 60 to 240 while accelerating the Polaris submarine IRBM system.[47] To protect the missiles, the committee also urged hardened bases for the ICBMs be "phased in as rapidly as possible."[48]

Second, active defenses had to be built up. That meant strengthening Strategic Air Command by reducing response time and increasing warning time. It had to be less vulnerable. To lessen its vulnerability, reaction time had to be reduced by implementing Strategic Air Command's "alert" concept, improving tactical warning by extending the early warning lines, and building a missile defense system around Strategic Air Command bases.[49] Further suggestions included the widest possible dispersal of Strategic Air Command aircraft, even to commercial airfields, and constructing shelters on the bases for planes, weapons, supplies, and personnel.[50] In addition, an effective air defense system was imperative and had to be strengthened continually. Keeping up this invulnerable deterrent through ensuring the survival of Strategic Air Command and hardening and dispersing missiles had also been emphasized in the Killian report.

Third, although the following suggestions were designed to help protect the civilian population, the committee members concluded that to ensure survival, a nationwide fallout shelter program was the "only feasible protection for millions of people who will be increasingly exposed to the hazards of radiation." The report went on, "The Panel has been unable to identify any other type of defense likely to save more lives for the same money in the event of a nuclear attack."[51] Ye the report said the government should not adopt the $32 billion Federal Civil Defense Administration's proposal for blast and fallout shelters. There was a cheaper way. The committee saw blast shelters as less likely to be effective since one had to get into a blast shelter before an attack, but those surviving an attack would have "adequate time (one to five hours) to get into fallout shelters."[52] Fallout shelters made more sense and were cheaper than the blast shelters as they did not have to be as reinforced to withstand the blast and heat from an explosion.[53] The committee estimated that half the population might be saved with fallout shelters and that a national program might only cost $25 billion—$5 billion a year over a five-year period.[54]

Finally, the committee concluded by discussing the expansion of the military's capability to wage limited war. This direction stemmed in part from the Committee members' lack of enthusiasm for the policy of massive retaliation, and from the personal bias of the authors. The committee recommended an augmentation of American and Allied forces for limited war and provision of greater mobility for those forces. It also said that a national, not Service level, study should be undertaken to "develop current doctrine on when and how nuclear weapons can contribute to limited operations."[55] Although this section was underplayed within the report, its inclusion is significant in that it was a contentious point between Eisenhower and the Democrats like Nitze who sought to implement limited war capabilities. Eisenhower had fought with his own national security team to discard limited war as an option and NSC 5707/8 reflected the administration's policy to not engage in limited war.[56] The issue for Eisenhower was moot.

Not surprisingly, the Gaither committee recognized, like the Killian Committee before it, that strategic warning was needed particularly in light of the reduced warning times created by missile technology. Although the Gaither committee members suggested no specific measures for improved strategic warning, it did imply that the U.S. at present had no sound way to receive strategic warning.[57] The committee members were unaware of the current U-2 program because of its top-secret status. Even when information derived from U-2 missions could have been helpful to Eisenhower in dispelling the missile-gap myth that emerged out of the Gaither report, the President refused to compromise the secrecy of the program.

In short, the committee's report concluded that a shelter program alone was not enough to ensure survival, nor was an air defense system. Instead, a combination of national fallout shelters and air defense was the optimum way to allocate resources to protect the nation against nuclear attack.[58] In other words, even if active defense measures delivered a 100% kill-ratio, the committee believed shelters were still needed to protect the population from fallout generated from American missiles or the detonation of weapons from enemy aircraft shot down.[59] In addition, the authors of the report assured that, "If deterrence should fail, and nuclear war should come through miscalculation or design, the programs outlined . . . would . . . go far to ensure our survival as a nation . . . . The next two years are critical. If we fail to act at once," they warned, "the risk . . . will be unacceptable."[60]

The total cost for its recommendations was $44 billion over five years—$25 billion on civil defense and $19 billion for deterrent and offensive capabilities.[61] Seeing as the American people were capable of shouldering the costs for WWII and the Korean War, when 41% and 14% of the Gross National Product was devoted to defense respectively, the committee was confident that America could afford to increase its present spending on defense.[62] What the group did not acknowledge was that during those wars the United States took casualties. Without that provocation, the public had to be shown the need for such expenditures. In other words, public support in a period of hostilities cannot be likened to a period of peace.[63] However, it was conceded that an undertaking of all the programs would cause a larger Federal debt, higher taxes, the need for additional private investment, and the postponement or slowdown of the national highway construction, one of the few programs Eisenhower enthusiastically supported.[64] These consequences were not in line with Eisenhower's New Look strategy or the Great Equation. As such, Eisenhower did not accept the majority of the recommendations nor change his strategic thinking, as many members had desired.

Missiles Yes, Shelters No: Reactions and Implementations

The crux of the report was that the focus for survival had to be on deterrence, and strengthening American deterrence depended both on reducing the vulnerability of Strategic Air Command and maintaining nuclear superiority. However, the Gaither committee overestimated the capabilities of the Soviets. For example, the Soviet Union had only four operational ICBMs by 1961, not the hundreds the committee had predicted. The committee members also exaggerated the vulnerability of Strategic Air Command. In 1957 it was the Soviet Union that was vulnerable, not the United States. Eisenhower understood this and was not about to accept the report lock, stock and barrel.

Eisenhower believed that the American strategic forces were stronger than the committee reported and that the overseas bases offered excellent dispersal capacity for American power. He conceded dispersal was important at home and that things did seem to move slowly in that area, but things were not all that dire. In fact, Eisenhower stressed to the group that the United States was in no way behind the Soviets. The President agreed with the committee that shelters on the Strategic Air Command bases for supplies and weapons were a good idea, but reminded them that many weapons were already dispersed.[65] However, in a budget meeting a few days later, Eisenhower did note the importance of providing additional defense funds for the dispersal and alert of Strategic Air Command. Although, he was quick to remind his defense secretary that should the Department get the additional funds requested, "they must be prepared to give up such things as excessive executive aircraft, etc."[66] He thought they could find $600 million or more this way.

Eisenhower was open to the idea of accelerating the missile program, but not to the crash program levels that the Gaither committee recommended. As a former military commander, Eisenhower was worried that the act of preparing for war, such as a crash program for missiles, can make the avoidance of war rather difficult.[67] Instead of authorizing the crash program, he relied on the "good judgment" of his new Secretary of Defense Neil McElroy to keep the pace from becoming excessive.[68] McElroy did propose IRBM and Polaris acceleration, but was able to keep the requested additional costs for each program well below the figures given by the Gaither committee.[69] Keeping up a strong retaliatory force remained the key element for defense. Eisenhower would not consider implementing measures for limited war capabilities.[70] "Maximum massive retaliation," he said, "remains the crux of our defense."[71] Dulles agreed with the President, saying that a deterrent capability had to be maintained at all costs. "With such a deterrent capability," he said, "we would be in a position to conduct our foreign policy in such a manner as to assure victory in the cold war."[72]

Overall, Dulles was as upset about the report as Eisenhower. During the committee's presentation, Dulles frequently interrupted and openly disagreed with the recommendations. He knew in advance the conclusions of the report, having seen a memorandum in late October from his Policy Planning Staff, which had been briefed by members of the Gaither committee. The Policy Planning Staff had been impressed with the committee's report and had certainly given the Gaither committee's members reason to believe that the State Department was in line with their thinking. Nitze, who was at the briefing, certainly thought that the State Department endorsed the report. When Dulles came out against its conclusions, Nitze was so disgusted at Dulles for ignoring the opinions of his staff he sent a letter to Dulles calling for his resignation.[73] "I should ask you to consider," wrote Nitze, "in the light of events of recent years, whether there is not some other prominent Republican disposed to exercise the responsibility of Secretary of State in seeking a balance between our capabilities and our unavoidable commitments, equipped to form persuasive policies, and able to secure the confidence and understanding of our allies."[74]

The question of shelters remained open for study, but Eisenhower rejected the committee's recommendations here. Construction of fallout shelters was a lower priority in the report, but nonetheless they were still recommended. As indicated in the report, the strongest defense combined both active and passive defense measures. Eisenhower agreed that, "shelters rank rather low in the list of priorities" and commented that the money spent on shelters would be better spent on "other things," like improving active defense programs and accelerating the missile programs.[75] In fact, Eisenhower was just plain opposed to spending billions on shelters.[76]

Dulles agreed. He recognized that the United States was better off with shelters, "if it were possible by a wave of the hand to create shelters," but such a program would have serious effects on America's economy and ability to provide allies with economic aid. He also feared that a shelter program would "bring home to the people our lack of faith in our capability to deter war."[77] This viewpoint greatly differed from the report's conclusions which stated that shelters would "symbolize our *will to survive*," and augment American deterrent power by discouraging an enemy attack because the U.S. was prepared and ready to use its "strategic retaliatory power."[78]

Dulles also thought shelters might disrupt the effectiveness of deterrence. As he explained to Eisenhower, he thought these matters of shelters were "largely a matter of temperament, and that [he] was temperamentally unsympathetic to such defensive measures."[79] Atomic Energy Committee chairman Lewis Strauss also agreed, believing shelters might actually provoke the Soviets to launch a preemptive attack on the United States before it could finish a truly effective shelter program. This thinking goes back to strategist Bernard Brodie, who argued that too much deterrence could be seen as aggressive by one's enemy. Dulles even suggested, "perhaps the United States and the U.S.S.R. should conclude a disarmament agreement under which neither would build shelters."[80]

Another concern was Allied perception. Both Eisenhower and Dulles worried about the consequences if the U.S. embarked on a shelter program and American allies could not afford to do the same. Dulles figured allied support would be lost. "It might be argued theoretically," he said, "that the United States as the arsenal of the Free World requires the protection of shelters but to say that the American people must be saved from the effects of radiation and not the British or French and the others was tantamount to losing our Allies."[81]

Yet even if the shelters were deemed a good idea militarily, diplomatically, and economically, the administration still needed maximum support from the public. Eisenhower was skeptical he would get that support. A federally funded program was bound to run into problems and jealousies. For example, to obtain national support, the urgent need for the program would have to be explained, which might frighten the public into panic. Furthermore, in deciding how much funding each state received, some states might feel slighted.[82] There were too many logistics to figure in, and the recommendations of the Gaither committee did not take into account the total picture.

In addition to shelters, there was still the option of evacuation. The new Federal Civil Defense Administration director, Leo Hoegh, wanted to see a balanced program between evacuation and shelters and not a wholesale decision for one or the other.[83] Evacuation to outside fallout shelters was likely to work if an area had two to three hours of warning. In densely populated areas like Washington, D.C. and New York, he suggested a combination of fallout and blast shelters, with an evacuation strategy. Although Hoegh agreed with Eisenhower that a partnership between the Federal government and the States and local authorities was needed, he also thought there had to be in the near future a "greater emphasis on the leadership role of the Federal Government in this partnership."[84] Overall, Hoegh, like Peterson before him, sought a greater federal role and a continued effort to provide shelters to the American public.

Despite the position of the Gaither committee and the Federal Civil Defense Administration, Eisenhower did not enlarge the role of the federal government in regards to civil defense, but the issue of shelters never completely went away for Eisenhower. In many instances, the shelter question revolved around the kind of existence one might live after a nuclear exchange.[85] One committee reported that it was unable to say that, even given improvements made to active defenses, a nationwide fallout shelter program could save enough citizens to ensure the survival of the nation.[86] Eisenhower even privately questioned who would want to survive such a devastating war.[87] The grim reality of a post nuclear war world further influenced Eisenhower to not allow a federally funded national shelter program. The furthest he went was to officially introduce a National Shelter Policy in 1958, but it merely continued to emphasize the notion that each individual was responsible for his own protection.[88]

In addition to the four primary recommendations put forth by the Gaither committee, Eisenhower had other concerns that the recommendations went against his 'Great Equation.' He expressed to the Gaither committee that the difficulty with a democracy was how to keep up interest and support of the people without creating hysteria and a "government by crisis." In other words, he could not just accept the report without regard for its impact on the public, since "we have before us a big job of molding public opinion as well as avoiding extremes."[89] The people had to be motivated to take up the cause of defense. For example, the country needed people educated in science and technology, so the country had to educate the people why that was required in order to gain their support. In fact, Eisenhower began a series of speeches aimed at calming the public and directing their attention towards education.[90] Eisenhower explained that the difficulty was to stress the need for scientists and engineers enough to garner support without creating a crisis or garrison state. Furthermore, he said that to retain a free enterprise system "we must retain incentives," and, he noted, "the group's study had not embraced these complications."[91] He recognized that America needed to "carry a challenging load for a couple of years," but said it was "very hard to obtain the commitments to indefinite burdens."[92] So while the Gaither report described a nation in grave danger, Eisenhower was not willing to let such a notion move the country into a direction of crisis government, hysteria, and excessive military spending.

It seemed to Eisenhower that the committee had not looked at the problem in its entirety. Further matters needed to be explored. For example, he asked, "what can the American people be expected to put up with in terms of the allocation of the Gross National Product over the next several years? Was the Panel proposing to impose controls on the U.S. economy now? Are we now to advocate the re-introduction of controls?"[93] Before anyone could respond, the President explained that if this group were sitting in the Kremlin, surely their recommendations would be adopted "in total, regardless of the effect of such action on our people."[94] He did not have that luxury as the president of a democracy. The bottom line was that the recommendations cost too much, provided what Eisenhower saw as an unnecessary defense element, and was likely to sap the public's spiritual resolve. The recommendations did not uphold the Great Equation.

In the end however, Eisenhower realized he had asked the wrong question of the committee. He had asked the committee to study a course of action in the event of a nuclear war, but he had no intention of ever fighting a nuclear war. "You can't have this kind of war," he said. "There just aren't enough bulldozers to scrape the bodies off the street."[95] So while he agreed to some moderate increases in missile production and remedies to reduce Strategic Air Command vulnerability—recommendations that complimented his strategic thinking—he rejected the bulk of the report's recommendations.

Leaks and Headaches

Eisenhower should have been able to put the report into a file cabinet without the greater public knowing what the report said. He should have been able to say thank you to the committee members for a job well done and expect them to return to their civilian lives. Unfortunately for Eisenhower, the report was leaked to the press and many committee members became active lobbyists campaigning for the recommendations within the report to be implemented. These two developments, neither of which occurred during the Solarium or Killian exercises, caused Eisenhower to reevaluate the usefulness of civilian committees.

Parts of the report and its grim conclusions were made public, making it even more difficult for the President to reassure the public in light of Sputnik.

Within weeks of the report's submission to the NSC, leaks about it began to appear in the press. The November 23 weekend edition of the *New York Herald Tribune* ran a somewhat complete account of the report.[96] In what was an understatement, Sprague said to Killian that it was "bad security on our study" and thought it might distress the President "enormously."[97] He was right. In part, no doubt, of the pressures created from Sputnik and the Gaither Report, Eisenhower was distressed to the point of suffering a mild stroke on November 25.[98] Sprague also worried that such a leak was going to hinder rather than help the implementation of the recommendations made by the report.[99] Again, he was right.

On December 20, the *Washington Post* ran a story by Chalmers Roberts that was a substantial summary of the report and remained the most complete public record of the report until it was declassified in 1973.[100] It began by saying that the Gaither report portrayed the U.S. "in the gravest danger in its history," and that America was well on its way "in frightening course to the status of a second-class power." It also reported that many of the members of the committee, "prominent figures in the Nation's business, financial, scientific, and educational communities," were truly "frightened" and "appalled" at the state of the American military posture compared to the Soviet Union.[101] In addition, the press also reported from the Gaither report that in the event of war, 60 to 100 million Americans would likely be killed by radioactive fallout without a national shelter program.[102]

These startling revelations led Congress to scream for the report to be released. For example, Holified, who was investigating civil defense, requested a copy of the report or, at the very least, a briefing by someone in the Executive branch. Senator Lyndon Johnson (D-TX), chairman of the Senate Subcommittee on Preparedness, asked the president to release both the Killian and Gaither reports to Congress, primarily because he thought they would be helpful in making a case to increase defense appropriations and for ulterior political reasons.[103] Others in Congress agreed. One senator argued that the report should have forced the administration into a sense of urgency and said that Roberts' article described the "critical situation which confronts our country, and which I must say in all good conscience the President's budget does so little to remedy."[104] Given that Eisenhower had recently asked Congress for a higher defense budget than Congress was willing to grant, Eisenhower was again facing unwarranted criticism for his defense budget, and he was furious.[105]

Cutler later said that his most difficult time with the president arose from the Gaither report leaks.[106] Since it was Cutler who approved the expanded mandate of the report, he was aware that the President ought to have been furious with him. "The fracas ensuing from discreditable leaks to the press of parts of the Committee's report dealing with aspects of military defenses of the nation," Cutler later recalled, "would have caused a less understanding President to lop off the head of his Special Assistant."[107] Fortunately for Cutler, Eisenhower deeply respected him and was not about to get rid of one of his most trusted assistants.[108]

During a period when Eisenhower was trying to reassure the American public in the aftermath of Sputnik and deal with a Democratic Congress accusing the administration of inadequate defense budgets, it was natural that Eisenhower was not receptive to the charges being made in the papers that the U.S. was in grave danger. To release the report might panic the public, which Eisenhower likely feared would result in wild demands for massive spending on all kinds of programs, ruining the economy and creating a garrison state and government by crisis. The report contained figures of estimated American casualties from a Soviet attack that were hypothetical, but still disturbing. Sherman Adams, the President's Assistant, explained that Eisenhower reasoned that, "public knowledge of these speculative conclusions, based on assumptions that could be challenged, would do the nation much more harm than good."[109] Acting on his convictions about the Great Equation, Eisenhower refused to make the report public.

He explained his reasons to Senator Johnson. Eisenhower told Johnson that the report was not going to be released to the public or to Congress because, from time to time, groups of civilian advisors that were called upon to advise the President did so with the understanding that their advice would be kept confidential and he intended to honor that understanding. Furthermore, their reports were official documents of the National Security Council and never before had documents of the NSC been furnished to Congress. Eisenhower did remind Johnson that the information given to the study groups was the same information that had been available to Congressional committees studying the same problems and that the committees drew their own conclusions. However, Eisenhower was careful to also mention that he had carefully considered the conclusions of the Gaither report, along with those opinions from other advisors and study groups.[110] However, since the conclusion made by the Gaither committee that the United States was in grave danger was public knowledge through press leaks and Congressional debates, Eisenhower had to explain to the American people why he found the recommendations unpersuasive. To complicate matters further, his refusal to release the report fueled rumors in Washington that the administration was unwilling to face the realities of the security situation.[111] It was a position the President did not enjoy.

However, Eisenhower was aware that the public release of some of the information in the report might be helpful to clarify the inaccuracies being reported in the press. For example, the committee did recommend fallout shelters, but it did not place shelters on its highest priority list and recognized the limits of shelters in providing protection against an attack. It also rejected the price tag the Federal Civil Defense Administration had suggested for shelters of $32 billion. If the public were made aware of these limitations and findings of the report, Eisenhower might convince the public that money for shelters would be better spent on other defenses. As one military friend wrote to Eisenhower in response to the articles he had read about the Gaither report, "I think the recommendation of a long-term program of shelter construction is absurd, the costs are absurd, and the fact that we have the best Strategic Air Command in the world is not even mentioned . . . [and] it seems to me that this report should be released so that the people have a chance to read it."[112] Eisenhower explained that the release of the report was impossible because of its classified material but agreed if some of its contents could be made public it would "be helpful to a sound public approach to our defense and civil defense needs."[113]

While Eisenhower wanted to alleviate the fears of the public, ultimately the members of the Gaither committee wished to see the report's contents made public to arouse public demand that all the recommendations be implemented. After the Gaither report was submitted, Sprague told Eisenhower that the group was a most dedicated bunch and offered that many of the members were "extraordinarily well informed" on many areas in national security and all were available individually or collectively "for consultation . . . to explain or enlarge on any of the recommendations made in the report."[114] Emphasizing the recurring theme that time was running out, Sprague also recommended the establishment of another study group to recommend what should be done to take advantage of the "very modest time" America had to make the "most effective efforts."[115] Eisenhower politely agreed to consider the idea and Sprague encouraged Killian to mention it to the President so that he might take action on the suggestion.[116] But Dulles discouraged the idea, pointing to the "complications of having independent groups dealing with segments only of the total problem."[117] Cutler agreed and was frustrated by Sprague, saying that all of Sprague's work on continental defense seemed to have blinded him into a narrow view and that Sprague's views about Strategic Air Command alertness and vulnerability were his "stock-in-trade." The trouble with Sprague, Cutler went on to say, was that he "brushes all other considerations aside—foreign relations, foreign repercussions, whether what we do to beef up etc., will actually bring war nearer, etc. He has a single track mind of great capacity."[118] Eisenhower had to agree and thought that the usefulness of such advice and committees was limited, especially in light of the recent events surrounding the Gaither committee.

Stories about the Gaither report continued to be published in the papers. Eisenhower, Cutler, and Killian held the committee members responsible for the stories and decided not to let the Gaither committee reconvene to review and comment on the various department remarks about the report. Instead, the Science Advisory Committee was asked to review those remarks. Cutler met with a number of members of the Gaither committee, including Sprague, E.P. Oliver, and Jim Perkins, in February to convey the President's "exasperation" with the leaks and Congressional pressures. Cutler also explained to the group that the function of the study group was completed with its report; it was not a continuing body.[119]

Many committee members were outraged by these developments and believed that since their work from June through November had proceeded without any leaks, the responsible parties for the leaks were those who received the report *after* the report had been submitted. One member, writing to Killian, described himself as "distressed" over the accusations and believed that silencing the committee was a mistake. It was a mistake because *Sputnik*, he believed, had frightened "a largely uninformed and hence easily alarmed American public," and the public had therefore to be educated about issues of national security to allay their concerns. Bringing these issues into the arena of public debate was something many members of the Gaither committee sought to do.[120]

By January, committee members were making many efforts to circulate the contents of the report to a wider public to raise public opinion and force the administration to act. In particular, three reports were circulated which reflected the perseverance of some members to see their recommendations implemented. Nitze wrote one report which Foster found so impressive that he suggested to Killian that it be added to the supplementary papers for staff personnel in relevant departments like the Joint Chiefs of Staff, State, and NSC.[121] Nitze also co-authored with Lincoln a 13-page paper submitted to the NSC executive secretary, which continued to push for limited war options. In it, they outlined various approaches to limited war and stated the views of every conceivable department on the subject in attempts to demonstrate the support within the policymaking community for limited war.[122] The technical advisor to the committee, Oliver of the RAND Corporation, wrote the third report. Oliver's nine-page memo advised the committee to take full advantage of what he called a "favorable environment" created by the leaks of the report. He argued that the committee members had to "impress the highest levels of Government and all concerned with the unanimity of their belief in at least the highest priority category of recommendations."[123] Reflecting the tone of the original report, Oliver told his colleagues that the United States "had entered into a period of mortal danger" and reiterated the point that time was running out.[124] Like his other peers lobbying for more action, Oliver believed that *Sputnik* indicated the advances being made in the Soviet Union and was most alarmed by the slowness of the administration's responses.

Oliver also held the same misinformed opinion of many others—that the Soviets had surpassed the U.S. in weapon systems and that they had better intelligence information about American weapon systems. He also believed the Soviets were likely to initiate a war and surmised that war would come as a surprise air attack which Strategic Air Command was painfully ill prepared to withstand. Particularly striking about Oliver's report is that he saw no room for compromise; the recommendations with the highest priority from the Gaither report had to be implemented in their entirety. He accused the administration of having an inadequate and inflexible decision-making process that impeded these implementations. As such, Oliver said that the President had better have a "sober understanding" of the situation to speed through these recommendations or else Eisenhower would be forced to act because of an "external crisis of an aroused public opinion."[125] A government by crisis was something Eisenhower had dismissed earlier and would not tolerate. Oliver was trying to create such an aroused public opinion.

Sprague, Gaither, and Perkins also set about trying to bring the contents of the report to a wider public. Meeting in mid-January, the three spent an entire day discussing strategies and sent their recommendations to Killian for action. The three agreed that the report should not be released verbatim as it did contain classified information that might be valuable to the Soviets. However, after trying to write a sanitized version, the three decided such a version was not effective enough and even misleading. They did think that the summary report presented to the President was appropriate for public release and recommended that Eisenhower hold a press conference soliciting the "widest possible discussion and debate of matters vital to our national security" and promising the release of relevant information vital to such a debate.[126] Finally, the three thought that the members of the Gaither committee ought to be permitted to testify before the appropriate subcommittees of the Congress.[127] However, Eisenhower, in declining to furnish either the Gaither or Killian reports to Johnson's Senate Preparedness Subcommittee, made it impossible for members to testify. In fact, Gaither was asked in March to testify to the Military Operations Subcommittee on the relative importance of shelters in an overall program of defense against modern weapons, but he had to decline, noting that "it would be impossible for me to separate my views on this important subject from the conclusions and recommendations of the Security Resources Panel . . . [and] that my testimony cannot with propriety be given without violating the fundamental principles and considerations" of Eisenhower's decision to keep the report classified.[128] The influence of the civilian advisors had been greatly diminished.

Nitze complained about this weakness in the ability of civilian consultants to wield any real power in making policy. He explained a serious problem facing the Gaither committee was that "the committee may be too far removed from executive branch responsibilities to be fully effective. Those members of the executive branch who are actually responsible for carrying out policy . . . feel, perhaps rightly, that such groups are out of touch with the real problems with which the officials, in the end, must always deal. In any case, it is obvious that the committee, once its report has been presented, is in a poor position to help fight its recommendation through the decision stage."[129] Nitze missed the point that the civilian committees during the Eisenhower administration were never asked to make policy. The reports were never intended to be policy papers. They were, in the role of outside experts, simply advising the policymakers. Killian understood this more than anyone else.

In his memoirs as Science Advisor, Killian reflected on the aftermath of the Gaither report. He thought the credibility of the report was severely damaged by the newspaper leaks and limited Eisenhower's ability to make policy. Had the report not been leaked, Eisenhower might have been "in a better position to follow through on its recommendations."[130] Furthermore, the public maneuvering and politicking that many of the members engaged in to make the report public deeply concerned Killian. He reflected that it is arguable "that a study group of this kind had a responsibility to abide by the terms of reference given to it at the start of the study, to present its report in the most persuasive possible manner, and then to leave to the administration the decisions about what should be done about it and whether it should be made public."[131] Such public activism by the participants, Killian concluded, "tends to inhibit presidents from using this highly valuable advisory process."[132] Eisenhower agreed and concluded that the whole episode had proved the imprudence of calling in outside groups.

The Gaither Committee was not a success like the Solarium Exercise and Killian Committee before it. It failed for a number of reasons. The committee went too far in expanding its mandate. Rather than simply determining technically and economically what kinds of shelters could be built compared to what kinds of active defense systems could be built, the committee made judgments about the administration's overall passive and active defense measures.[133] As civilian experts, they were called upon for their expertise, not for their policy-making agendas. Where Eisenhower failed was in his leadership. His lack of attention to the group allowed the mandate to expand and its membership to grow.

Eisenhower had firmly established both the membership and narrow assignments of the Solarium Exercise and had fully backed the mission of the Killian Committee. George Kennan's appointment as chair of Task Force A predetermined the outcome of the group's report. James Killian often mirrored Eisenhower's own thinking and Killian was able to successfully organize and manage a relatively large group. Yet Rowan Gaither, coming from RAND, which often held differing opinions from that of Eisenhower, was an odd choice. Furthermore, Gaither established a sprawling group with no manageable subcommittees. At first glance, it would seem that Eisenhower and his aides dropped the ball by failing to monitor the process. However, had the report never been leaked to the public, and had the committee members dispersed after the report was completed rather than lobbying for the report, Eisenhower could have quietly put the report into a file cabinet, and claimed he carefully considered the recommendations but ultimately found them unpersuasive. Had the committee agreed with Eisenhower's views that the money spent on passive defense would have been better spent on active defenses, the President could have pointed to a diverse group of civilian experts in explaining why he rejected the idea of a national shelter program—the group would have been made complicit in the decision. Either way, Eisenhower probably did not feel that he had to be on top of the Gaither committee since he had his mind made up already that the Federal Government was not going to foot the bill for a national shelter system. The process backfired on the President when the Gaither report became public.

The Gaither committee also failed because the committee members were not seeing the entire picture. Unlike with the Solarium and Killian committees, the Gaither Committee did not have full access to all the reports that were relevant to their new, self-expanded mandate. In addition, Eisenhower did not personally get involved in the success of the committee as he had with the Killian committee, and the consequence was that the committee faced restrictions to classified information. For example, Admiral Radford declined one request from the Gaither committee for two classified Joint Chiefs of Staff reports because he said it was not relevant to their study—the original study as he understood it.[134] In addition, important classified information gathered from U-2 missions was not made available to the committee members. These restrictions compromised the ability of the committee to successfully carry out their expanded mandate. As a result, the authors of the report had suggested that a missile gap existed and proposed massive spending for both aggressive and passive defense. Eisenhower rejected parts of the report because he would not allow runaway spending to appease alarmists, and neither he nor Dulles thought spending billions on shelters was wise.[135]

What Eisenhower did accept from the Gaither report, strengthening deterrence and the security of second strike capabilities—the heart of his strategic thinking—was already in the works at some level, largely because of the recommendations made by the Killian committee. The Gaither report failed to convince Eisenhower to shift that thinking. He was unmoved by the arguments to increase limited war capabilities; he simply would not consider the issue.

In the end, Eisenhower's use of civilian committees in his decision-making process came to a close with the Gaither committee. Both the Solarium Exercise and Killian report reflected the ideas captured by the 'Great Equation' and Eisenhower's strategic thinking. The Gaither report did neither of these things. However, this experience alone was not why Eisenhower became unenthusiastic to the use of committees. As demonstrated, he could use a committee's report to make its members complicit in the policymaking process or reject a report while claiming to have looked at all sides. He also used them to bring his team on board with his policies. What soured Eisenhower to civilian groups after the Gaither report was the lack of anonymity the members displayed and their persistence in trying to make policy by exploiting the fears of the public. Eisenhower respected the views of civilian experts, but he did not tolerate their wanting to assume more power and influence than they had—a position made clear in his Farewell Address. When Eisenhower controlled the process of civilian committees, when they were organized from within and born out of internal initiative, he found them useful in his decision-making process. When the Gaither committee was organized because of outside pressures, Eisenhower left the process alone resulting in the failure that was the Gaither committee.

Notes

1. Memorandum of Conversation with President, 12/26/57, EL, JFD Papers, WH Memorandum Series, Box 5, "Meetings with the President 1957 (1)."

2. Memorandum of Conversation with the President, 11/25/57, EL, JFD Papers, WH Memorandum Series, Box 5, "Meetings with the President 1957 (1)."

3. Memorandum for File: Gaither Panel, 06/28/57, EL, WHO OSANSA, NSC Series, Briefing Notes Subseries, Box 8, "[Fallout Shelters](3) 1957-60."

There is no indication that Eisenhower had any hand in preparing or approving this list.

4. For a complete membership list of the Gaither Committee, see Appendix C.

5. Killian and Fisk directed the Killian Committee and Hill worked part-time on the Defensive Power panel. McCormack chaired Task Force B on the Solarium Exercise.

6. Colonel George Abe Linclon, who ended up writing part of the final Gaither report, had served with George Kennan on Task Force A of the Solarium Exercise. Dr. Richard Emberson and Dr. Brockway McMillan were two scientists who served on the Defensive Power panel of the Killian Committee.

7. The TCP Report, 186.

8. David Snead, *The Gaither Committee, Eisenhower, and the Cold War*, (Columbus: Ohio State University Press, 1999), 48.

9. Baxter had been the official historian of the Office of Scientific Research and Development during WWII and wrote *Scientists Against Time*, (Cambridge: MIT Press, 1946), a history of the OSRD.

10. Richard Immerman, review of *The Gaither Committee, Eisenhower, and the Cold War*, by David Snead, *H-Net Reviews*, November 2000, <http://www2.h-net.msu.edu/reviews/>

11. Gregg Herken, *Counsels of War*, (New York: Oxford University Press, 1987), 113.

12. Nitze himself wrote that he "spent long hours working on his [Stevenson's] behalf in the presidential race of 1956." See Paul Nitze, *From Hiroshima to Glasnost: At the Center of Decision*, (New York: Grove Weidenfeld, 1989), 160.

13. Memorandum of conversation with General Draper, 12/1/58, EL, JFD Papers, General Correspondence and Memo series, Box 1, "Memos of conversation- General A-D (4)," 1.

14. David Callahan, *Dangerous Capabilities, Paul Nitze and the Cold War*, (New York: HarperCollins, 1990), 167-168.

15. Memo for the Honorable Bernard Shanley, 07/15/57, EL, WH Central Files, Confidential File, Box 23, "Defense Mobilization, Office of (5)."

16. Eisenhower quoted in Herken, *Counsels of War*, 113.

17. Robert Cutler, *No Time for Rest*, (Boston: Little Brown, 1966), 354-355.

18. Spurgeon Keeny in an interview with John Newhouse, 07/9/87, quoted in John Newhouse, *War and Peace in the Nuclear Age*, (New York, Knopf, 1989), 119.

19. Letter from Steering Committee to Eisenhower, 11/7/57, in *Deterrence and Survival in the Nuclear Age* (The "Gaither Report"), 11/7/57, (Washington DC: US Government Printing Office, 1976), 9.

20. Security Resources Panel, Schedule of Briefings, 07/23/57, MIT, AC 4, Box 195, "SAC, Security Resources Panel (Gaither Panel), 1957."

21. Herken, *Counsels of War*, 114.

22. Roman Kolkowicz, *The Soviet Military and the Communist Party*, (Princeton: Princeton University Press, 1967), 27.

23. Arnold Horelick and Myron Rush, *Strategic Power and Soviet Foreign Policy*, (Chicago: University of Chicago Press, 1966), 18; 27-28.

24. SNIE 11-10-57, "The Soviet ICBM Program," in *Intentions and Capabilities*, Donald Steury, ed., (Washington, DC: US Printing, 1996), 63.

25. Memorandum Aurand to Cutler, 8/14/57, EL, Evan Aurand Papers, Box 11, "Special Folder (1)," 1.

26. See chapter 5.

27. James Killian, *Sputnik, Scientists, and Eisenhower*, (Cambridge: MIT Press, 1977), 7.

28. NIE 11-5-57, "Soviet Capabilities and Probable Programs in the Guided Missile Field," in *Intentions and Capabilities*, Donald Steury, ed., 62.

29. Eisenhower, *Public Papers of the President*, 1957, (Washington, DC: Government Printing Press, 1958), 730.

30. Paul O'Neil, "U.S. Change of Mind," *Life*, March 3, 1958.

31. For a discussion on science education pre and post-Sputnik, see Valerie Adams, "Ensuring the Ivory Tower Did Not Fall Behind an Ivory Curtain," *Essays in Arts and* Sciences, 33:1 (Summer 2004), 19-36. Michael Beschloss, *MayDay: Eisenhower, Khrushchev, and the U-2 Affair*, (New York: Harper & Row, 1986), 148.

32. Robert Divine, *The Sputnik Challenge: Eisenhower's Response to the Soviet Satellite*, (New York: Oxford University Press, 1993), 205.

33. Nitze, Public Statements of Deputy Secretary of Defense Paul H. Nitze, 1967, (Washington, DC: Department of Defense, n.d.), 306, quoted in Callahan, *Dangerous Capabilities*, 169.

34. Nitze, *From Hiroshima to Glasnost*, 167.

35. Letter Dwight Eisenhower to Milton Eisenhower, 04/6/63, EL, Milton Eisenhower Manuscripts, Box 15, "Correspondence 1963." Back in 1947, when Eisenhower was Army Chief of Staff, Lincoln decided to retire to an academic career. Eisenhower begged him to stay on at the Pentagon because of the "high value I placed upon his knowledge, thoroughness and good sense." Ibid.

36. Memorandum of Conversation with the President, 08/23/57, JFD Papers, WH Memorandum Series, Box 5, "Meetings with the President (4);" Memorandum for the Record, 08/02/57, EL, JFD Papers, General Correspondence and Memorandum Series, Box 2, "Strictly Confidential- L (1)."

37. The 1956 group reported to Nelson Rockefeller, a study group often called the Quantico II Panel, see *FRUS*, 1955-57, XIX:153-154.

38. George A. Lincoln, *Economics and National Security: Managing America's Resources for* Defense, 2nd ed., (Englewood Cliffs, NJ: Prentice-Hall, 1954); Colonel G. A. Lincoln and Lt. Colonel Amos Jordan, Jr., "Technology and the Changing Nature of General War," *Military Review* 36 (May 1957). Lincoln quoted in Snead, *Gaither Committee*, 68.

39. Memorandum Cutler to Gray and Goodpaster, 10/30/57, EL, WHO OSANSA, NSC Series, Briefing Notes Subseries, Box 16, "Security Resources Panel (2) 1957-58."

40. Letter Cutler to Eisenhower, 11/04/57, EL, AWF, Administrative Series, Box 11, "Cutler, Robert 1956-57(1)." Gaither headed this initial presentation to the President on November 4th before the NSC meeting on November 7, 1957. Others present were Sprague, Foster, Killian, McCloy, Doolittle, Frank Stanton, and Carney. See Memorandum of Conference with the President on November 4, 1957, 11/6/57, EL, AWF, DDE Diary, Box 28, "November 1957 Staff Notes."

41. Quoted in Newhouse, *War and Peace*, 119.

42. *Deterrence and Survival in the Nuclear Age* (The "Gaither Report"), 11/7/57, (Washington DC: US Government Printing Office, 1976), 16-18. (Hereafter the Gaither Report).

43. Ibid., 19.

44. Ibid., 15.

45. Memorandum of Conference with the President on November 4, 1957, 11/6/57, EL, AWF, DDE Diary, Box 28, "November 1957 Staff Notes."

46. Gaither Report, 16.

47. The Report's recommendations for missile acceleration were substantially greater than present Defense plans. For example, the Gaither Report recommended 600 ICBMs be operational by 1963, whereas the Defense Department plans only called for 130 by that time. See Memorandum of Discussion at the 350th Meeting of the NSC, 1/6/58, *FRUS*, 1958-60, 3:5.

48. Gaither Report, 17-18.

49. Both Killian and Sprague had been told in 1955 that an "alert" system which would get at least 25% of SAC's aircraft off the ground was to be implemented. By 1957 that system had not yet been implemented because of lack of funds and trained personnel. As of September 1957, Sprague was told by SAC Commander General Curtis LeMay some improvements had been made, but that "not a single plane could have left the ground within six hours except for a few that were by chance in the air on a test at the time." See Memorandum of Conference with the President Following NSC Meeting, 11/7/57, EL, AWF, DDE Diary, Box 28, "November 1957 Staff Notes."

50. Gaither Report, 17.

51. Ibid., 19.

52. Ibid., 19.

53. The FCDA report (NSC 5709) estimated $100 per occupant for group fallout shelters compared to $235 per occupant for blast shelters. See A Federal Shelter Program for Civil Defense, 03/29/57, NA, RG 273, Box 44, "NSC-5709," A-6.

54. Gaither Report, 31.

55. Ibid., 18.

56. NSC 5707/8 was approved June 3, 1957. It was vital to Eisenhower that a limited war option not be included in a Basic National Security Policy. If it were an option, then he feared limited war would result in general nuclear war. See Craig, *Destroying the Village*, 62-67. NSC 5707/8 is printed in *FRUS*, 1955-57, 19:509-524.

57. The Gaither Report, 21.

58. Ibid., 33.

59. Memorandum for Cutler: Gaither Recommendations on Shelter, 02/14/58, EL, WHO OSANSA, NSC Series, Briefing Notes Subseries, Box 8, "[Fallout Shelters](3) 1957-60."

60. Gaither Report, 24; 25.

61. Ibid., 22.

62. Ibid., 23. In 1957, the U.S. spent 8.5% of its GNP on defense and 10% on all national security programs.

63. Memorandum to Fredrick Dearborn from R.V. Mrozinski, 12/27/57, EL, WHO OSANSA, OCB Series, Subject Subseries, Box 6, "Security Resources."

64. The Gaither Report, 23. The Federal National Highway Act was passed in 1956 and it was a program Eisenhower had been interested in since taking a cross-country trip by Army convoy in 1919. Impressed by the German *Autobahnen*, Eisenhower felt a highway program "was an ideal program for the federal government to undertake." For more see Ambrose, *Eisenhower: Soldier and President*, 387.

65. Memorandum of Conference with the President on November 4, 1957, 11/6/57, EL, AWF, DDE Diary, Box 28, "November 1957 Staff Notes."

66. Memorandum of Conference with the President on November 11, 1957, 11/16/57, EL, AWF, DDE Diary, Box 28, "November 1957 Staff Notes." Defense was asking for $200 million more for SAC dispersal and reduction time proposals.

67. Newhouse, *War and Peace*, 120.

68. Memorandum of Conference with the President on November 11, 1957, 11/16/57, EL, AWF, DDE Diary, Box 28, "November 1957 Staff Notes."

69. McElroy did not request any of the missile programs be accelerated to match the levels of the Gaither report in either cost or number. See ibid.

70. Although the matter was closed for Eisenhower, it was still discussed and studied. Cutler brought forth memos indicating support and programs from civilian and military men. Even the PSAC decided to set up a Panel on Limited

Warfare, in part because the TCP report said there was a need for a study of the technology of limited warfare. See Memorandum for the President from Cutler on Limited war in the Nuclear Age, 08/07/57, EL, AWF, Administrative Series, Box 11, "Cutler, Robert 1956-57(1);" Record of Meeting of PSAC, 05/18/59, EL, USPSAC Records, Box 5, "Records of Action and Meetings- PSAC."

71. Memorandum of Conference with the President on November 4, 1957, 11/6/57, EL, AWF, DDE Diary, Box 28, "November 1957 Staff Notes."

72. Memorandum of Discussion at the 343d Meeting of the National Security Council, 11/7/57, *FRUS*, 1955-57, 19:634.

73. Memorandum from Gerald Smith to Dulles: Discussion of Preliminary Views of Some Members of the Security Resources Panel, 10/23/57, NA, RG 59, Records of the Policy Planning Staff, 1957-61, Box 128, "National Security."

74. Letter Nitze to Dulles, 11/16/57, quoted in Callahan, *Dangerous Capabilities*, 173.

75. Memorandum of Conference with the President on November 4, 1957, 11/6/57, EL, AWF, DDE Diary, Box 28, "November 1957 Staff Notes."

76. Memorandum of Conversation with the President, 12/26/57, EL, JFD Papers, JFD Chronological Series, Box 15, "December 1957 (1);" Letters Mrs. Allan Jones to Eisenhower, 9/19/61 and Eisenhower to Freeman Gosden, 9/25/61, EL, DDE Papers, Post Presidential, 1961-69, Special Name Series, Box 4, "Gosden, Freeman, 1960-61."

77. Memorandum of Discussion at the 351st Meeting of the NSC, 01/16/58, *FRUS*, 1958-60, 3:14-15.

78. Gaither Report, 33. Italics in original.

79. Memorandum of Conversation with the President, 12/26/57, EL, JFD Papers, JFD Chronological Series, Box 15, "December 1957 (1)."

80. Historian Neal Rosendorf saw this exchange as a precursor to U.S. strategic policy under future president Richard Nixon. He writes, "in suggesting that stability and security might best be preserved by allowing a degree of vulnerability on both sides of the superpower confrontation, [Dulles] had hit upon the fundamental principle of Mutual Assured Destruction." See Rosendorf, "John Foster Dulles' Nuclear Schizophrenia," 82.

81. Memorandum of Discussion at the 343d Meeting of the NSC, 11/7/57, *FRUS*, 1955-57, 19:634.

82. Memorandum to Cutler from Fredrick Dearborn, 12/18/57, EL, WHO OSANSA, OCB Series, Subject Subseries, Box 6, "Security Resources."

83. Val Peterson had stepped down from the FCDA in June 1957 to accept an ambassadorship to Denmark.

84. Memorandum for the Record, Interview with the Federal Civil Defense Administrator in Mr. Lay's Office on 12/11/57, NA, RG 273, Box 44, "NSC 5709- Background Documents."

85. Letter Cutler to Robert Sprague, 03/19/58, EL, WHO OSANSA, NSC Series, Briefing Notes Subseries, Box 8, "[Fallout Shelters](3) 1957-60."

86. The committee was the Interdepartmental Shelter Committee and its report was designated NSC 5807. Memorandum to Cutler: Interdepartmental Shelter Committee Report, 03/14/58, EL, WHO OSANSA, NSC Series, Briefing Notes Subseries, Box 8, "[Fallout Shelters](3) 1957-60." Shelters continued to be studied through the end of Eisenhower's term. For example, Eisenhower asked the OCDM, State, and Defense departments in 1960 to re-examine policies and programs for passive defense of the population, with particular reference to fallout shelters. Their report continued to emphasize individual and private construction of shelters, but concluded such efforts fell short of protecting the entire population. Tax credits of $25 per shelter space and a requirement that all Federally-supported housing construction include shelters were suggested. Briefing Note for the PB, OCDM Shelter Paper, 12/9/60, EL, WHO OSANSA, NSC Series, Briefing Notes Subseries, Box 8, "[Fallout Shelters](1) 1957-60."

87. When he and his wife were planning to build a home at a California country club, a resident wrote to Eisenhower asking if he might join her and her husband in a group effort to build a community bomb shelter for the country club to "set a good example." Eisenhower clearly did not want to offend the woman, but neither did he take her proposal very seriously as he wrote to a friend about it: "So far as I am personally concerned, I am not sure whether I would really want to be living if this country of ours should ever be subjected to a nuclear bath. But even if I were persuaded that the building of a shelter would be good, I would most certainly insist that it would have to be ample to take care of all the caddies, the workmen on the golf course, together with everybody that works in the clubhouse, including waitresses, maids, janitors and all the rest." Letters Mrs. Allan Jones to Eisenhower, 9/19/61 and Eisenhower to Freeman Gosden, 9/25/61, EL, DDE Papers, Post Presidential, 1961-69, Special Name Series, Box 4, "Gosden, Freeman, 1960-61."

88. The "National Plan for Civil Defense and Defense Mobilization," stated that the Federal Government's responsibilities were only the "direction and coordination of the total national effort," and that "individuals and families are responsible for sustaining themselves in an emergency and for contributing to the general survival and recovery effort." See The National Plan for Civil Defense and Defense Mobilization, October 1958, EL, WHO OSANSA, NSC Series, Briefing Notes Subseries, Box 4, "[Civil Defense and Defense Mobilization][1957-60]." Many Americans did build their own shelters and, by the end of 1960, there were an estimated one million family shelters in place. John F. Kennedy continued the policy of offering advice and direction on shelters, going as far as to writing a letter to the American public in *Life* encouraging all to use the blueprints provided in that issue to build a shelter. But after the Cuban Missile

Crisis and a relaxation in cold war tensions, interest in constructing back yard shelters declined. "A Message to You from the President," *Life*, 09/15/61.

89. Memorandum of Conference with the President on November 4, 1957, 11/6/57, EL, AWF, DDE Diary, Box 28, "November 1957 Staff Notes."

90. See Eisenhower, "Radio and Television Address to the American People on Science in National Security, 11/7/57," and "Radio and Television Address to the American People on 'Our Future Security,'" 11/13/57, *Public Papers of the President*, 1957, 230; 234.

91. Memorandum of Conference with the President on November 4, 1957, 11/6/57, EL, AWF, DDE Diary, Box 28, "November 1957 Staff Notes."

92. Ibid.

93. Memorandum of discussion of 343d meeting of NSC, 11/7/57, *FRUS*, 1955-57, 19:632.

94. Ibid., 634.

95. Eisenhower quoted in Herken, *Counsels of War*, 116.

96. Morton Halperin, "The Gaither Committee and the Policy Process," *World Politics*, 13:3 (April 1961), 376.

97. Letter Robert Sprague to James Killian, 11/25/57, EL, WHO OSAST, Box 14, "Security Resources Panel [June 1957-Nov. 1960]."

98. Eisenhower recovered from what his doctor called a minor stroke within three days. See Ambrose, *Eisenhower*, 455-457; Beschloss, *MayDay*, 149.

99. Killian to Sprague, 11/29/57, EL, WHO OSAST, Box 14, "Security Resources Panel [June 1957-Nov. 1960];" *New York Herald Tribune*, November 23, 1957, p 1:8.

100. Chalmers Roberts, *Washington Post*, December 20, 1957, 1:6. The article was inserted into the *Congressional Record* by Senator Clark of Pennsylvania with the comment that "It so happens that the withholding of the conclusions of the Gaither Report has been only partially effective, because in the brilliant article written by Chalmers Roberts . . . the substance of the report has already been made available." Clark quoted in Killian, *Sputnik, Scientists, and Eisenhower*, 98.

101. Roberts, *Washington Post*, 12/20/57, copy in EL, WHO OSANSA, NSC Series, Briefing Notes Subseries, Box 16, "Security Resources Panel (1) 1957-58."

102. "Fallout Shelters Are Part of Our Defense," *The Providence Journal*, 01/22/58, found in EL, WHO OSANSA, NSC Series, Briefing Notes Subseries, Box 8, "[Fallout Shelters](3) 1957-60)."

103. Letter Lyndon Johnson to Eisenhower, 12/4/57 and Letter Chet Holifield to Eisenhower, 01/6/58, EL, WH Central Files, Official File, Box 676, "OF-133-R" (Gaither Report). Also see Killian, *Sputnik, Scientists, and Eisenhower*, 99; Halperin, "The Gaither Committee," 378.

104. Senator Clark, Congressional Record, quoted in Halperin, "The Gaither Committee," 378.

105. The criticism was unwarranted in part because Eisenhower had recently asked Congress for a higher defense budget than Congress was willing to grant. In fact, Eisenhower reminded the Gaither Panel of that fact in the November 7th NSC presentation. The NSC minutes recorded that: "Enlarging on a comment made in the course of the presentation about the 38-billion dollar ceiling on the Defense Department program, the President reminded those present that he had urged upon the Congress appropriations amounting to 39.5 billion rather than the 38 billion. In spite of a number of meetings with members of Congress on the budget, in spite of the fact that he had gone on television to urge the validity of his proposed appropriation, Congress nevertheless cut the figure." *FRUS*, 1955-57, 19:632.

106. Killian, *Sputnik, Scientists and Eisenhower*, 97. Biographer Stephen Ambrose wrote that by the winter of 1957-1958, the President was "noticeably more irritable and short-tempered, and complained about his job more than he ever had." The series of criticisms over the past two years, including Suez, Hungary, the Middle East, Little Rock, and Sputnik, had taken their toll. See Ambrose, *Eisenhower*, 457.

107. Cutler, *No Time for Rest*, 355.

108. Eisenhower often expressed his deep appreciation for Cutler and complimented his work in letters to him. In one particular letter, Eisenhower equated Cutler's resignation to losing his right arm. See Letter, Eisenhower to Cutler, 3/8/55, EL, AWF, Administrative Series, Box 10, "Cutler, General Robert, 1952-55 (2)."

109. Sherman Adams, *First Hand Report*, (New York: Harper & Brothers, 1961), 413-414.

110. Letter Eisenhower to Lyndon Johnson, n.d., (1/22/58), EL, WHO OSS, Subject Series, Alphabetical Subseries, Box 13, "Gaither Report [November 1957-January 1958](1)."

111. Adams, *First Hand Report*, 414.

112. Letter General Robert Wood to Eisenhower, 12/30/57, EL, WH Central Files, Official File, Box 676, "OF-133-R" (Gaither Report).

113. Letter Eisenhower to General Robert Wood, 01/10/58, EL, WH Central Files, Official File, Box 676, "OF-133-R" (Gaither Report).

114. Letter Robert Sprague to Eisenhower, 11/14/57, EL, WHO OSAST, Box 14, "Security Resources Panel [June 1957-Nov. 1960]."

115. Ibid.

116. Letters Eisenhower to Sprague, 11/18/57 and Sprague to Killian, 11/25/57, EL, WHO OSAST, Box 14, "Security Resources Panel [June 1957-Nov. 1960]."

117. Memorandum of Conversation with the President, 11/25/57, EL, JFD Papers, WH Memorandum Series, Box 5, "Meetings with the President 1957 (1)."

118. Letter Cutler to Admiral Radford, 07/9/58, EL, WHO OSANSA, NSC Series, Briefing Notes Subseries, Box 8, [Fallout Shelters](2) 1957-60."

119. Memorandum for Cutler: Attendance at Meeting on Gaither Report, 02/12/58 and Gaither Procedure, n.d., EL, WHO OSANSA, NSC Series, Briefing Notes Subseries, Box 8, "[Fallout Shelters](3) 1957-60."

120. Letter James Perkins to James Killian, 01/07/58, EL, WHO OSAST, Box 14, "Security Resources Panel [June 1957-Nov 1960]."

121. Letter William Foster to Killian, 01/13/58, EL, WHO OSAST, Box 14, "Security Resources Panel [June 1957- Nov. 1960].

122. Paul Nitze and Abe Lincoln, Limited Military Operations, 12/26/57, EL, WHO OSANSA, Special Assistant Series, Subject Subseries, Box 11, "Security Resources Panel." The report includes the views about limited war from the Air Force, Army, Navy, State, SACEUR, ORO, and the RAND Corp.

123. E.P. Oliver, Memorandum to the Security Resources Panel Steering Committee and Advisory Panel: Two Months Later, 01/14/58, EL, WHO OSAST, Box 14, "Security Resources Panel [June 1957- Nov. 1960]," 1.

124. Ibid., 1.

125. Ibid., 4.

126. Letter Gaither to Killian, 01/14/58, EL, WHO OSAST, Box 14, "Security Resources Panel [June 1957-Nov 1960]."

127. Ibid.

128. Letter Gaither to Chet Holifield, 3/19/58, EL, WHO OSAST, Box 14, "Security Resources Panel [June 1957-Nov 1960]."

129. Paul Nitze, "Organization for National Policy Planning in the United States," reprinted in U.S. Senate, Subcommittee on National Policy Machinery, Committee on Government Operations, *Organizing for National Security, Selected Materials*, 86th Congress, 2nd Session, Washington, DC, 1960, 168, quoted in Halperin, "The Gaither Committee," 373.

130. Killian, *Sputnik, Scientists, and Eisenhower,* 101.

131. ibid.

132. Ibid.

133. Scholar and scientist George Rathjens explained: "There is a serious problem in asking the right questions. If the president has the interest, the background, and the ability, perhaps he will ask the right questions. If he doesn't, however, others have to ask the questions for him and sometimes try to answer them, even if the questions are more encompassing than their own narrow discipline." See George Rathjens, "Science Advising: Eisenhower to the Present," in Kenneth Thompson, *The Presidency and Science Advising*, Vol. VIII, (New York: University Press of America, 1991), 45.

134. Memorandum for the Deputy Secretary of Defense from Radford, 07/31/57, NA, RG 218, Admiral Radford Files, Box 36, "381(Continental Defense)(1957)."

135. Dulles told Eisenhower, "A strong offensive capability as a deterrent was more effective [than shelters] in many ways." Both opposed spending billions on shelters because they "felt it would have an adverse effect in many respects." See, Memo of conversation with the President, 12/26/57, EL, JFD Papers, WH Memo Series, Box 5 "Meetings with the President 1957 (1)," 1.

Conclusion

Eisenhower oversaw eight years of the Cold War—eight years that not only witnessed a leadership change in Moscow, but also a technological revolution that directly shaped U.S. national security policy. Eisenhower skillfully led the country by adhering to the principles behind his Great Equation, by creating a team of advisors he trusted, and by periodically calling on a fine group of fellows to offer solutions and advice on national security. A great irony is that he left office under the cloud of a "missile gap," leading his successor to request and receive one of the largest increases in military spending, greatly disrupting the balance of the Great Equation. Another irony is that in the span of his eight years in office, Eisenhower had come to appreciate and respect the work of scientists such as Killian, yet the Gaither Committee experience left Eisenhower warning the American public about technocrats when he left office. He warned of the powers of the military-industrial complex, even though a consequence of the Solarium and Killian Committees had been the unleashing of this complex.

In his farewell address, Eisenhower warned the nation of becoming captive to the scientific-technological elite, but the address was not directed at his science advisors. It was directed at what Herbert York called the "hard-sell technologists and their sycophants" who invented the missile-gap and tried to exploit Sputnik and the Gaither report leaks and the fear both caused within the American public.

Specifically, Eisenhower warned in his Farewell Address that "public policy could itself become the captive of a scientific-technological elite," and "in councils of government we must guard against the acquisition of unwarranted influence, whether sought or unsought, by the military-industrial complex."[1] What Eisenhower was warning against was not so much his own science advisers within the President's Science Advisory Committee, but rather the special interest groups that were springing up from the emphasis on military research and development in industry, the press, and universities.[2]

Historian H. W. Brands wrote that Eisenhower's farewell address was more of an admission of defeat rather than a warning about the future, since it was Eisenhower who promoted the growth of the military-industrial-complex.[3] Yet that is not completely accurate. It was not that Eisenhower believed that there was no place for a relationship between the military and industry to foster new technologies. Indeed, he did think there was a place for such relationships, as evidenced by his promotion of such growth. Eisenhower was worried about the potential certain people had within this military-industrial complex to gain power and dominate policy by playing upon the ignorance of the public through scare tactics. Eisenhower was saying to the public "be wary of accepting their claims, believing their analyses, and buying their wares."[4] These hard-selling technocrats filled the public with fear and then offered expensive technological solutions that were more loaded, said York, with "engineering virtuosity than with good sense."[5]

It seemed to Eisenhower that many of the Gaither Committee members, who actively campaigned for the implementation of the Committee's recommendations and made false claims that American security was vulnerable, were endangering the balance of the Great Equation. They were creating fear and calling for aggressive defense spending. Since these men were perceived as experts in their fields, it was easy for the public to become captivated. Certainly the world had recently witnessed the miracles these experts created through science and technology: radar had saved Britain in WWII, the atomic bomb ended the war, and even antibiotics were saving the world's children. But the problem lay not only with the public believing that these men could solve problems if only unleashed, the scientists and engineers themselves believed it and believed that only they understood the problem. "As a consequence," wrote York, "many of them believed it was their patriotic duty to save the rest of us whether or not we wanted them to," and "anyone who did not immediately agree with their assessments of the situation and who failed to recognize the necessity of proceeding forthwith on the development and production of their solutions was said to be unable to understand the situation, technically backward, and trying to put the budget ahead of survival."[6] People like Sprague and Nitze certainly felt that way, and Nitze had his chance to implement his policies during the Kennedy Administration, where many of the Gaither Committee's recommendations were eventually implemented, driving up the defense budgets.

So Eisenhower's farewell warnings were not targeted against his own Science Advisory Committee or a response to his experiences with the Solarium or Killian Committees.[7] Rather, his warnings were, in part, rooted in the experiences he had during Sputnik and the Gaither Committee. His message to the people in 1961 also reflected eight years of strategic planning and focused leadership. Explaining that the current arms build-up and defense industries were unique to American peace-time history, Eisenhower implored upon his audience members to remember that the total influence of the Cold War was "economic, political, even spiritual" in nature and that they should not sacrifice one over the other. To the new leadership in Washington, Eisenhower asked them to "mold, to balance, and to integrate these and other forces," so that the American way of life should not be jeopardized.[8] No doubt Eisenhower worried that eight years of teambuilding, strategic planning, budget balancing, and spiritual development might be drastically changed with the new administration. And certainly he was right. John F. Kennedy revised strategy to embrace limited war, briefly considered spending billions on a national shelter program, saw defense budgets increase, and brought the Cold War to the brink of nuclear war in 1962.

In June 1965, Eisenhower wrote a piece on leadership for the *Reader's Digest*. Within the article, Eisenhower spoke to the many common traits one expects from a leader: selfless dedication, courage and conviction, fortitude. In addition to these traits, Eisenhower also identified "Thorough Homework" and "Power of Persuasion" as essential traits for a leader. Here we see Eisenhower advising from the heart, as he operated as a leader. The idea of thorough homework goes back to what General Andrew Goodpaster once said of Eisenhower: "he liked to have very thorough, comprehensive evaluations made, targeted ultimately on specific options and specific lines of policy."[9] To get these evaluations, he often turned to advisory committees of experts. Their reports were not meant to be policy; they were only meant to help in the preparation of policy. Eisenhower made the final decisions, but he used this decision-making process to learn from experts and to achieve his own ends. Eisenhower was no expert in science and technology, but he learned from those who were so that he could ultimately make the best informed decisions. Doing your homework was a trait admired by Eisenhower and one that he took to heart.

The leadership trait of persuasion was the basis of the team-building ability Eisenhower mastered early in his career. Eisenhower wrote that, "whenever men can be persuaded rather than ordered—when they can be made to feel that they have participated in developing the plan—they approach their tasks with understanding and enthusiasm."[10] This is reminiscent of his days at West Point, where his classmates looked up to him as a natural leader who was continually looking for ways to organize a group's efforts toward a common goal. This trait is also reflected in his organization of the National Security Council and his use of civilian advisors. He used both to create consensus and build a sense of teamwork.

Eisenhower's experiences with civilian committees ended with the Gaither Committee, but they continue to serve as valuable models. Former Policy Planning Staff member Robert Bowie suggested in the 1980s that, "incoming presidents may well be advised to emulate 'Operation Solarium' as a means for developing an integrated strategy on the basis of competing analysis."[11] Former national security advisor, Zbigniew Brzezinski, also saw the Solarium Exercise as a creative process that was orderly, rigorous, and effective.[12] Killian believed that the government, to deal with the many complex problems facing the foreign policy, could effectively use the techniques of his committee.[13] An exercise such as the Killian Committee can provide valuable information to the current administration on the feasibility of a National Missile Defense or on solutions to the AIDS epidemic in Africa. However, to make the most of such committees, the top experts need to come together unselfishly to serve their country and be welcomed by the administration.

The end of the Cold War made it more difficult to solicit civilian experts to give up their time for national security. During WWII, the Manhattan Project and the radiation laboratory at MIT had assembled the nation's top scientists who temporarily set aside their academic and scientific careers to help win the war. After the war, when the Cold War heated up and it seemed that the Soviet Union was an immediate threat, those scientists and their students for the most part willingly rolled up their sleeves again for the sake of their country. The members of the Science Advisory Committee, for example, were dedicated, brilliant men, tops in their fields, willing to sacrifice their time and energy for a cause greater than themselves. And it was a relatively small group. Killian estimated that the core group of scientists active in government advising by the end of the 1950s numbered only 200. According to MIT physicist Jerrold Zacharias, everyone knew each other; it was "just us boys."[14]

This fine group of fellows helped Eisenhower understand and apply the new science and technologies of the day to improve national security, all the while maintaining the Great Equation. This constant emphasis on strong defenses, fiscal responsibility, and the fostering of a positive public morale is perhaps the most important legacy of Eisenhower's presidency. Few presidents have mastered the Great Equation, and the nation has suffered for it. Cold War spending after 1961 continued to increase, with little effort to balance budgets. Leaders have often forgotten Eisenhower's plea to the world to remember that the cost of one modern heavy bomber was a modern brick school in more than thirty cities, two electrical power plants and two fine, fully equipped hospitals. Hard choices have to be made, in spite of political opposition, to prepare the country for the long haul. Leaders today, in this age of terrorism, can learn from Eisenhower. Today's war on terror will very much be like the Cold War—an era lasting decades with limited hot wars. We must prepare for that—be able to sustain our defenses, but also continue to enjoy the American way of life. We must remember that there are a finite number of resources. Ronald Regan said in his inaugural address, "You and I, as individuals, can, by borrowing, live beyond our means, but for only a limited period of time. Why, then, should we think that collectively, as a nation, we are not bound by that same limitation?" Leaders understand the scarcity of everything. Dwight Eisenhower understood this best of any of the 20th century presidents. The legacy of Eisenhower is in his devotion to teamwork and his devotion to educating himself and those around him. Most important, his legacy is crafting a strong national security policy while adhering to the Great Equation.

Notes

1. Eisenhower, "Farewell Address to the Nation," *Public Papers of the President*, 1960-61.
2. James Killian, *Sputnik, Scientists, and Eisenhower*, 237.

3. H.W. Brands, "The Age of Vulnerability: Eisenhower and the National Insecurity State," *American Historical Review* 94 (October 1989), 988-89.

4. York, *Race to Oblivion*, 11.

5. Ibid.

6. Ibid., 11-12.

7. James Killian wrote that "in this period, when Sputnik panic was being used to support an orgy of technological fantasies and a speed-up in the arms race, PSAC was a voice of sense and moderation, and that this was one of the reasons it commanded the confidence of its beleaguered chief." Killian, *Sputnik, Scientists, and Eisenhower*, 239.

8. Dwight Eisenhower, "Farewell Address to the Nation," *Public Papers of the President*, 1960-61.

9. "Project Solarium: A Collective Oral History with General Andrew Goodpaster, Robert Bowie, and Ambassador George Kennan," 2/27/88, Princeton University, Mudd Library, Woodrow Wilson School, Box 93, folder 10, 10-11.

10. Dwight Eisenhower, "What is Leadership," *Readers Digest* June, 1965.

11. Robert Bowie, "The President and the Executive Branch," in *The Making of America's Soviet Policy*, ed. Joseph Nye, (New Haven: Yale University Press, 1984), 93.

12. Zbigniew Brzezinski, "NSC's Midlife Crisis," *Foreign Policy*, 69 (Winter 1987-88): 80-99.

13. James Killian, Oral History, Columbia Oral History Project, 32-33.

14. Daniel Kevles, *The Physicists*, (Cambridge: Harvard Press, 1995), 394.

APPENDIX A

Solarium Exercise

Task Force A:
>George F. Kennan - Chairman
>Colonel C. H. Bonesteel
>Rear Admiral H. P. Smith
>Colonel G. A. Lincoln
>C. T. Wood
>J. Maury
>Captain H. S. Sears, USN

Task Force B:
>Major General J. McCormack - Chairman
>Major General J. R. Deane
>J. K. Penfield
>P. E. Mosely
>Calvin Hoover
>J. C. Campbell
>Colonel E.S. Ligon

Task Force C:
>Admiral R. L. Conolly - Chairman
>Lieut. General L. L. Lemnitzer
>G. F. Reinhardt
>Colonel K. Johnston
>Colonel A. J. Goodpaster
>Leslie Brady
>Colonel H. K. Johnston

APPENDIX B

Technological Capabilities Panel

Steering Committee

James R. Killian, Jr.	(Director of TCP)	Massachusetts Institute of Technology
James B. Fisk	(Deputy Director)	Bell Telephone Laboratories
Marshall G. Holloway	(Director of Project 1)	Los Alamos Scientific Laboratory
Leland J. Haworth	(Director of Project 2)	Brookhaven National Laboratory
Edwin H. Land	(Director of Project 3)	Polaroid Corporation
Lee H. DuBridge	Member-at-Large	California Institute of Technology
James H. Doolittle	Member-at-Large	Shell Oil Company
James P. Baxter, III	Member-at-Large	Williams College
Robert C. Sprague	Consultant	Sprague Electric Company

Project 1

Marshall G. Holloway, Director	Los Alamos Scientific Laboratory
E. Peter Aurand	Commander, U.S.N.
Robert L. Belzer	The RAND Corporation
Stuart C. Hight	Sandia Corporation
Burke Horton	Office of Defense Mobilization
Ruben F. Mettler	Office of Assistant Secretary of Defense (R&D)
Ernst H. Plesset	The RAND Corporation
William R. Stratton	Los Alamos Scientific Laboratory
Julian M. West	Bell Telephone Laboratories
Carroll Zimmerman	Strategic Air Command

Project 2

Leland J. Haworth, Director	Brookhaven National Laboratory
Edward Barlow	The RAND Corporation
Daniel Dustin	Lincoln Laboratories

Richard Emberson	Associated Universities, Inc.
Robert Gilruth	National Advisory Committee for Aeronautics
Albert G. Hill (part time)	Lincoln Laboratories
Brockway McMillan	Bell Telephone Laboratories
J. L. Morton	Commander, U.S.N.
James C. Mouzon	Operations Research Office, Johns Hopkins Univ.
Ragnar Rollefson	University of Wisconsin
Herbert Scoville, Jr.	Armed Forces Special Weapons Project
Merle A. Tuve	Carnegie Institution of Washington

Project 3

Edwin H. Land, Director	Polaroid Corporation
James G. Baker	Harvard University
Joseph W. Kennedy	Washington University
Allen Latham, Jr.	Arthur D. Little, Incorporated
Edward M. Purcell	Harvard University
John W. Tukey	Princeton University

Communications Working Group

Jerome B. Wiener, Chairman	Massachusetts Institute of Technology
G. W. Gilman	Bell Telephone Laboratories
H. T. Friis	Bell Telephone Laboratories
W. H. Radford	Massachusetts Institute of Technology

Subcommittee

H. A Affel	Bell Telephone Laboratories
W.B. Davenport, Jr.	Lincoln Laborites
R. H. Scherer	Central Intelligence Agency

Consultant for Technical Personnel

H. D. Chittim	Strategic Air Command

Military Advisory Committee

Lt. Gen. L. L. Lemnitzer	U.S. Army
*Rear Adm. H. D. Felt	U.S. Navy
*Brig. Gen. B. K. Holloway	U.S. Air Force

---

*With Maj. Gen. H. McK. Roper, U.S. Army, constitute military consultant group.

Executive Staff

David Z. Beckler	Office of Defense Mobilization
Lt. Col. Vincent T. Ford	U.S. Air Force

Administrative Staff

William W. Brazeal, Jr.	Atomic Energy Commission
Marie Comerford	Central Intelligence Agency
Enes M. Hockett	Office of Assistant Secretary of Defense (R&D)
Carlene Klett	Office of Defense Mobilization
Dorothy H. Lewis	Atomic Energy Commission
Kathryn Weichold	Atomic Energy Commission
Lois Wiesner	Atomic Energy Commission

APPENDIX C

Security Resources Panel

Steering Committee

Mr. Robert C. Sprague	Sprague Electric Company
Dr. James A. Perkins	Carnegie Corporation
Mr. William C. Foster	Olin-Mathieson Chemical Corp.
Dr. Robert C. Prim	Bell Telephone Labs.
Dr. James P. Baxter, III	Williams College
Dr. Hector R. Skiter	Airborne Instruments Labs.
Dr. Robert D. Calkins	Brookings Institution
Mr. William Webster	New England Electric System
Mr. John J. Corson	McKinsey and Company
Prof. Jerome B. Wiesner	Massachusetts Institute of Technology

Technical Advisor - Mr. Edward P. Oliver
Rand Corporation

Advisory Panel

Mr. H. Rowan Gaither, Jr.	Ford Foundation
Dr. Ernest O. Lawrence	Radiation Laboratory University of California
Adm. Robert B. Carney	Westinghouse Electric Co.
Mr. Robert Lovett	Brown Bros., Harriman
Gen. James H. Doolittel	Shell Oil Company
Mr. John J. McCloy	Chase Manhattan Bank
Gen. John E. Hull	Manufacturing Chemists Assoc.
Dr. Frank Stanton	Columbia Broadcasting System
Dr. Mervin J. Kelly	Bell Telephone Laboratories

Science Advisory Committee - Subcommittee

Dr. James B. Fisk	Bell telephone Laboratories
Dr. I. I. Rabi	Science Advisory Committee
Dr. James R. Killian, Jr.	Massachusetts Institute of Technology

Executive Staff

Mr. David Z. Beckler   Science Advisory Committee
Lt. Colonel Vincent T. Ford   United States Air Force

Institute for Defense Analyses Officers

Gen. James McCormack, Jr.   President
Dr. Albert G. Hill   Vice President and Director of Research

Project Members

Dr. Sidney S. Alexander   Massachusetts Institute of Technology
Mr. Donald Y. Barrer   IDA / WSEG
Dr. Lloyd V. Berkner   Associated Universities
Mr. Richard M. Bissell   Central Intelligence Agency
Dr. Eugene T. Booth   Columbia University
Mr. Richard P. Booth   Bell Telephone Laboratories
Dr. Willard G. Bouricius   International Business Machines
Dr. William E. Bradley   Philco Corporation
Mr. William E. Butler   Chase Manhattan Bank
Mr. Leonard Carulli   McKinsey and Company
Dr. Joseph M. Clifford   IDA / WSEG
Dr. George A. Contos   IDA / WSEG
Mr. James E. Cross   Center for International Study
Dr. John H. Daniel   IDA / WSEG
Dr. Edwin O. Elliott   Operations Evaluation Group
Dr. Richard Emberson   Associated Universities, Inc.
Mr. William J. Frantz   Boeing Aircraft Corporation
Dr. J. Wayne Fredericks   Ford Foundation
Mr. Edwin B. George   Office of Defense Mobilization
Dr. William M. Hall   Raytheon Manufacturing Corporation
Dr. Robert J. Hanson   Massachusetts Institute of Technology
Dr. Joseph O. Hanson   U.S. Information Agency
Lt. Colonel James Hartgering   Walter Reed Medical Center
Mr. Robert A. Hawkins   AVCO Manufacturing Company
Dr. William A. Higinbotham   Brookhaven National Lab.
Mr. H. Burk Horton   Office of Defense Mobilization
Mr. William R. Hutchins   Raytheon Manufacturing Corporation
Mr. Chandler W. Jones   Narragansett Electric Company
Mr. Spurgeon M. Keeny, Jr.   Office of Sec. of Def. (R&E)
Mr. John W. Klotz   Office of Sec. of Def. (R&E)
Col. Omar E. Knox   USAF / IDA / WSEG

Mr. Dalimil Kybal	Lockheed Aircraft Corporation
Dr. Joel S. Lawson	University of Illinois
Dr. Stanley J. Lawwill	Strategic Air Command
Col. George A. Lincoln	United States Military Academy
Mr. Franklin A. Lindsay	McKinsey and Company
Dr. Andrew Longacre	Syracuse University
Dr. Andrew W. Marshall	Rand Corporation
Dr. Brockway McMillan	Bell Telephones Laboratories
Dr. Edwin M. McMillan	University of California
Dr. Vincent V. McRae	Operation Research Office
Dr. Melvin L. Merritt	Sandia Corporation
Dr. Donald N. Michael	Dunlap & Associates
Mr. William H. Minshull, Jr.	Hughes Aircraft Corporation
Mr. Anthony J. Navoy	IDA / WSEG
Gen. Otto L. Nelson, Jr.	New York life Insurance Co.
Dr. Nathan M. Newmark	University of Illinois
Mr. Guy W. Nichols, Jr.	New England Electric System
Mr. Paul H. Nitze	School of Advanced International Studies
Dr. Joseph H. Pechman	Committee for Economic Development
Mr. Oliver Popenoe	Office of Defense Mobilization
Dr. Franklin A. Rodgers	Lincoln Laboratory
Dr. Bruce W. Rohrbacher	McKinsey and Company
Mr. Luis R. Sanchez	Rand Corporation
Dr. William McC. Siebert	Massachusetts Institute of Technology
Lt. Colonel Glen A. Smith	Central Intelligence Agency
Mr. Robert Stockley	Fed. Civil Defense Admin.
Dr. Donald C. Stone	Springfield College
Mr. Walmer E. Strope	U.S. Naval Radiological Lab.
Mr. Norman H. Taylor	Lincoln Laboratory
Dr. Lester Van Atta	Hughes Aircraft
Mr. Lawrence R. Walters	IDA / WSEG
Mr. William L. White	Stanford Research Institute
Dr. Robert Whitmer	Ramo-Wooldridge Corporation
Mjr. Paul H. Wine	USAF / NORAD
Mr. Marshall K. Wood	Office of Sec. of Def. (S&L)
Dr. Herbert F. York	University of California

BIBLIOGRAPHY

Archival Collections

Dwight D. Eisenhower Library (EL)
Sherman Adams Oral History
Evan Aurand Papers
Virgil Couch Papers
Dwight D. Eisenhower Papers as the President of the United States, 1953-1961
Ann Whitman File (AWF)
    Administrative Series
    Cabinet Series
    Dwight D. Eisenhower Diary Series
    Legislative Meetings
    NSC Series
Dwight D. Eisenhower Papers, Post Presidential, 1961-69
    Special Name Series
John Foster Dulles Papers (JFD)
    Chronological Series
    General Correspondence and Memo Series
    Subject Series
    White House Memorandum Series
C.D. Jackson Papers
James Killian, Jr. Oral History
White House Office Files (WHO)
    Central Files
        Confidential File
        Official File
        NSC Staff (NSCS)
            Disaster File
            Executive Secretary Subject File
            Special Staff File Series
        Office of the Staff Secretary (OSS)
            Cabinet Series
            L. Arthur Minnich Series
            Subject Series
    Office of the Special Assistant for National Security Affairs: Records, 1952-61
    (OSANSA)
        NSC Series

OCB Series
Special Assistant Series
Office of the Special Assistant for Science and Technology (OSAST)

National Archives of the United States (NA)
Record Group 59 - Department of State
    Deputy Assistant Secretary for Politico-Military Affairs
        Subject Files of the Special Assistant for Atomic Energy, 1950-66
        Participation in OCB/NSC, 1947-63
        Records of the PPS, 1947-53
            Working Papers
            PPS Members Chronological File
    Records of the PPS, 1935-62
Record Group 218 - Joint Chiefs of Staff
    Chairman's File
        Admiral Radford, 1953-57
    Geographic File
Record Group 273 - National Security Council

Massachusetts Institute of Technology Archives (MIT)
James R. Killian, Jr. Papers (Collection 423)
Compton-Killian Papers (Collection AC4)

Princeton University Mudd Library
John Foster Dulles Papers
Richard Bissell Oral History

Government Publications

Condit, Kenneth. *History of the Joint Chiefs of Staff.* Vol. VI. Washington DC: GPO, 1992.
Deterrence and Survival in the Nuclear Age (The "Gaither Report"). 11/7/57. Washington DC: GPO, 1976.
Public Papers of the Presidents of the United States: Franklin D. Roosevelt. Washington, DC: GPO.
Public Papers of the Presidents of the United States: Dwight D. Eisenhower. Washington, DC: GPO.
Steury, Donald, ed. *Intentions and Capabilities.* Washington, DC: US Printing, 1996.
Sturm, Thomas. *The USAF Scientific Advisory Board: Its First Twenty Years, 1944-1964.* Washington, DC: GPO, 1967.

U.S. Senate, Subcommittee on National Policy Machinery, Committee on Government Operations, *Organizational History of the National Security Council*, 86th Congress, 2nd Session, Washington D.C., GPO,1960.

United States Department of State. *Foreign Relations of the United States, 1948. (FRUS)* Volume 1. Washington, DC: GPO.

————. *Foreign Relations of the United States, 1949.* Volume1. Washington, DC: GPO.

————. *Foreign Relations of the United States, 1950.* Volume 1. Washington, DC: GPO.

————. *Foreign Relations of the United States, 1952-54.* Volume 2. Washington, DC: GPO.

————. *Foreign Relations of the United States, 1952-54.* Volume 8. Washington, DC: GPO.

————. *Foreign Relations of the United States, 1955-57.* Volume 19. Washington, DC: GPO.

————. *Foreign Relations of the United States, 1958-60.* Volume . Washington, DC: GPO.

Diaries, Memoirs, Books, and Articles

Acheson, Dean. *Present at the Creation: My Years in the State Department.* New York: Norton, 1969.

Adams, Sherman. *First Hand Report: The Story of the Eisenhower Administration.* New York: Harper & Brothers, 1961.

Adams, Valerie. "Ensuring the Ivory Tower Did Not Fall Behind an Ivory Curtain." *Essays in Arts and* Sciences, 33:1 (Summer 2004).

Alexander, Charles. *Holding the Line: The Eisenhower Era, 1952-1961.* Bloomington: Indiana University Press, 1975.

Alperovitz, Gar. *Atomic Diplomacy: Hiroshima and Potsdam.* New York: Simon and Schuster, 1965.

Ambrose, Stephen. *Eisenhower: Soldier and President.* New York: Simon and Schuster, 1990.

Baxter, James Phinney, III. *Scientists against Time.* Cambridge: MIT Press, 1946.

Beschloss, Michael. *MayDay: Eisenhower, Khrushchev, and the U-2 Affair.* New York: Harper & Row, 1986.

Bissell, Richard, Jr. *Reflections of a Cold Warrior: From Yalta to the Bay of Pigs.* New Haven: Yale University Press, 1996.

Boyer, Paul. *By the Bomb's Early Light: American Thought and Culture at the Dawn of the Atomic Age.* Chapel Hill: University of North Carolina Press, 1994.

Bowie, Robert and Richard Immerman. *Waging Peace: How Eisenhower Shaped an Enduring Cold War Strategy.* New York: Oxford University Press, 1998.

Bowie, Robert. "The President and the Executive Branch," in *The Making of America's Soviet Policy*, ed. Joseph Nye. New Haven: Yale University Press, 1984.

Brands, H.W. "The Age of Vulnerability: Eisenhower and the National Security State." *American Historical Review* Vol. 94 No. 4, (October 1989).

Broscious, S. David. "Longing for International Control, Banking on American Superiority: Harry S Truman's Approach to Nuclear Weapons." in John L. Gaddis, Philip Gordon, Ernest May, Jonathan Rosenberg eds., *Cold War Statesmen Confront the Bomb: Nuclear Diplomacy Since 1945.* New York: Oxford University Press, 1999.

Bradley, David. *No Place To Hide.* Boston: Little Brown, 1948.

Brodie, Bernard. *Strategy in the Missile Age.* Princeton: Princeton University Press, 1965.

Brzezinski, Zbigniew. "NSC's Midlife Crisis." *Foreign Policy*, 69 (Winter 1987-88).

Buhite, Russell and William Christopher Hamel. "War for Peace: The Question of an American Preventive War against the Soviet Union, 1945-1955." *Diplomatic History*, 14 (1990).

Bundy, McGeorge. *Danger and Survival: Choices About the Bomb in the First Fifty Years.* New York: Random House, 1988.

Burrows, William. *Deep Black: Space Espionage and National Security.* New York: Random House, 1986.

Burns, James McGregor. *The Crosswinds of Freedom.* New York: Knopf, 1989.

Callahan, David. *Dangerous Capabilities: Paul Nitze and the Cold War.* New York: Harper Collins, 1990.

Churchill, Winston. *The Second World War.* Vol. 3 *The Grand Alliance.* New York: Houghton Mifflin, 1950.

Clarfield, Gerard. *Security With Solvency: Dwight D. Eisenhower and the Shaping of the American Military Establishment.* Westport, CT.: Praeger, 1999.

Craig, Campbell. *Destroying the Village: Eisenhower and the Thermonuclear War.* New York: Columbia University Press, 1998.

Cutler, Robert. *No Time For Rest.* Boston: Little Brown & Co., 1965.

Damms, Richard. "Eisenhower's 'Scientific-Technological Elite.'" *Diplomatic History*, 24 (Winter 2000).

Day, Dwayne. John Logsdon, Brian Latell, eds. *Eye in the Sky: The Story of the Corona Spy Satellites.* Washington: Smithsonian Institution Press, 1998.

Dinerstein, Herbert. *War and the Soviet Union: Nuclear Weapons and the Revolution in Soviet Military and Political Thinking.* New York: Praeger, 1962.

Divine, Robert. *Blowing on the Wind: The Nuclear Test Ban Debate, 1954-1960.* New York: Oxford University Press, 1978.

———. *Eisenhower and the Cold War.* New York: Oxford University Press,

1981.

———. *The Sputnik Challenge: Eisenhower's Response to the Soviet Satellite.*
New York: Oxford University Press, 1993.

Dockrill, Saki. *Eisenhower's New Look National Security Policy, 1953-61.* New
York: St. Martin's, 1996.

Eisenhower, Dwight. *Mandate for Change, 1953-1956.* New York: Double Day
and Co., 1963.

———. "What is Leadership?" *Readers Digest,* June 1965.

———. *At Ease: Stories I Tell to Friends.* New York: Double Day, 1967.

———. "The Central Role of the President in the Conduct of Security Affairs."
in Col. Amos A. Jordan, Jr., ed. *Issues of National Security in the 1970s:
Essays Presented to Colonel George A. Lincoln on His Sixtieth Birthday.*
New York: Praeger, 1967.

Ermath, Fritz. "Contrasts in American and Soviet Strategic Thought." in Derek
Leebaert, ed., *Soviet Military Thinking.* Boston: George Allen & Unwin,
1981.

Ferrell, Robert, ed. *The Eisenhower Diaries.* New York: W.W. Norton, 1981.

———. *Off the Record: The Private Papers of Harry S Truman.* New York:
Harper and Row, 1980.

Fowler, John ed. *Fallout: A Study of Superbombs, Strontium 90, and Survival.*
New York: Basic Books, 1960.

Foyle, Douglas. *Counting the Public In: Presidents, Public Opinion, and Foreign Policy.* New York: Columbia University Press, 1999.

Freedman, Lawrence. *The Evolution of Nuclear Strategy.* New York: St. Martin's Press, 1983.

Gaddis, John Lewis. *The United States and the Origins of the Cold War.* New
York: Columbia University Press, 1972.

———. *Strategies of Containment: A Critical Appraisal of Postwar American
National Security Policy.* New York: Oxford University Press, 1982.

———. *We Now Know: Rethinking Cold War History.* New York: Oxford
University Press, 1997.

Garthoff, Raymond. *Soviet Strategy in the Nuclear Age.* New York: Praeger,
1958.

Gilpin, Robert. *American Scientists and Nuclear Weapons Policy.* Princeton:
Princeton University Press, 1962.

Gilpin, Robert and Christopher Wright, eds. *Scientists and National Policy-
Making.* New York: Columbia University Press, 1964.

Greenstein, Fred. *The Hidden Hand Presidency: Eisenhower as Leader.* New
York: Basic Books, 1982.

Halperin, Morton. "The Gaither Committee and the Policy Process." *World Politics,* 13:3 (April 1961).

Herken, Gregg. The Winning Weapon: The Atomic Bomb in the Cold War,
1945-1950. New York: Vintage, 1981.

————. *Counsels of War.* New York: Oxford University Press, 1987.

————. *Cardinal Choices: Presidential Science Advising from the Atomic Bomb to SDI.* New York: Oxford University Press, 1992.

Hershberg, James. *James Conant: Harvard to Hiroshima and the Making of the Nuclear Age.* New York: Knopf, 1993.

Hixon, Walter. *George Kennan: Cold War Iconoclast.* New York: Columbia University Press, 1989.

Hogan, Michael. *A Cross of Iron: Harry S. Truman and the Origins of the National Security State, 1945-1954.* New York: Cambridge University Press, 1998.

Holloway, David. *The Soviet Union and the Arms Race.* New Haven: Yale University Press, 1984.

Horelick, Arnold and Myron Rush. *Strategic Power and Soviet Foreign Policy.* Chicago: University of Chicago Press, 1966.

Hughes, Emmet John. *The Ordeal of Power: A Political Memoir of the Eisenhower Years.* New York: Atheneum, 1975.

Hughes, Thomas. *Rescuing Prometheus: The Story of the Mammoth Projects.* New York: Pantheon Books, 1998.

Immerman, Richard. "Confessions of an Eisenhower Revisionist: An Agonizing Reappraisal," *Diplomatic History*, 14 (Summer 1990), 328.

————. Review of *The Gaither Committee, Eisenhower, and the Cold War.* by David Snead. *H-Net Reviews*, November 2000. <http://www2.h-net.msu.edu/reviews/>.

Kaplan, Fred. *The Wizards of Armageddon.* New York: Simon and Schuster, 1983.

Kennan, George. "The Sources of Soviet Conduct." in *American Diplomacy*, Chicago: University of Chicago Press, 1984.

Kennedy, David. *Over Here: The First World War and American Society.* New York: Oxford University Press, 1980.

Kennedy, John F. "A Message to You From the President." *Life*, September 15, 1961.

Kevles, Daniel. *The Physicists: The History of a Scientific Community in Modern America.* Cambridge: Harvard Press, 1995.

Killian, James. *Sputnik, Scientists, and Eisenhower: A Memoir of the First Special Assistant to the President for Science and Technology.* Cambridge: MIT Press, 1977.

————. *The Education of a College President.* Cambridge: MIT Press, 1985.

Kistiakowsky, George. *A Scientist at the White House: The Private Diary of President Eisenhower's Special Assistant for Science and Technology.* Cambridge: Harvard University Press, 1976.

Kolkowicz, Roman. *The Soviet Military and the Communist Party.* Princeton: Princeton University Press, 1967.

Lambeth, Benjamin. "How to Think About Soviet Military Doctrine." Rand Corporation, February 1978.

LeFeber, Walter. *The American Age.* Vol. 2, 2nd ed. New York: Norton, 1994.

———. "Technology and U.S. Foreign Relations." *Diplomatic History,* 24 (Winter 2000), 1-19.

Leffler, Melvyn. *A Preponderance of Power: National Security, the Truman Administration, and the Cold War.* Stanford: Stanford University Press, 1992.

Lyon, Peter. *Eisenhower: Portrait of the Hero.* Boston: Little Brown, 1974.

Maddux, Thomas. *Years of Estrangement: American Relations with the Soviet Union, 1933-1941.* Tallahasee, 1980.

McDougall, Walter. *Promised Land, Crusader State: The American Encounter with the World Since 1776.* Boston: Houghton Mifflin, 1997.

Nelson, Anna Kasten. "The 'Top of Policy Hill': President Eisenhower and the National Security Council." *Diplomatic History,* 7 (Fall 1983).

Newhouse, John. *War and Peace in the Nuclear Age.* New York: Knopf, 1989.

Nitze, Paul. *From Hiroshima to Glasnost: At the Center of Decision.* New York: Grove Weidenfeld, 1989.

Nogee, Joseph and Robert Donaldson. *Soviet Foreign Policy Since World War II.* Fourth ed., New York: Macmillan Publishing, 1992.

O'Neil, Paul. "U.S. Change of Mind," *Life,* March 3, 1958.

Parmet, Herbert. *Eisenhower and the American Crusades.* New York: Macmillian, 1972.

Patterson, James. *Mr. Republican: A Biography of Robert A. Taft.* Boston: Houghton Mifflin, 1972.

Paterson, Thomas ed. *Major Problems in American Foreign Relations.* Vol. II, 4th ed. Lexington, MA: DC Heath, 1995.

Porter, David. "American Historians Rate Our Presidents," in *The Rating Game in American Politics,* ed. William Penderson and Ann McLaurin. New York: Irvington Publishers, 1987.

Prados, John. *The Soviet Estimate: U.S. Intelligence Analysis and Soviet Strategic Forces.* Princeton: Princeton University Press, 1986.

Rabe, Stephen. "Eisenhower Revisionism: A Decade of Scholarship." *Diplomatic History,* 17 (Winter 1993).

Rathjens, George. "Science Advising: Eisenhower to the Present." in Kenneth Thompson, *The Presidency and Science Advising.* Vol. VIII, New York: University Press of America, 1991.

Reichard, Gary. *The Reaffirmation of Republicanism: Eisenhower and the Eighty-Third Congress.* Knoxville: University of Tennessee Press, 1975.

———. "Divisions and Dissent: Democrats and Foreign Policy, 1952-1956." *Political Science Quarterly,* 93 (Spring 1978).

Rhodes, Richard. *Dark Sun: Making of the Hydrogen Bomb.* NY: Simon & Schuster, 1995.

Richardson, Elmo. *The Presidency of Dwight D. Eisenhower.* Lawrence, KS: University Press of Kansas,1979.

Rosenberg, David Alan. "Origins of Overkill: Nuclear Weapons and American Strategy." in *The National Security: Its Theory and Practice,* ed. Norman Graebner. New York: Oxford University Press, 1986.

———. "A Smoking Radiating Ruin at the End of Two Hours:' Documents on American Plans for Nuclear War with the Soviet Union, 1954-55." *International Security,* Vol. 6 (Winter 1982), 3-17.

Rosendorf, Neal. "John Foster Dulles' Nuclear Schizophrenia." in John L. Gaddis, Philip Gordon, Ernest May, Jonathan Rosenberg eds., *Cold War Statesmen Confront the Bomb: Nuclear Diplomacy Since 1945.* New York: Oxford University Press, 1999.

Rostow, W. Walt. *Europe After Stalin: Eisenhower's Three Decisions of March 11, 1953.* Austin: University of Texas Press, 1982.

Schelling, Thomas. *Arms and Influence.* New Haven: Yale University Press, 1966.

Scott, Harriet Fast and William Scott. *Soviet Military Doctrine: Continuity, Formation, and Dissemination.* Boulder, CO: Westview Press, 1988.

Sherwin, Martin. *A World Destroyed: Hiroshima and the Origins of the Arms Race.* New York: Vintage Books, 1987.

Shute, Nevil. *On the Beach.* New York: Morrow, 1957.

Smith, Bruce. *The Advisers: Scientists in the Policy Process.* Washington: Brookings Institute, 1992.

Smith, Gaddis. *American Diplomacy During the Second World War, 1941-1945.* New York: John Wiley & Sons, 1965.

———. *The Last Years of the Monroe Doctrine, 1945-1993.* New York: Hill & Wang, 1994.

Snead, David. *The Gaither Committee, Eisenhower, and the Cold War.* Columbus: Ohio State University Press, 1999.

Snyder, Glen H. "The 'New Look' of 1953." in *Strategy, Politics, and Defense Budgets.* New York: Columbia University Press, 1962.

Steiner, Barry. *Bernard Brodie and the Foundations of American Nuclear Strategy.* Lawrence, KS: University Press of Kansas, 1991.

Stern, Philip. *The Oppenheimer Case: Security on Trial.* NY: Harper Row, 1969.

Talbott, Strobe. *The Master of the Game: Paul Nitze and the Nuclear Peace.* New York: Knopf, 1988.

Taubman, Philip. *Secret Empire: Eisenhower, the CIA, and the Hidden Story of America's Space Espionage.* New York: Simon and Schuster, 2003.

Trachtenberg, Marc. *History and Strategy.* Princeton: Princeton University Press, 1991.

Truman, Harry S. *Memoirs.* Volume 1. *Year of Decisions.* Garden City, NJ: DoubleDay, 1956.

Wang, Jessica. *American Science in an Age of Anxiety: Scientists, Anticommunism, and the Cold War.* Cambridge: MIT Press, 1999.

Winkler, Allan. *Life Under a Cloud: American Anxiety about the Atom.* Chicago: University of Illinois Press, 1999.

Wells, Samuel Jr. "The Origins of Massive Retaliation." *Political Science Quarterly*, 96(1981).

York, Herbert. *Race to Oblivion: A Participant's View of the Arms Race.* New York: Simon and Schuster, 1970.

Zubok, "Vladislav M. "Stalin and the Nuclear Age." in John L. Gaddis, Philip Gordon, Ernest May, Jonathan Rosenberg eds., *Cold War Statesmen Confront the Bomb: Nuclear Diplomacy Since 1945.* New York: Oxford University Press, 1999.

Index

Acheson, Dean, 22, 25, 85, 148, 149, 151
Adams, Sherman, 116, 134, 150, 187
Alaska, 90
Alsop, Joseph, 150
Anderson, Dillon, 28, 112
Atomic Energy Commission, 113, 126
Aurand, Evan, 149, 176

Baker, James, 128
Baxter, James Phinney III, 92, 121, 172, 173, 174, 177
Beckler, David, 115
Bohlen, Charles, 24
Bowie, Robert, 61, 205
Bowles, Charles, 148, 151
Bradley, David, 154
Brodie, Bernard, 83–84, 101n14, 183
Bronk, Detlev, 110, 113
Buckley, Oliver, 111, 135n11
Bulganin, Nikolai, 84, 175–176
Bull, Harold, 91
Bush, Vannevar, 110, 113, 117

Caldwell, Millard, 156
Camp David, 26
Canada, 95
Chance for Peace, 30–33, 39
China. *See* People's Republic of China
Churchill, Winston, 14, 17, 20
civil defense, 94, 97, 147, 152–156, 164
Civil Defense Act of 1950, 156, 157

civilian committees, 42, 88, 92, 96, 117, 135, 147, 161, 172, 187, 190, 192, 205
Civilian Consultants Board, 112
Clay, Lucius, 111
Compton, Karl, 113, 117
computer, 131–132
Conant, James, 24, 113
Conolly, Richard, 50, 57–58
continental defense, 87–88, 95, 96, 120, 126–127, 164
continental defense committee, 91–95
Cutler, Robert, 28, 29, 40, 45, 49, 60, 92, 112, 113, 121, 122, 160, 162, 163, 164, 174–175, 178, 186, 188, 200n108

Deane, John, 50
Democratic Advisory Council, 151
Dinerstein, Herbert, 85–86
Dodge, Joseph, 41–42, 64
Doolittle, James, 48, 121, 129, 172
Doolittle Committee, 49, 50
Douglas, James, 175
DuBridge, Lee, 97, 109, 110, 112, 114–116, 117, 121, 133
Dulles, Allen, 45, 60, 90, 116, 129
Dulles, John Foster, 27, 32, 39, 44, 45–46, 49, 60, 62, 64, 148, 160, 172, 174, 182–183, 188, 192

early warning system, 92, 97, 99, 109, 126–127, 179
Edwards, Idwal, 89, 90
Eisenhower, Dwight, 1, 36n65, 92, 117, 127, 134, 141n123, 147, 151, 174, 186, 189, 190, 203–